# Mexico City's Alternative Futures

# Mexico City's Alternative Futures

*Bruce Nord*

**University Press of America, Inc.**
Lanham • New York • London

Copyright © 1996 by
University Press of America,® Inc.
4720 Boston Way
Lanham, Maryland 20706

3 Henrietta Street
London, WC2E 8LU England

**Library of Congress Cataloging-in-Publication Data**

Nord, Bruce
Mexico City's alternative futures / Bruce Nord.
p.    cm.
Includes bibliographical references and index.
1. Economic forecasting--Mexico--Mexico City.   2. Social prediction-
-Mexico--Mexico City.   3. Mexico City (Mexico)--Economic
conditions.   4. Mexico City (Mexico)--Social conditions.   I. Title.
HC138.M4N67   1995      303.497253 --dc20      95-40217 CIP

ISBN 0-7618-0172-3 (cloth: alk: ppr.)

## Dedication

Most of us will be alive in the year 2010 and we will want all of human life to improve.

People of good vision and hope will want to avoid what Carlos Fuentes described in the introduction to his collection of stories that center on Mexico City.

"By the end of the century, it will, fatally, be the largest city in the world: The capital of underdevelopment."

*Burnt Water, 1980*
*The Noonday Press*

# Contents

# Introduction

Prediction, forecasting, prognosticating, and so forth, are risky and sometimes rewarding activities. They can also be self-fulfilling (after the sociologist Robert Merton). If the latter means that doomsday predictions could also bring themselves into reality, then we should probably only predict positive futures.

A philosopher of such epistemological enterprises may question what is knowable, given the many paths and contingencies that can occur. A person of certain religious persuasion may write the effort off as blasphemous at best. A wise man may point out that we are living in our own future, and given our previous blindness to the present outcome, then we should be very humble indeed. Another view would be to try to master our fates by anticipating probable outcomes that we wish to avoid. The chart on the following pages plots 5 or 6 such worst case outcomes with the present being offered as ''business as usual.''

As a tactic one could ask whether one should seek to avoid worst cases or seek fervently the best cases—especially if they are not on a continuum of some sort. The best cases offered in this table are not all that utopian with respect to Mexico City's future. The local populations deserve to control their political destinies. Economic power should be decentralized and shared. The nation and city can be objects of productive identification rather than a narrow (perhaps incestuous or at least parochial) one. In a world where local identifications are equated with pluralism or democracy and national units are associated with the norm of illegitimacy, coercion or compromise, our social goal may be suspect.

The cultural, best scenario involves another chance for Mexico and Mexico City to undo its own past. Governmental units as well as people (Echeverria?) may deserve a second chance even when mass homicide is involved. As the first Olympiad in the third world, Mexico in 1968 was trying to avoid the telling questions which the students were asking.

Perhaps Mexico and its leaders have matured enough to let the world see its accomplishments as well as its failures. One must remember that the world as a whole is still struggling with this condition. The contradiction here is seen as a basic cultural one rather than only a political one.

Environmentally, Mexico City can and must clean up its act. No doubt all the Mega Cities have environmental problems that match their lopsided growth patterns. It is not too utopian to assume improvements in transportation, as low pollution forms become available. Mexico City's smog-producing buses and factories can be tamed. The author has spent Easter weekend in Mexico City and in the near absence of cars, with fewer factories and buses in operation, the air is greatly improved. As this volume is intended to be a case study in change there are scenarios that can be noted, some of which may take root as plan or policy. Perhaps an unplanned event, as an environmental crisis like the great London fog in the 1950's could galvanize a change in the current condition. The air quality index offered in the Mexico City News shows levels of ozone with readings calibrated up to 500. Readings from 100– 200 are found almost daily and these are classified as being "poor." Zones of the city often go into the "very poor" classification, and may at one point be seen as "dangerous." Will Mexico City's pattern of change be stimulated by such a crisis?

The bottom column in our introductory table sees the current condition as involving "technocratic non-solutions." This cynical sounding aphorism sees both current tinkering and grand plans (The central region plan of the 1970's) as being part of the problem. But much *does* work in Mexico City. The worst cast scenario may be found in the collapse of plans and functions now in place. It is true that plans proposed are possible plans not implemented. Probably more true is that the quality of life in Mexico City never was given a high priority in development strategies. There is sufficient pride and concern for Mexico City to regain its mythic or real past as "El Gran Tenochtitlan." The current author agrees with Geisse and Sabatini in their article on "Latin American Cities and their Poor," that these mega cities do confer advantages to the national unit, but that the costs of such urban concentration fall too heavily upon some groups. "The problem of giant cities is not their large size but the pace of their growth and the social mechanisms through which the benefits of concentration in space are accessible only to a minority, whereas costs must be borne by the whole of society and, particularily by the poor." (Geisse and Sabatini, 322.)

The authors note the "survival mechanisms" of the poor and the obstacles to "alternative urban development." Self-help and an informal economy are examples of the former, and the urban land and housing markets as well as access to resources are examples of the latter. Needless to say, the existing political system can play a role in either category. The model of change we plan to follow in the volume sees all groups as coping with survival mechanisms against obstacles built into the "system."

Before we preview our plans for this effort, let us discuss the worst cases. These could have been set up to represent the end of the game, but our assumption is that only nuclear war could do that. Actually, the status quo may be the worst case and under the political heading we used a subtitle from an article by Peter Ward to note that some changes could be made so that no improvements would be permitted! Under economic worst cases, we took a nationalistic tact by stressing an increase in economic dependency. The involvement of multinational corporations, it may be argued, has a variety of consequencews—not all negative. It's probably true that media imperialism from the outside has a variety of consequences—not all negative. These two worst case scenarios were chosen because they would distract from a decent, local dialogue that would effectively prevent movement to a best case outcome. As to social worst cases we assumed that social warfare that destroys any sense of community is the next to the last step before actual dissolution of social life as we could appreciate it.

## Mexico City Seen Comparatively

The poet Shelly (could have) said "Hell is a city just like Mexico City."
   Yet Samuel Johnson (could have) said "When man is tired of Mexico City, He is tired of life."

Mattei Dogan in the two-volume work on Giant Cities deals with Mexico City at a number of points. We want to establish a comparative perspective on this city for the purpose of assessing what traits will and will not affect its future. Dogan notes right off that "Mexico City, with its suburbs, is one of only two megalopolises in the world without direct access to the sea or an important river passing through it (The other is Teheran)," (p. 36). The advantages of Mexico City, according to Dogan, are its moderate climate on the tierra templada, its freedom from low-land diseases, and unleached soils suitable for crop production. The disadvantages include a lack of good water whose main supply will soon have to come from 300 kilometers away and 1000 meters below Mexico City. Sachs, in the Dogan-Kasarda volume (#1, page 344) cites the faulty, accident prone transportation and industrial systems in Mexico City. The 1984 explosion of a gas storage facility is noted as an example—perhaps foreshadowing things to come. Sach's chapter is on the "Vulnerability of the Giant Cities," and Mexico City is indeed in jeopardy.

In terms of problems, Mexico City shares a number given by Dogan and Kasarda (p. 19).

> These include high underemployment, insufficient housing, health and nutrition problems, inadequate water and sanitation, overloaded transportation, pollution generally, a financial crisis, crime and social upset, and a general deterioration.

Yes, these are all comparatively true for Mexico City. We will deal with each of these separatively later, even though Martha Schteingart and others have done some of this already. (See her article in volume 2 of the Dogan-Kasarda series; Sage Publications, 1988, p. 268.) Schteingart stresses "problems of hyperconcentration" as well as more general economic and environmental ones.

The current author, in teaching a comparative urbanization class, has used such materials as by Feagin and Parker (*Building American Cities: The Urban Real Estate Game*, 1990). Their edited chapters deal with issues of lack of affordable housing, the homeless, autocratic decision making, lack of local home rule, plant closings, capital mobility, gentrification, the impact of autos and suburban complications. Most of these apply to Mexico City, but perhaps plant closings and gentrification less so. From the above noted type of sources, we can construct a comparative grid, including not only problems but also general and more beneign traits. Comparative research can look for universals, but benefit from the absence of certain traits.

Our offhand comparison of Third World mega-cities shows many common traits. Mexico City stands out as being without home rule, having an appointed mayor (see Peter Ward, 1988). It clearly has a primate status (see Browing, 1972). The strong class vote increased in the previous election between PRI, PAN, and the Frente (see Molinar Horcasitas and Peter Ward, 1989). Hostility from the hinterland has been observed as "Chilangos" are perceived as being arrogant (Riding, 1985). Obviously, the citizens of Mexico City and the Federal District can and do vote in the presidential elections and seem to have voted for the slightly left of center "Frente." Vote fraud seems to occur more in the hinterland than in the more sophisticated capital. As to the nature of the voting majority, the Cardenas Frente must have represented a non-business oriented coalition within which the "left" dominated. The PRI manipulaiton of the 1983 "elections" is noted by Riding (1985, p. 211) as a very alienating experience for Chilangos.

As to economic traits, Mexico City holds the plurality of the cards with respect to manufacturing, finances and probably technology or technology-transfer. In the latter case, transfer of petro-chemical or steel producing technology does not physically come to Mexico City, but finds its function elsewhere. As a labor force magnet, Mexico City probably draws as much from non-skilled as skilled pools of workers. Both of these groups can and do head for the Rio Brava and yankee territory, but have Mexico City high on their choice list.

Most Mexican states now have their own universities, but those in Mexico City have much more prestige and program strength. Studies by people like Roderick Camp show the dominance of institutions like UNAM and IPN in the production of the TECHNICOS—at least in the early levels of their advanced education. Many high level political leaders also cap-off their educations abroad, but the intelligentia in general matriculate in Mexico City's big three universities.

Concerning social traits, all of the mega cities seem similarily blessed with respect to great inequalities (Giesse and Sabatini, 1987). Economists using lorenze curves and Gini coefficients find Mexico in general as having great disparities and would find Mexico City as representing those extremes. Alan Riding notes how real estate practices as in San Angel force the poor to leave that neighborhood (1985, p. 266). Hence augmenting class-neighborhood segregation, although Coyoacan persists (for now) with rich and poor living side by side.

Mexico City has a fairly large middle class, which is probably also true of Guadalajara, but less true elsewhere. Most of the affluent and well educated are in Mexico City or nearby. Riding observes (1985, p. 273), "The largest concentrations of rich, middle class, and poor are to be found in Mexico City, each with a potential to destabilize society if their expectations were permanently disappointed." Our view of Mexico and Mexico City in particular, is that there is no aggrevating caste or racial separation. Riding (1985, p. 199) notes the overall situation as one in which they are "proud of its Indian past, (but) seems ashamed of its Indian present." With 8–10 million "Indios" divided into 56 recognized cultural-language groups, they find protection int he INI.

The Mestizos and Criollos remain dominant and Indians in Mexico City are treated with "Contempt, curiosity or pity," (Riding, 1985, p. 208). In Mexico City, at least the Indian can escape the slavery of the Cacique system.

Concerning out-migration, much does occur, but numbers are impossible to achieve. Mexico City probably does not contribute much to the "silent invasion" and "informal reconquest" of land north of the border. As Riding observes, "90% (of the Mexican migrants studied by President Carter's select commission on immigration) come from the mainly arid states north of Mexico City," (1985, p. 331).

Concerning local identifications, it is obvious that local communities have preserved this attribute—although there are pressures to the contrary. In our section on Mexico City as a cultural fountainhead, we will deal with the overall contribution to popular-high culture as well as to the Mexican National identity. Riding believes that:

> Mexico City has lost much of its staid-turn-of-the-century elegance, but its soul has survived the metamorphosis. (Page 265)

A "handful of old communities" maintain traditions having to do with architecture, family life, the pace of life, the music and food. There is identification with their own colonia. These pueblos live, even though real estate manipulation forced many out. Some communities have enough self respect and verve to stand off alien, outside authority. Overall, there is an identification with the city itself and the nation, (witness the proliferation of museums) and we will try to weigh these in affecting alternative futures.

Comparatively, Mexico City is not like any other large Mexican city. Monterrey has a smaller middle and upper class. The latter is composed of a relatively few families who dominate industry and commerce in such areas as steel, cement, and brewing. Over 90% of the firms were home owned Groupos, and multinationals were not as obiquitous as elsewhere (Menno Vellingia, 1979). Guadalajara is probably closer in social structure to Mexico City and allows us to say "yes" to the question of similarities. Nothing matches the size of the various elite, middle and lower class groups in Mexico City, however.

As to cultural comparisons, we said "No" to massive heterogeniety. Mexico City is not New York, Los Angeles or London in this regard. Its composition is (depending on definitions) about 65% mestizo, 20% criollos, 5% Indian (at most) and the remainder "foreigners." One must remember that in the 17th century Mexico City and Puebla were centers of criollo power (Riding, 1985, p. 31). Mexico City is open to the world, but being a non-port, and being set in a poor country means it is not to say that Mexico City is not a "world city" or that it lacks international representation.

The focus of Mexico City is culturally on secular matters despite its colonial and modern Catholic churches. Three centuries of church dominance were severed by the Revolution, even though most Mexicans claim a Catholic background. Mexico City is not as secular as the Federal Triangle in Washington, D.C., and only on religious holidays does Mexico City radiate religiosity. And then, many take a very secular vacation. Carlos Fuentes may complain that Mexicans went from one church to another (Catholicism to Marxism) without giving up on dogma, but political culture seems more omnipresent than other-worldly matters.

Mexico City is the primate center of Mexican popular culture. Journals like *Studies in Latin American Popular Culture* cover the mass media in Mexico (centered in Mexico City, of course) and such additional areas as music production, magazines, and printed materials (volumes 5 and 6, 1986–87). We will have a chapter later which will try to evaluate the impact of this popular-mass culture on alternative futures.

As to high culture, the intelligentsia are royalty. They are "cultural caudillos" but they disdain popular culture and the mass media so they fail to have a broad impact. (The latter is left to such as Televisa.) With much government support and occasional bones from the private media (The cultural inserts in *Novedades*, for example) they thrive in an involuted fashion. Although the worldly impact of this "housebroken intelligentsia" (not my term) is slow in coming, they have national status. To quote our favorite source, Alan Riding: (1985, p. 303)

Artistic expression remains peculiarly Mexican, but it is freer than in the past, able to develop new techniques and address universal themes without re- nouncing Mexico as a font of inspiration.

Perhaps only the "Mexican school of painters" has had complete acceptance abroad. Literature, of course, is catching the hearts and minds of the world literati as well. National television really obliterates Mexican high culture as it does almost everywhere else. Folk culture is reinforced in some high culture from Mexico City, and the museums and stores help as well.

# The Plan of This Project

The best laid plans of mice and men, oft gang aglay. (Misquoted from Robert Burns.)

The goals of this volume are at least three in number. First, to summarize materials on Mexico City which might be relevant to its future. Next by focusing on substantial groups within the population and their institutions, not finally, but with hopefulness, we will contrast our best prognostications with those of the major students of Mexico City.

Both hard and soft methods will be chosen to help in this endeavor. The former will, for example, examine statistical "trends" for Mexico City and other, possibly comparable, mega cities. An example of a soft method would include speculations about possible futures for the next generation. The latter may resemble the biased, overly dramatized kind of "mega trend" of the kind Naisbitt has spawned. Our batting average in either case may be near the level of chance of a trained chimpanzee coming up with a Shakespearian sonnet on a typewriter!

Predictions in separate areas (economic, political, social, environmental or cultural) may not be so difficult to achieve—as some outcomes must come about. One consideration that we must entertain is that a "scenario of no change" has a high probability in some areas. Alan Knight in commenting on materials in *Mexico's Alternative Political Futures* (Cornelius, Gentleman and Smith, Editors, 1989) seems to exhibit a "bias in favor of continuity," (p. 456). He sees several of the writers in this volume as stressing "scenarios of no change." And, although "history is full of surprises," we can only "favor winners," but not predict their occurance. Linear routes between dichotomous ends (Authoritarianism versus democracy) are not necessarily ones we can follow, and democracy has not been a favored outcome in the past in any case. "The Anti Reelectionists of the 1920's, Vasconcelos "crusade of 1929," the liberal protest of 1940, the student movement of 1968, the Panista opposition of the 1960's and 80's" never transformed the system, (p. 460). The "opportunity costs of rebellion (also) have increased," (p. 461) and the repressive hardware is much greater than in the past. Perhaps a crisis (of current and past sorts) can be permanent. Just because Gorbachev seems to have changed Russia via Glasnost and Perestroika does not mean it can happen in Mexico.

We entertained these thoughts because one of the obvious alternative futures is of *no* significant change, and their current volume is relevant to our concerns about Mexico. We agree with Knight that when change possibilities do occur, (as with Madero in the early years of the Revolution) they may defy explanation. The ''apertura'' for change may be opening right in front of our eyes, however. The ''democratic current'' with the middle class siding with the Cardenista Frente has been around for over a decade. The ''New politics of prosperity'' did not suddenly emerge in 1988. Attitudes toward authority, toward wanting a better level of living, toward uniting with citizens of diverse sorts have been in transition for several decades.

Lastly in this introduction we want to see Mexico and its great metropolis as it exists in the world system. World quakes can occur as well as earthquakes and these are equally unpredictable at this juncture. A change in the per barrel price of oil might be such a ''world quake,'' but these are beyond man's ken at this point. Let us examine Mexico City in a variety of manners and then return to our task of prediction. We do not know whether a change in national leadership, joining a North American common market, or massive oil scarcity would be a ''3'', a ''5'', or a ''9'' on our ''Richter scale'' of change.

# MEXICO CITY'S ALTERNATIVE FUTURES PATHS AND OUTCOMES

|  | Best Senario | "Business as Usual" | Worst Case |
|---|---|---|---|
| **Political** | Home Rule<br>----------<br>Opposition<br>Consolidation | Representative,<br>but not Autonomous | Change to Effect<br>No Change* |
| **Economic** | Viable,<br>Decentralized | Primate Status<br>----------<br>Captive Markets<br>Persist | Multi-National<br>Control Increases<br>----------<br>Overdoing<br>Austerity |
| **Social** | Identification with<br>Colonia and City<br>and Country | Continued Flight<br>----------<br>Class Warfare<br>Unabated | Crime Already<br>Perceived as<br>Signaling Death of<br>the Community<br>(Like L.A. 1992?) |
| **Cultural** | An Olympiad<br>without a Tlateloco | Kitsch, Mexican<br>Style<br>----------<br>Chilango Arrogance | Media<br>Imperialism |
| **Environmental** | "Where the Air is<br>Clear" | Illusion of Progress<br>----------<br>Photochemical Soup | Dead Zone<br>----------<br>Evacuation of the<br>Vulnerable |
| **Overall** | "El Gran<br>Tenochtitlan" =<br>Local and National<br>Role | Technocratic<br>Non-Solution<br>----------<br>Development<br>Strategy Persists | Gridlock<br>----------<br>Collapse of<br>Central Region<br>Plan |

\* Peter Ward, 1989

*Chapter 1*

# Mexico City as a Mega-City

Large cities of undeveloped countries like Mexico tend to be general receivers rather than generators of capital, industrial products, culture and so on. Because of this phenomenon, they cannot really be considered world cities. Mexico City, nonetheless, is the dominant center of Central America and fulfills an important function at a regional level. (Martha Schteingart, 1988, page 273.)

A mega city need not be a "world city," it seems, but it clearly will dominate a regional hinterland. The metropolitan zone including Mexico City is over 1000 square kilometers and will shortly contain 20–25 million people. These statistics qualify Mexico City as a super or mega-city, and there are other elements involved which we will discuss.

Dogan and Kasarda, in their two volumes on mega-cities, have a table based on U.N. data showing Mexico City as being the 17th world's largest metro area in 1950, while it was number one in the year 2000 at 24 million people. Apart from the trends which we will attempt to deliniate, as 486 world cities are expected to be over 1,000,000 in the year 2025, (vs. only 31 in 1950) we must note probable reasons for this explosion of the mega-urban form. A giant urban form is defined as one over 4 million, and these authors see the bulk of these as being (114 of 135) in the "developing countries." The latter largely being in Africa and Latin America and most of them having common problems, namely:

unemployment, housing shortages, health problems, transportation overload, pollution, budget problems, crime and general decreptitude. (p. 19)

The main cause of urban growth is cited as being "overruralization" or having more rural residents than rural areas can sustain. The latter sounds like an ecological theory stressing "carrying capacity" rather

1

than a notion of political-economy stressing the exploitive class relations in much of the world. The actual rub in the rural to urban press is the need to absorb the young and vigorous (as via industrialization or reintensified, extended agriculture.) (p. 19)

In this Dogan-Kasarda work on "Super Cities," a number of hypotheses are tried out regarding this exponential growth. As to the lack of rural opportunities, many countries with super cities still have rural capacity (as in the Philippines or Indonesia). (p. 20) Disease, vile climates, violence, and pitiless exploitation will drive people away from noxious rural environments en masse. Push factors are many and so are pull factors, so migration is probably overdetermined. Dogan and Kasarda note (p. 21) how the uneven pattern of government (and certainly private) investments augment the push and pull factors leading to urban migration.

Early on, Mega-cities are seen as growing out of such functions as being maritime gateways or on major rivers, (p. 30). The rub was that one could not easily predict which port would eventually grow to such mammoth proportions, out of many in extant. No single geographic characteristic or function will account for the growth of mega cities, but few are exempt from the prerequisite of a good transportation linkage. Even landlocked Mexico City has the access routes to funnel people and commerce into its inner core. Dogan notes physical factors in contradistinction to sociological ones (p. 31). Rich hinterlands are prerequisites for the demographic growth. Mexico obviously lacks rivers, and its ports are in very poor hinterlands, so far. As Dogan observes (p. 36) only Mexico City and Teheran, of the world's largest cities, are "without direct access to the sea or an important river. . . ." A moderate climate is claimed as explanation for the gargantuan status, although the lowland Mayas did farily well in the tierra caliente. Soil characteristics, disease potential, water supply, and other local resources play various roles with respect to the growth of mega status.

Ultimately, small or super large cities must meet human needs in order to persist or grow. Urban growth then contributes to growth in productivity and the extension of the internal market. Linkage of large urban centers within the national unit will step up the flow of new technology and innovations generally. Almost all factors seem to lead to growth, endless growth—when we know decline is quite possible (as in Western Europe). It seems true that cities have continuously been associated not only with the meeting of human needs, but with the overall enhancement of people's lives. Later we'll try to measure this economic enhancement, and assume that its extension tracks close to demographic, political and cultural indicators. As Martha Schteingart and others have noted (Chapter 9 in Dogan and Kasarda, Vol. 2, 1988, p. 278), there are dozens of problems as well, which include housing shortages, inefficient use of resources (financial and natural), grossly maldistributed income, etc. The latter stem not "simply in terms of population growth."

> The problems may also be seen in the context of a model of dependent and unbalanced national development which presents problems of structural unemployment and working force exploitation, and works for the benefit of the land-owning, industrial, financial, and real estate sectors (who also profit from the concentration of population and economic activities.)

As a major theme of this volume, the growth of Mexico City has seldom been the result of "natural," spontaneous, unconscious forces. Our historical-demographic chapters will note the repetitive and unique interventions that have often guided Mexico City's growth trends.

One must remember the first incentive for mega-cities in South America, namely control of the hinterland's resources. The origins of the dualism in the form of metropolis and satellite or periphery set forth a chain of forces making primate and mega cities much more likely down the line. Inca and Aztec cities were demolisheed to be replaced by Iberian forms which deliberately aimed at concentrated regional power. Centrapedal processes were unleashed that would, on an irregular basis, stimulate urban growth.

Two processes (with some similarities) noted by Gilbert and Gugler, lead to urban and regional concentration which they see as "basically distorted." An "export oriented phase" and an "inward-oriented industrialization phase" are described. (*Cities, Poverty and Development: Urbanization in the Third World*, 1982, p. 38.) In the first phase, cities grew if they were in proximity to the export trade as with ports or places near the production. Hence, Singapore or Manila are central to their regional export networks, and grew appropriately. Independence may accentuate the primacy (and concentration) as well, according to Gilbert and Gugler (p. 41). The level of profits remaining locally was a key variable in expanding urbanization in this export phase.

As countries learned that development could be accelerated by import substitution, industrialization, and modernization, they implemented this strategy. By the early 1960's, many third world countries, including Mexico, had become so oriented, even though it was obvious to some that the benefits would be unevenly distributed. The main point about this latter policy is that it would blossom in the larger urban areas, thus spurring these toward gargantuan size and further unbalance.

Gilbert and Gugler note about this second phase that it may not be the result of industrial expansion per se that is the main source of urban and regional growth. Rather, being near the government and the sources of modernization may be more central to the concentration of population. "Modern administration" and planning have a way of being self-fulfilling and self-enhancing also (p. 47). Much of primate or super city growth came at great cost to regional towns and cities.

Back of the growth of mega cities has to be, of course, the huge population increase in general. However, alternative outcomes rather than unbelievable large primate cities are possible with or without policy interventions.

Policy approaches can include:

1. A decentralized urban outcome (by augmenting local incentives and functions via conscious decisions).

Or

2. Draconian limitation of entry to the super city (as Russia and China have tried).

Much theorizing assumes "natural" (therefore deterministic, predictable, and, perhaps, interveneable) phenomenon. Are policy interventions "natural"?

A counter "theory" to one stressing the "natural" growth of super cities must stress the role of a human decision making process. In this case, one or a series of decisions can have the direct or the latent function of concentrating national population. Examples of the latter include:

A) Plant location by private concerns or governments.
B) Citizens seeking the enhanced amenities which mega cities may provide.
C) Gerrymandering of populations and population boundaries for various gains.
D) Protection from the hostilities unleashed with the forced commercialization of rural agriculture.

Let us now turn to a list of traits of mega cities and try to see what their potential for change is. Alternative futures for Mexico City are rooted in these traits and their maleability.

Table II attempts to list universal and less universal traits of mega cities. Columns 2 and 3 try to assess the relative importance of these traits for Mexico City and also the routes by which they may change. In some instances, the potentials for change are speculated upon. The top examples refer to traits that are probably universal and functional for mega cities wherever they are, and the bottom examples are not necessarily present or "functional." It is implied that there may be more potential for change in the bottom level of traits or more generally accepted motivation at least.

# TRAITS OF MEGA CITIES UNIVERSALITY
## (1 = UNIVERSAL, 5 = LESS S0)

| TRAIT (Functional) | Universality* | Paths and Potential for Change in Mexico City |
|---|---|---|
| High Population | #1 | — War? Social Dissolution? <br> — Decentralization? |
| High Density | #3 | — Zoning — Planning <br> — Birth Control <br> — Housing Arrangements |
| Multiple Funtions (Service Types: Health, Education, etc.) | #2 | — Growth elswhere on a regional basis |
| Many "Master" Functions (Pol., Financial; via Added Production) | #1 | — Decentralization, but a friendly hierarchy probably will persist |
| Transportation Hub | #2 | — New ports may change this pattern and focus <br> — Hard to achieve this |
| Center of Government | #2 (but Brazil differs) | — PRI hierarchy giving way to regionalism? |
| Communication Center | #1 | — Satellites will/can change the pattern (the Morelos system) |
| Industrial Center | #3 | — Policy changes likely, but multi-national and "groupos" have their own interests |
| Financial Center | #1 | — Government policy very protective of this function |
| Cultural-Generation Center | #2 or 3 | — Indigenous culture centered elsewhere, but popular/high culture likely to remain |

| TRAIT | Universality* | Potiential for change |
|---|---|---|
| Link to Outside World | #2 | — Vulnerable as 1985 earthquake showed<br>— Geographically isolated<br>— New ports would change this<br>— Also satellite communication |
| **TRAITS—Not Necessarily Present or Functional** | **Likely, but Not Necessary** | **Probably Greater than All of the Above** |
| Goal of Migrants (More Services) | #2 | — Services can easily be decentralized |
| Great Social Inequality | Has long historical linkage with urbanization— not universal #2 | — Many moves to redistribute currently shelved (?) |
| Environmental Degradation | #5 | — Moves to clean air now strong (media campains, closing of Pemex refinery) |
| World Political Role | #5 | — Not like London, New York, Paris, Hong Kong, Los Angeles and never will be (?) |
| World Cultural Role | #5 | — Same as above |
| Crime and Deviance | #5 | — Increasing frequency related to over-conforming with respect to economic and political policy |
| Information-Expertise Monopoly | #2 | — One would assume that new technology could decentralize, except for private information |

*Universality as trait of a mega city versus being less "necessary" as part of this form.

# Chapter 2

# Our Theoretical and Practical Problems

## Theories of urbanization with special reference to Latin America

Some social theories are more universalistic in their implication than others. This is true of theories about the growth of urban places. The more "natural" the process is seen to be, the more universalistic it could be presumed to represent. The idea of the "natural" has been better examined in other disciplines than "urban studies," but relativistic-regional approaches cite local disparate experiences. In this section, we will try to lay out both universalistic and more locally relevant urban "theories." (Tabb and Sawyer)

We must specify which aspect of the urban process we are concerned with; that is urban origins, growth, dominance or decline. All of these are separate concerns that could be addressed by "nomothetic," or generalizing types of intellectual behavior. All of the above concerns should be dealt with in common or near common "theoretical" frameworks. Theoreticians worry themselves about single, key, cyclical, interactive, or deterministic factors—as well they might. Some "theories" turn out to be mostly descriptive, and therefore only slightly predictive in your investigations. Other theories can give an intellectual underpinning to your observations forward and backward in time; and are more difficult to dismiss when particularistic local elements offer themselves.

Let us outline possible models (less restrictive than theories because they do not insist on specific causal connections) and theories which, if lacking in perdictive qualities, may lead us to at least diagram the urban experience: First, there must be a "theory" that stresses spontaneous growth of urban places. If the author understood correctly about what "growing up Topsy" meant, then this first model sees "urban places" as growing autonomously, or at least congeneally within their environ-

# VARIETIES OF URBAN THEORIES

| NAME OR DESCRIPTION OF THEORY | MAIN CONCEPTS | ASPECTS OF PREDICTION | KNOWABLE OUTCOMES |
|---|---|---|---|
| DEPENDENCY THEORY | DISTORTION OF LOCAL INTERESTS VIA INTRA- AND INTER-NATIONAL FORCES | NOT HIGH IF IT FAILS TO SEE LOCAL CLASS STRUCTURE. STRESSES EXCHANGE MORE THAN PRODUCTIVE RELATIONS | CRITICIZED FOR FAILING TO EXPLAIN PAST, SO LESS USEFUL FOR PREDICTION? % OF MULTINATIONALS IN CUT-TING EDGE AREAS HAS BEEN NOTED. |
| WORLD SYSTEM THEORY | A HIERARCHY OF EXPLOITATION VIA METRO EXPANSIONISM | AS MUCH BEHAVIOR IS SEEN AS PASSIVE, LOCAL ACTION MAY BE MISSED? | CAN BE AUGMENTED BY OUR SOCIAL INCLUSION APPROACH (BELOW) |
| LOCATION THEORY | OPTIMIZING DECISIONS "RATIONALITY" IN THE ABSTRACT | IT NEGLECTS LOCAL & INTER-SYSTEM POLITICAL ECONOMY SO CAN'T PREDICT REAL ACTION? | DECISIONS WILL BE MADE HOWEVER; THESE CAN BE NOTED, AS AFTER THE EARTHQUAKE OF 1985 |
| MODERNIZATION THEORY | NOTES SELF CONTAINED REGIONS WHICH WILL GROW ON THEIR OWN, BUT NEEDS DIFFUSED ASPECTS, HOWEVER | NEGLECTS REASONS FOR HISTORICAL INEQUALITY. CAN'T ACCOUNT FOR ROLE OF WORLD SYSTEM | USED WISELY IT COULD DEPICT GREATER DEPENDENCY VIA "MODERNIZATION" M.C.'s PROBLEM IS NOT MODERNIZATION! |
| STRUCTURALIST (MARXIST, ETC.) THEORY | CAPITALIST ACCUMULA-TION WITHIN, VERSUS RELATIVE "AUTONOMY OF THE STATE" | INHERENT FUNCTIONALISM ARGUES IN A CIRCLE; CAN'T MAKE UP ITS MIND ABOUT ROLE OF THE STATE | WAKE US WHEN THE REVOLUTION OCCURS. P. G. CASANOVA SEES MEXICO AS "PRECAPITALIST", BUT CERTAINLY NOT MEXICO CITY |
| GRASS ROOTS "THEORIES" A) SOCIAL EXCLUSION | STRUGGLE AT COMMUNITY OR HOUSEHOLD LEVELS | SOCIAL MOVEMENTS WILL STIMULATE CHANGE—CAN ENLIST INTERMEDIATE INSTITUTIONS | POLITICAL SYSTEMS IN MEXICO CITY AND COUNTRY AS A WHOLE ARE MASTERS WITH THESE GROUPS. DIRECTION OF ANY CHANGE IS UNCLEAR. |
| β.) SOCIAL INCLUSION | MARGINALITY OF SORTS DOES EXIST AS IN CON-SUMPTION, POLITICS, AND CULTURAL SUPPORT | FLUCTUATIONS ARE NOTED. OPPOSITION PARTIES MUST MOBILIZE THESE GROUPS. | CAN BE MEASURED AS TO TRENDS. MANY ASPECTS ARE VISIBLE IN FEDERAL DISTRICT THAT WOULD NOT BE IN THE HINTERLAND. |

ments. In this mode of thinking, this type of urban development could hardly be stopped, short of dead-fall interference by nature, as with Pompeii.

R. J. Holton in the volume on *Cities, Capitalism and Civilization*, mentions Adam Smith's attempts and also those derived from political theory such as those of Karl Marx, of Henri Pirene, and Max Weber. Many central-urban places can be distinguished in the world, and they clearly differ from rural-countryside places. Can or should we go back to models based on the experience of the western world in its depiction of Mesopotamia, Egypt, the Indus Valley and China as a way to view urban place origins and development in the rest of the world? We know that all indigenous New World and Third World (the Americas, Asia, and Africa) urban places except China were impacted by intervention from the outside. Latin American cities were typically leveled by the European interventionists and then proceeded under dependent ties for subsequent centuries. If this scenario is "natural" so-be-it; but it is not to be seen like the unfolding of internal, organic, plant-like growth. These plant-like growth theories also linked urban growth with "civilization, progress, and freedom" (R.J. Holton, 1986, p. 303). We can, perhaps, see contradictory values appreciating from the urban experience. Thus, progress, innovation and "modernity" are clearly linked to "disorder," "pathology," "disorganization" and the decline of community. The city benign or brutish? There has been precious little autonomous, spontaneous development in the formative periods of Mexico City or indeed any of the imperially dominated Latin American cities.

R. J. Holton warns (p. 5) against "any simplistic attempt to derive modern categories from those of the classical world as this would represent indifference toward explicitly economic relations as these are now understood within ancient conceptions of urban and rural.

Holton notes that later Roman authority destroyed the autonomy of the early self-governing polis. In this regard the cities of Latin America were treated to imperial control and were overwhelmed at the governmental level, and elsewhere. Holton doesn't want cities to be seen as the bearers of civilization or a "New Jerusalem." This author doubts the supposed truism that "town air makes (people) free" (p. 7) (stadtluft nacht frei), but our concern is not with metaphors about urban growth effects and character. The danger of improper comparisons will damage our attempts at understanding Mexico City, and we stand apologetic at the offset.

The classical world's urbanization process cannot be thrown out as sources of inspiration. The likelihood of universal processes of change in diverse societies and epics cannot be dismissed. Marxist views, for instance, relate "transformation of social institutions as a product of complex conditions and forces operating throughout society in its entirety." We will get to a variety of "Marxist" perspectives later in this section. (From Judith Adler Hellman, p. 219, *LAAR*, 1983). But, if the author's logic does not fail him, common processes allow for comparability despite and because of expected differences in settings. The next approach we will examine on urban studies is that of the "Chicago school" and its various contributors.

Tabb and Sawyers offer us a full review of what they call "The fetishism of Space," (*Marxism and the Metropolis*, 1978, Oxford). Our approach, which is not in urban ecology, still can consider the spatial dimension. These authors cite Burgess' 1925 article on "The growth of cities" and the concept of "zones of deterioration" in order to note applicability of such spatial approaches. These authors offer criticisms by way of pinning down the simplicity of the Burgess model, although this has been done before. The focus on "deterioration," "disorganization," and "vice" may have missed the intellectual boat, however, and one can suspect that the urban ecologists were interested in highlighting problems, and may well have been part of the "social pathology" approach.

Tabb and Sawyers bluntly observe that Engels had a "clearer sense of the causes and effect relationships behind the urban concentric configuration." Stressing workers as "victims rather than as inferior beings" this group was shut out of the benefits. "The self-regulating market leads to such results," these authors declare, (p. 13). The Burgess, Chicago-ecological "school was a product of a major midwest scholastic center funded by large capitalist inputs. The autonomy of universities and their academic-intellectual components may well be a myth. This author, having been a graduate student there, was aware of events at this citadel that deny its academic-intellectual autonomy. The latter had to do with the highly conflicted late 1960–early 1970 period. But one suspects that obtuseness of academic-intellectual approaches kept university contributors and faculty marching in a somewhat parallel direction. Perhaps the totality of university complicity in suspect academic-intellectual activities should not come to light—as this might destroy other progressive urges associated with universities since the middle ages. What if today, moral regulators such as the Nader groups or even local neighborhoods, etc. all condemned what author James Ridgeway called the "closed corporations." If a more neutral body of knowledge were our task here, then we might wonder how such a basically biased perspective got so well established in American urban studies. Even in the relatively honest midwest, the brokers of knowledge had geographers telling us about the specifics of American urban places in terms of modificaitons of spatial theories. The latter stressed how space was dominated by such impersonal forces as transportation, communication, and environmental clines. Where did the social reality of cities go? The concepts of "invasion, conquest and retreat" are used to avoid the underlying class struggles, we must be led to believe. Tabb and Sawyers note how General Motors with its obvious interests in busses and cars, destroyed the trolley car as a alternative form of urban transport. This conspiracy was no doubt capable of authentication, but does not bother those who offer the simple description of the spontaneous development of urban forms.

This simple geography turned on itself with corrective notions of multiple nuclei and sector "theories." The particular outranged the general, yet the correlations of problems with concentric zones could not be denied. Thus, problems of people were located at least, and would you not expect such people who are impacted by this political-economic-geography to exhibit these qualities? Much was not drawn out in these simple geographic models. Capitalism as an historic urban form had *destroyed* many genuine forms of expression. There were other ways to describe to the urban experience than merely geographic locationalism, and human ecology overstressed the physical relationship between people and land use—ignoring the real political economy of this relationship. The concentric zone model describing cities as a series of expanding circles beyond the central core has some descriptive relevance to many American cities. It really does not explain why this structuring of urban space as opposed to some other (sectoral, quadrant, etc.) form is arrived at. Mexico City certainly has a central core, but it is not so clear that the receeding circles bear much relationship to the patterns of US cities. Even the US has cities like Pittsburgh and New Orleans which have cultural or physical features which establish a sector pattern.

The neoclassical premises of harmony and naturalism involved in the typical utilization of such models as the concentric zone theory are challenged by such writers as Tabb and Sawyers (*Marxism and the Metropolis*, 1978). The latter two writers stress how productive relations and ownership patterns yield the particular urban patterns which we perceive (p. 18). They stress that urban problems are generated by these factors and will not be relieved until capitalistic relationships are ended or modified. Their volume goes beyond conventional views that urban growth stems from such benign elements as technological changes and consumer preferences (p. 23). Instead, class conflicts against militant workers was more likely to have dictated urban central politics. Mexico City has a unique separation of its industry from workers' housing and it may be instructive to investigate whether such labor-control motives by owners played a role in this particular process. It seems that suburban relocation of the well-to-do served another major class function in that it may have allowed elite groups to avoid paying for the costs of running the metro core or of maintaining its surplus labor supply which they benefited from. All city (social?) forms *proceed* from previous forms of political, social economy, and Marxism implies minimally a *dynamic* approach where the analyst starts with the forces of production and how this generates a peculiar socio-spatial-political "order." Who could doubt the general validity of this model?

## Continuation of the Marxist Perspective

David Gordon writing on "capitalist development and the history of American cities" relates the three stages of perceived urban growth, namely commercial accumulation, industrial or competitive accumulation, and advanced or monopoly accumulation. The stages are determined by the nature of "class control in production" (p. 28, Gordon). Gordon sees US cities as more uniquely capitalist than others, and this continues the issue of the universality of urban "theories."

A hyphenated approach that stressed political-social-economy could hardly miss a globally crucial variable unless it were ideosyncratically described as "cultural," and therefore a given that we must offer "special," non-universal status to. The notion that "cultural" variables can account for the overwhelming political-economic similarities must be bred of political-academic desperation. Gordon (in Tabb and Sawyer's) notes how economics, rather than efficient use of space, spawned that urban grid north of Houston street in Manhattan (based on a Commission's map and admission in 1811). While it would be hard, short of intense historical analysis, to pin down the "real" motives for Mexico City's street pattern, we might suggest just such a range of motives.

The growth of cities, according to Gordon, saw "uneven development among buyers and sellers'' (p. 36) in the commercial accumulation period. Industrial accumulation demanded ''continual homogenization of the labor process''; craft jobs were (p. 37) ''compressed into semi-skilled operative work and almost all factory workers were subjected to the same discipline of factory control'' (Gordon, p. 37). The parallel demand for a reserve army of the unemployed bolstered factory control, adn kept wages low, and the squeezed out ''surplus value'' at the desired levels. Mexico City seems to have had two periods involving moves toward industrial accumulation, during the Porfirio Diaz years and after 1940. To understand the effect on the structure of Mexico City will be one of our tasks; clearly industrialization in its peculiar form had lasting effects on both social outcomes and spatial usage. Workers in large towns were more vulnerable to factory control because of the lack of sympathy from the other class groups and this meant that factory work would not decentralize (Gordon, p. 41). Gordon notes how large factories became concentrated, working-class neighborhoods became segregated and the middle- and upper-classes fled ''as far as finances permitted'' (p. 43). Shopping centers followed the convenience of the consuming classes, first to the center, then to the suburbs. The city now contained dependent wage earners instead of independent property owners, according to Gordon (p. 44). The Mexico City squatting experience gives this observation a different twist, however. The working classes were isolated and suffered the ''increasingly intense, impersonal and assaulting street life, and they had little choice'' (p. 44). Mexico City's Barrios, Tugurios, and Colonias Proletarias were isolated but may not have deteriorated into modern urban jungles at this early point.

Gordon sees the third major change in the 20th century as involving political fragmentation. It was not the result of residential decentralization, nor the technology of the street car, but more mundanely from the desire to escape central city taxes. Annexation by the central city ceased, and outlying autonomy was achieved for industrial-class interests. The creation of several layers of governmental authority in the valley of Mexico must be examined to see if this is analogous to Gordon's observation.

In these past paragraphs we have sampled Marxian perceptions about urban growth. There are ''classical'' theories about urban growth of all sorts and we would not negate the value of ''naturalness'' nor of any of the supposed deterministic forces—if they shed light on our problems of explanation.

The main structural transformation of all the urban units we are discussing has been their horizontal expansion. Urban sprawl, suburbanization, conurbation are features of the cities that we are interested in, especially Mexico City. As noted earlier, this explosion is recent for Mexico City. The central area had its own dynamics, and perhaps there must be a somewhat different model to account for more recent growth. The shortage of land, the influx of migrants, the accumulation of urban functions, the expansion of transportation and related technological innovations are clearly involved. A national policy that neglects agriculture and centralizes economic development elsewhere must be inviting this implosion. The idea of naturalness must nevertheless supply us with a more predictive set of hypotheses. What Patrick J. Ashton writes about as ''The political economy of Suburban development'' may have relevance for Mexico City's expansion. Ashton generrralizes about the ''spatial distribution of privilege.'' The ''free market for space in the metropolis has produced a pattern of suburban sprawl.'' Large scale consumerism was needed in the 1950 to 1980 period both in the US, Canada and Mexico to keep the capitalist dynamic going. We have already noted the motive of political independence and for a way to avoid paying for the externalities needed by underpaid working classes. If we are to understand urban growth patterns we need a rhetoric of motives of those clearly involved. Suburbs are not the mere outcome of changes in consumer preferences or of transportation, whereas factories and their energy sources had fostered centralization and the consolidation of capitalist political power in orer to control state investments. Other forces were at work. The polluted cities pushed out those who could afford to go outward—if only in non-working hours. Trains and streetcars on a subsidized basis allowed upper middle-class groups an exodus to a sheltered life style, and real estate profits fueled further decentralization. The availability of ''loose'' capital that needed to be invested was a further stimulus to urban horizontal development.

The move to outlying areas introduced a selectivity and a structuring of the labor force, and a similar process in residential choices. Ashton believes that these ''choices'' were not so much conscious, but were the results of the motive to protect one's interests as these manifest themselves in the flow of activities. We will discuss some of these processes again in our chapters on politics, on housing, and on geography and infrastructure. We can discuss what Ward calls the ''reproduction of inequality'' to see if one of these models deserves more credibility than the others. Let us next discuss some of the methodological concerns that may be related to these theories and models. How can we generate data that may help in our predictive and theory testing activities?

# Practical or Methodological Problems

Prediction can be based on extrapolation, on comparisons with appropriate current or historic cases, on requests to the knowledgeable who have monitored general or specific trends, or on completely A-PRIORI methods. We will use all four of these "methods" in this volume. Demographic extrapolation will be an example of the first method. Old world mega cities could be the basis for comparisons about what occurances have been the historic example or could be in the process of becoming elsewhere. (Is home rule for a national capital inevitable?) Our third approach asking experts would involve a modified Delphi technique where we could request a panel involvement with a group of people familiar with aspects of Mexico City such that they will interact with their previous collective responses and then modify their judgements if they feel it to be necessary. This older technique could be "grounded" by asking for a validating idea or fact which is part of the basis for their prediction. Lastly, we will use an A-PRIORI method by establishing a range of possible outcomes within which the future scenario is likely to occur. Which of these methods we might use to test a theoretical question will be a judgement call, as most theories try to explain what did happen causally, not typically what might occur in the near future.

In our table entitled "Methods of Prediction" we have made a judgement (an hypothesis?) about the level of predictability (high, medium, or low) of a given method in a specific area of concern. Unless we have cause to go to the extremes of high or low predictability, we might better assume a medium level—which should not deter the effort in any case. Specific historical events, almost random, can lead to low levels of predictability. Demographic growth, given its almost inexorable quality (as opposed to demographic dispersal, which might come about as a result of one time events) seems to warrant a high level of predictability. We will refer to this table at various times in this volume. Some of our urban theories just discussed have more affinity than others with some of these particular methods. Theories emphasizing decisions (location theory and world-systems theory) may lead to lower levels of predictability because the decisions affecting change are made outside of the action we are concerned with, and, perhaps, are more arbitrary in terms of the direction taken. Theories stressing natural growth (modernization, or the Chicago School) might relate better to comparisons (assuming that universal processes were at work) or to extrapolation. (The

# METHODS OF PREDICTION

| A-PRIORI RANGES | DELPHI PANEL | COMPARISONS | EXTRAPOLATION | H = HIGH PREDICTABILITY<br>M = MEDIUM =<br>L = LOW = |
|:---:|:---:|:---:|:---:|:---|
| M | M | M | H | SIZE, DENSITY |
| M | H | H | H | PRIMATE STATUS |
| L | H | H | H | SPRAWL - FLIGHT |
| L | M | M | L | HOME RULE |
| M | M | M | M | ECON. VIABILITY |
| L | M | L | M | ECON. REDISTRIBUTION |
| M | M | M | L | SECTOR BALANCE |
| L | M | M | L | MEDIA INDEPENDENCE |
| M | M | M | L | SUITABLE ENVIRONMENT |
| M | M | M | M | PLANNING EFFICACY |
| L | M | L | L | HUMAN RESOURCES |
| M | M | L | M | REPRESENTATIVE CULTURE |
| M | M | M | L | UNIT IDENTITY |

trends being "natural," and, therefore predictable? Is entropy predictable then?)

The intent of this table is to begin to have expectations of where we can have higher levels of accuracy, and with what kinds of "evidence."

The four methods noted in our table were compared with the types of prediction used in the Cornelius, Gentleman, and Smith volume on "Mexico's Alternative Political Futures" on a chapter by chapter basis (p. 31). In this volume comparisons (rather thinly sketched) were the most common basis for predictions. Extrapolations of "trends" (historical comparisons?) were often made without quantitative accompaniment. In a sense their whole volume represented a kind of Delphi panel, as the authors interacted over a several year period. A-Priori ranges of analytical sorts (four fold tables, with several permutations, were also used—see the introduction). Other methods of prediction were used, especially when significant departures were observed.

The belief in the existence of dynamic, dialectical processes was offered as explanation for various outcomes. The radical departures were seen as being the result of "critical Masses" or from Marxian contradictions, which snapped like over-stretched rubber bands. Portentous signs, like the warnings before an erupting volcano, were offered at times. Unforeseen events, like the "eternal return" were alluded to. In all, we probably should remain confident with medium levels of predictability where this is appropriately linked to policy decisions. We will try to increase the interaction between theory and methods throughout this volume. In each section we have tried to present a model for the analysis of the identified ingredients. We hope to rise beyond chance in our predictions, especially of the expected ranges of outcomes.

*Chapter 3*

# The Historical Demography of the Valley of Mexico

## The Historical Demography of Mexico City

In 1977, a National Urban Development Plan projected optimistically that by the end of the century Mexico City would have 20 million inhabitants. . . . By 1984, with the capital's population already 17 million, these projections seemed unrealistic. (Riding, 1984, p. 272)

Peter Ward in 1990 notes that the new Master Plan of 1980 had already upped the ante (p. 124). He observes that: "The new Master Plan applied only to the Federal District and referred to the Metropolitan Area in so far as it identified a total population target not in excess of 21.3 million by the year 2000, 14 million of whom were to be accommodated within the Federal District. Although human satisfaction is a more important goal than merely restriction of numbers, densities, characteristics and quality of the population are obviously central to the former. From about 540,000 in 1890 on 25 sq. km.s, to about 3,000,000 in 1950 on 270 sq. km., to about 8,500,000 on 584 sq. km. in 1960, it kept on the march to nearly 17,000,000 in 1985 on 700 sq. km. Our statistical appendices will present an array of data on this growth pattern, but there are more people in the ZMCM than in the 31 other state capitals, and the density has been many times that in the second largest cities. Probably about half of the growth has been due to in-migration. Alan Riding (1984, p. 254) observes:

People flocked to Mexico City because the country's economic strategy since the 1940's obliged them to do so. Resources were poured into industry, commerce and urban construction, while agriculture was neglected.

Riding notes that even after industrial jobs became scarcer, people kept coming because the city solved other problems for them.

# GROWTH BY UNITS

| DISTRITO FEDERAL DELEGACIONES | (pop. 1980) | % INCREASE 1950—1980 | GROWTH PROJECTIONS IN NUMBERS—%s | | | FACTORS OR % OF GROWTH |
|---|---|---|---|---|---|---|
| | | | 1990 | 2000 | 2010 | |
| 1. Alvaro Obregón | 663,156 | 497% | 795,787 | 875,365 | 962,902 | 20/10/10 |
| 2. Atzcapotzalco | 623,433 | 312% | 685,773 | 720,061 | 756,064 | 10/05/05 |
| 3. Benito Juárez | 563,996 | 158% | 535,797 | 535,797 | 535,792 | -3/00/00 |
| 4. Coyoacán | 621,193 | 851% | 776,491 | 854,140 | 896,842 | 25/10/05 |
| 5. Cuajimalpa | 95,059 | 924% | 104,564 | 115,020 | 126,523 | 10/10/10 |
| 6. Cuauhtémoc | 843,283 | −24% | 758,955 | 721,608 | 685,528 | −10/−5/−5 |
| 7. Gustavo A. Madero | 1,569,714 | 510% | 1,883,656 | 2,072,021 | 2,175,623 | 30/10/05 |
| 8. Iztacalco | 591,445 | 1496% | 650,589 | 715,647 | 751,429 | 10/10/05 |
| 9. Iztapalapa | 1,315,063 | 1672% | 1,578,075 | 1,656,978 | 1,739,836 | 20/05/05 |
| 10. Magdalena Contraras | 179,986 | 771% | 233,981 | 280,777 | 308,854 | 30/20/10 |
| 11. Miguel Hidalgo | 561,999 | 26% | 561,999 | 561,999 | 590,098 | 00/00/05 |
| 12. Milpa Alta | 58,796 | 289% | 83,694 | 111,592 | 122,751 | 2×2000/10 |
| 13. Tlánuac | 153,061 | 739% | 229,591 | 306,122 | 336,734 | 2×2000/10 |
| 14. Tlalpan | 384,613 | 1104% | 499,996 | 599,995 | 659,994 | 30/20/10 |
| 15. Venustiano Carranza | 717,221 | 80% | 681,360 | 681,360 | 717,221 | −5/00/+5 |
| 16. Xochimilco | 226,208 | 450% | 271,449 | 325,738 | 358,311 | 20/20/10 |

## ESTADO DE MEXICO MUNICIPIOS CONURBADOS

| | (pop. 1980) | % INCREASE 1950—1980 | 1990 | 2000 | 2010 | FACTORS OR % OF GROWTH |
|---|---|---|---|---|---|---|
| 17. Atizapán de Zaragoza | 211,624 | 4124% | 232,786 | 279,343 | 307,277 | 10/20/10 |
| 18. Coacalco | 102,204 | 4154% | 112,424 | 123,666 | 136,032 | 10/10/10 |
| 19. Cuautitlán | 41,296 | 809% | 61,994 | 74,332 | 89,198 | 50/20/20 |
| 20. Cuautitlán Izcalli | 179,920 | 1924% | 233,896 | 304,064 | 364,076 | 30/30/20 |
| 21. Chalco | 81,532 | 348% | 122,298 | 146,757 | 176,108 | 50/20/20 |
| 22. Chicoloapan | 26,548 | 832% | 39,822 | 47,786 | 57,343 | 50/20/20 |
| 23. Chimalhuacán | 64,510 | 825% | 77,412 | 85,153 | 93,668 | 20/10/10 |
| 24. Ecatepec | 819,578 | 5046% | 1,065,451 | 1,278,412 | 1,406,253 | 30/20/10 |
| 25. Huixquilucan | 81,395 | 569% | 97,674 | 117,208 | 140,649 | 20/20/20 |
| 26. Ixtapaluca | 81,043 | 705% | 121,564 | 145,876 | 160,463 | 50/20/10 |
| 27. La Paz | 103,765 | 2325% | 134,894 | 161,872 | 194,246 | 30/20/20 |
| 28. Naucalpan da Juárez | 759,457 | 2382% | 1,139,185 | 1,367,022 | 1,640,426 | 50/20/20 |
| 29. Netzahualcoyctl | 1,396,854 | 23,319% | 1,676,224 | 1,843,846 | 2,028,230 | 20/10/10 |
| 30. Nicolás Romero | 117,338 | 473% | 175,067 | 228,809 | 274,570 | 50/30/20 |
| 31. Tecamec | 87,954 | 910% | 131,931 | 158,317 | 189,980 | 50/20/20 |
| 32. Tlalnepantla | 809,967 | 2613% | 1,052,957 | 1,263,584 | 1,516,257 | 30/20/10 |
| 33. Tultitlán | 142,625 | 1452% | 213,937 | 256,724 | 308,068 | 50/20/20 |

In this chapter we will examine this growth phenomenon and its consequences. We will look at methods to predict growth and also examine this possible growth by units, delegaciones and municipios conurbados. We will note current estimates of total growth in terms of the Mega-City concept. The growth will be seen as a process, where different factors impact different sub-populations. We hope to note the areas of the valley that will be most impacted, but this effort approaches the limits of social science effort.

## The Demographic Growth of Mexico City And Its Spatial Pattern

> The major hypothesis for this research suggests that the residential growth of the Mexico City study area has not been substantially influenced by the above factors, rather almost singly by the availability of public lands for rapid occupation. (W. Collins, 1974, p. 10)

In a dissertation on "The evolving spatial patterns of Metropolitan residential growth in Mexico City" William F. Collins offers a theory of demographic growth, which if correct, will have a similar predictive value until the lands run out. Collins notes that many studies of third-world cities are in fact a-spatial, but concepts of density, sprawl, and land use can not preceed without the spatial context. Collins does note how Mexico City with its often illegal settlement and title problems may differ from other areas. But in any case, the availability of "open lands" along with other inducements does help to explain the City's growth in the period he studied, 1930 to 1970. Although we might view the availability of lands as a more or less necessary factor in demographic growth (previously used lands are often re-cycled), it is probably not a sufficient factor. Still the evolving demographic picture of the ZMCM is still one of availability of land, plus the usual push-pull factors, and the policy-planning elements that are in place.

What of the history of this demographic growth? We will cite the sources which Collins uses because he is sensitive to the spatial dimensions of demographic growth. Daniel Moreno (1918, p. 67) is noted to have estimated a pre-conquest population of 500,000. Flood waters certainly effected the amount of available lands for several centuries. Because of the drainage canals and the amenities of the colonial period (available to some peoples!) the population of the colonial capital grew (Collins, p. 52) slowly to 113,000 in 1790, 137,000 in 1804, and

# PERCENT POPULATION INCREASE IN DELEGACIONS & MUNICIPIOS, 1950–80

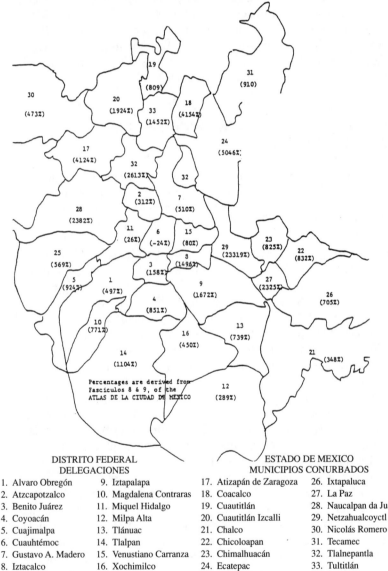

| DISTRITO FEDERAL DELEGACIONES | | ESTADO DE MEXICO MUNICIPIOS CONURBADOS | |
|---|---|---|---|
| 1. Alvaro Obregón | 9. Iztapalapa | 17. Atizapán de Zaragoza | 26. Ixtapaluca |
| 2. Atzcapotzalco | 10. Magdalena Contraras | 18. Coacalco | 27. La Paz |
| 3. Benito Juárez | 11. Miquel Hidalgo | 19. Cuautitlán | 28. Naucalpan da Juárez |
| 4. Coyoacán | 12. Milpa Alta | 20. Cuautitlán Izcalli | 29. Netzahualcoyctl |
| 5. Cuajimalpa | 13. Tlánuac | 21. Chalco | 30. Nicolás Romero |
| 6. Cuauhtémoc | 14. Tlalpan | 22. Chicoloapan | 31. Tecamec |
| 7. Gustavo A. Madero | 15. Venustiano Carranza | 23. Chimalhuacán | 32. Tlalnepantla |
| 8. Iztacalco | 16. Xochimilco | 24. Ecatepac | 33. Tultitlán |
| | | 25. Huixquilucan | |

# POSSIBLE GROWTH AREAS IN THE ZMCM 1990–2000?

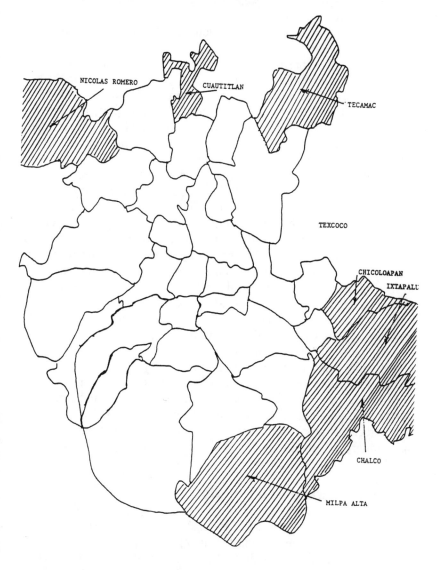

205,000 in 1838. Collins notes much conflict over public and private lands, but the point was that they were available, even if contested. The round number of 300,000 was offered for the year 1884. We won't contest any figures at this point.

Collin's scrupulousness in documenting the factors for leaving the rural areas and moving to Mexico City and environs, does diminish his single factor hypothesis about the availability of land. A clear rural crisis over living conditions and the alternative possibilities in the central valley made the migration over-determined, one might say! We have included Collin's Table I in our appendix on statistics, and one can observe different estimates being offered. We might note that so called "push" factors (rural destitution) may at one time be more efficacious than "pull" factors (such as economic opportunity). We should not neglect the high natural growth which the city has exhibited at various points. Citing a work by Stevens from 1966 Collins sees only 28% of the city's growth as being due to rural-urban migration.

Obviously Collins in focusing on land and its quality would note the preference for the better lands to the south as opposed to the alkaline soils of the old lake beds. The proximity of transportation routes and other pull factors affected all who moved within or to the city. The affluent moved to the south, and workers moved north and east. The proximity factors heavily impacted the decision to migrate itself, and will continue to do so. The social class basis of migration to the metro area, and within it are part of the demographic process. The affuent first moved south and then to the west beyond Chapultepec. The middle classes often moved to places like satellite city to the northwest, and the working class (who had already become established) moved east, northeast and northwest. Central tenements and tugurios have, of course, lost population. The uncounted Jacales and Ciudades perdidas still attract the most recent arrivals. Let us look closer at these relationships in terms of total growth and where it will occur.

## Urban Structure and Population

The Federal District consists of two sub-zones: The "Area de Desarrollo Urbano" includes 63,382 hectares or 42.6% of the total, and the "Area de conservacion Ecologia" includes 85,554 hectares or 57.4% of the total. (See "Programa General de Desarrollo Urbano, DDF, 1987–88.) The latter area is abbreviated as A.C.E. and if Mexico City is to grow enormously then it must be further invaded. Much of the

A.C.E. is to south of the city, and is being guarded by the Federal District. The vast lands to the south include the Sierra de Guadalupe and also uninhabitable barrancas (as in the Delegacion Alvaro Obregon). Maps of the population spread in the 20th century (as Peter Ward's, 1990, p. 36) show a crab-like growth growing from the north-central part of the Federal District, gradually absorbing contiguous areas in all directions. The 1988 *Atlas de la Ciudad de Mexico* (especially fasciculo 3 on "Origines y Evoluciones de la Ciudad de Mexico: Siglos XVI, XVII, XVIII, y XIX") shows the long term expansion of urban Mexico City and its population. Important for the modern expansion is Maria Delores Martinez's article in this atlas on the 1858–1910 period (Volume 3, p. 64). Colonias are shown developing in 3 sub-epochs as various class groups move from areas like the "Historic el centro." One must note the role of transportation, especially street cars (electric trolleys) in the latter part of this expansion. Public services also followed this expansion.

Mario Ramos Girault's 1971 volume "Distribution de population en la valle de Mexico" has data (as on p. 59) on the time period from 1921 to 1970, but largely relies on the 1960 Mexican census. This volume is especially important because of its "Anexo Aerofotographico." This volume shows the terrain of the city in relationship to the "Zona Forestal Publico" as well. The 120 aerial photos of the built up parts of the city are clear enough to compare with future developments. The A.C.E. or Area de Conservacion Ecologica, as this will emerge, has great meaning for the quality of life in the valley of Mexico. It will also, with restraint, delimit inhabited areas and impact the limits to demographic growth.

Peter Ward's point about social inequality being imbedded within the spatial structure of the city, country, and world systems (p. 42, for instance) can not be ignored. Basically, the present author assumes that policy decisions (what ever their genesis) are at the root of demographic spatial patterns. Ward observes how the 1954 DDF ban "stimulated a supply of plots in the state of Mexico." This policy decision spread individual housing decisions, and the current author remembers how a ban on further mobile home installation in Cook County, Illinois, meant that this University of Chicago graduate student had to take his trailer off into Indiana.

Ward (1990, p. 40) notes the spread into Ejido lands, up the southern slopes of the Ajusco, along the Puebla road, and into the rich agricultural lands to the south. Some areas have become saturated; some areas hold the line of policy against further expansion; some areas have covered up all of the usable land for habitation or other forms of "development" and some are surrounded by established park or open areas. We will try to surface assumptions about the processes at work until the year 2010 that may impact population levels and densities. Central areas, especially after the earthquake of 1985, have lost population relatively and absolutely. The policy decision to placate earthquake survivors by rebuilding in the central areas rather than dispersing the population, must be noted as having the effects of holding up population numbers in those zones. Rent control in the city center also reduced profitability, we are told, and, hence, reduced new construction there. Such are the kinds of factors involved, not to mention more distant forces of political-economy. The latter include such mega forces as debt service policy, IMF type loans, credit squeezes, and the manipulated price of world oil! A, so-called, "Free Trade Policy" might be seen as another, external mega-force. The ability to fully fund INFONAVIT AND FOVISSSTE in the 1970s led to a great increase in housing and population in various areas of the ZMCM. This was the results of decades of the "Mexican Miracle," where real growth could be passed along to the general population, and probably had to be—in order to avoid destabilizaiton of the body politic. Now, before attempting our magic act, let us examine some of the problems and forms of demographic prediction.

## Issues Of Method And Theory In Predicting For The ZMCM

Conventionally, projections into the future make no attempt to speculate about such possibilities (natural disasters, war, famine, epidemic, or mass migration) because they are essentially unforeseeable. (Shryock, 1976, page 439)

Apart from the kind of discontinuities noted in the above quote that author (and Jacob Snegel and associates) make distinctions beween populations projections, current estimates, and forecasts. We are probably more interested in the latter, namely attempting to describe the likely population and its characteristics at a future date. All projections are concerned with future growth, and it seems that back-casting is possible for "recensal" historical periods. Our goals of looking at Mexico City's alternative futures orients us toward special methodologies it seems. Our current mentors give us a framework of assumptions such as assuming that some background factors (economic conditions) will remain the same; a range of projections or a series of them may be desirable rather than just one shot in the dark; one series may be underlined as most likely; relatively simple methods can be used for middle range projections of the kind that we are undertaking; and that intermediate revisions can be helpful. As to specific methods, mathematical methods are seen as the "simplest conceptually" (p. 443), and most typically projections are sought by component methods with separate projections of fertility, mortality, immigration and emigration. We will not do the latter for lack of time, data, and our separate purposes. Projections for a city or urban area may represent other internal dynamics than for the nation as a whole, or some other sub-segment. It has only been recent that projections of urban areas have been attempted in the United States. As to the components of the ZMCM, we would expect to see a stable fertility rate, a declining mortality rate matching the country's, a continuing in-migration (at 28% or less as a result of de-centralization policies?), and perhaps greater emigration from the city than people might expect. Let us discuss forecasting in general, this time from an economic point of view, since we will also be attempting that magic act.

Forecasting usually implies numerical estimates in demography and economics. Planning is the gain, or sometimes an effort to change the outcome is attempted. The latter brings up the fantasy of control, but accuracies better than chance can occur with talented forecasting. Jeffrey Jarrett (*Business Forecasting Methods*, second edition, 1991, p. 6) discusses basic methods, both quantitative and qualitative. Extrapolative or projective methods involve such procedures as "moving averages" or "exponential smoothing." Time series decomposition techniques, as Jarrett defines it, can at least identify trends in algebraic terms. Regression models evidently are better for explaining the past. Such "econometric" models as the latter can both explain *and* predict we are told (Jarrett, p. 6). Advanced time series methods combine some of the specialized assumptions, and over time, by observing shortfalls in prediction and adjusting appropriately, more accuracy can be achieved. The idea is not to waste too much computer time when the macro-factors are uncontrollable and the micro-factors are self evident.

The present writer is equally, if not more impressed, by qualitative forecasting. Judgement must always be involved! Acquired wisdom can not be thrown out. Economic indicators, anticipation surveys, signals of recovery (as for example) are really qualitiative signposts used by economists, and there can be similar ones to light up the demographic process. The Delphi technique involving a panel of expert opinion feeding its aggregate responses back to itself may be seen as a multiplication of subjectivity by some. On the other hand, what passes for methematical certitude, may be a form of jibberish! There needs to be indicators of the macro situation in which demographic process works itself out. Unfortunately there are not too many indicators that would help to predict a world oil glut or a change in policy toward debt repayment. It may be true that much qualitative methodology is of short term use only, whereas the Delphi Technique may go beyond short and even medium horizons. As an "educated guess" the latter is not bound by any near-by signs or omens, (Jarrett, p. 407). In the latter technique, experts, so called, are kept apart except for the presentation of "averages" or typical opinions about likely futures. Repeated judgements on a panel basis may merely become a consensus making process, where truth or error will prevail. Perhaps it is less science than Ouiji board! Participants in such a panel must understand the common task, and the task of giving feedback from the coordinator is fraught with problems. This may be the most exhaustive procedure as well—surely not the quick and dirty extrapolation of numbers with a formula and a computer. Open subjectivity should not deter our prediction efforts rather than contending with hidden subjectivity. Let us go unit by unit (deligaciones and municipios conurbados), trying to surface the demographic process going on in them for the whole of the ZMCM. We will be using data from the *Atlas de la Ciudad de Mexico* (Volumes 8 and 9) on percent increase from 1950 to 1980 (derived from their census offerings), simplifying land uses, discussing future potential in terms of "saturation points" obtained, and then using any other intelligent projections we can lay our hands on in order to come up with numbers.

## Growth By Units In The ZMCM

Spatially this population growth has led to a 'wave' of rapid population expansion moving outwards, first through the DF and then into the surrounding State of Mexico. (Peter Ward, 1990, page 34)

David Drakakis-Smith in his book on the Third World City (1987, p. 1) starts out by saying that: "It must be admitted at the outset that there is little homogeniety in the nature of urban growth in the Third World. . . ." This "wave" of growth and expansion for Mexico City can not be that unusual, however. We want to understand this growth for the ZMCM by looking at the pattern in its subunits, knowing ahead of time that each of these units is different because of the more or less arbitrary manner in which the unit boundaries were drawn in relation to topography. Much of what Collins said about the role of available land is explicit in Ward's description above. In this section we will look at the characteristics of each of the major subunits of the metro area. It is in these units that the process will occur, as all of the individual decisions and those of much larger institutions work themselves out. The total increase will emerge arithmatically and in the final reality of the aggregate. The qualities of the total population will also emerge to the extent that our brief discussion allows. Ward stresses the "reproduction of social inequality" in this process, and we do not disagree with this assessment. Here we just want to get a handle on the growth (for sure?) process, by looking at what may happen in the subunits.

The *Atlas de la Ciudad de Mexico* details the 16 delegaciones and identifies an additional 17 "municipios conurbados." Using the census numbers they provide by decades from 1950 to 1980 we computed a total percent of change. (Cuauhtemoc in the old center lost 24%) Miguel Hidalgo (+26%) and Venustiano Carrenza (+80%) did not double. Amongst the delegaciones, and given the variety of existing land uses including about 50% of the area in habitation, they probably will not grow much in the next few decades. We have plotted this 30 year percent change on the accompaning map, and one can see the kind of changes that Peter Ward is refering to in the above quotation. Some observers talk about 3 or 4 rings of growth, but there are obviously other configurations. We are not convinced of the meaning of this statistic, because if an area previously had few people, then any substantial increase looks considerable. Certainly "trends" are not revealed directly by this statistic. The move amongst the delegaciones to the southeast (Iztacalco, Iztapalpa, and Tlalpan) seems to be "real" enough however. With 1100 to 1600% increases from a real base of 30,000 to 70,000 in 1950, this was a real settlement pattern. For different reasons including DF policy these three delegaciones might not be expected to grow outrageously. Tlalpan is up against open areas and protected forests it seems, and the other two delegaciones would have to see a change in residential densities—which is possible. The fifth highest growth rate amongst the 16 delegaciones was the southern one of Coyoacan with an 841% increase, doubling every decade from a 1950 base of 73,000. Given the type of housing in this area and the nature of the uses of the remaining open areas (also University-service related) it is not to be expected to double in coming decades. (It would be helpful to have the

1990 census at this point.) In our second column of this table we have given the percentage of land used for habitation and it ranges among the 16 delegaciones from 3% (Milpa Alta) to 78% (Alvaro Obregon). One area with a very small percent of land in habitation, to the south western barranca lands is Cuajimalpa which increases 924% but this meant only an increase from 10,000 to 95,000 people. The landscape would have to be greatly altered for an increase to occur here. One delegacion in el centro, Benito Juarez, showed a 158% increase from 1950 to 1980, but trendlike it dropped 10% from 1970 to 1980. No simple use of statics is being advocated here. How shall we then make our own projections? Two delegaciones, Milpa Alta and Tlahuac, are noted by Ward (from Partida, 1987) as doubling by the year 2000. We would be forced to bow to the expertise of a writer in the *Atlas* but also note that each area is up against the policy question on open areas in general. Pressure from campesinos has led to equivocation on Federal District policy, according toWard. One must remember the underlying pressures of residential density, which except for some Asian mega-cities, are the highest in the world, (see Ward, p. 40). Before looking at the changes in the Municipios conurbados, let us repeat that the sub-units have very different capacities for growth, whatever the total ZMCM becomes.

## Growth By Units In The ZMCM: Estado De Mexico

However, in terms of a planning process which embodies legislative plans, zoning, and regulations for the implementation of a plan, the process is nowhere as advanced in the State of Mexico. (Ward, 1990, p. 127)

It may be true that at this very minute the above situation is being remedied, or that a process has started. Our concern in this section is to look at the likely demographic growth in these adjacent "municipios conurbados," and we will look at the planning problems later. They are linked, of course.

In absolute terms the 17 munis range from 28,500 people (Chicolopan) to Netzahualcoyotl (1,396,854). The average size is about 180,000 people. About 3,050,000 people were recorded here in the 1980 census, and this will jump substantially in the 1990 report. However, only Tlalneplanta in the north and Netzahualcoyotl in the east grew tremendously, so far. The latter area my well be saturated although it more than doubled in the decade of the 1970s. As Nunez, et al (Atlas, p. 356) point out the latter muni constitutes as of 1980, over 28% of the part of the State of Mexico that is urban. The incredible population density of this area is reflected in the low level of services (40% without electricity) and the strength of the popular movements that have sought amelioration. What can we say about this range of munis and their potential for demographic change in the next decades?

As we have noted above, the growth in the State of Mexico seems to have been heaviest so far to the east and north of the center city. The largest land use in *all* of these 17 munis is non-urban, agricultural, park or generally "open." Ejidal lands are a significant part of these subareas, as with Chalco where many hectares were alienated. Much land is also described as of "no uso" or as "areas baldias." Commercial cores do in fact exist. The percentage of urban-type lands that are in to habitation ranges from 2% (Ixtapa) to 41% (Netzahualcoyotl), with the average being about 18%. At various points in Ward's volume the following are designated as of high growth potential for the 1990–2000 period: Nicolas Romero, Cuautitlan, and Tecamac in the north, and Chicoloapan, Ixtapaluca, Chalco and Milpa Alta in the south. (See our map, page 25.) Several of these areas had relatively small rates of growth from 1950 to 1980. Of the munis in 1980 only 3 had substantial populations: Ecatepec (819578), Tlalnepantla (809,967) and, of course, Netzahualcoyotl (at 1,396,854). Our table entitled "Growth by Units" shows great percentage increases from 1950 to 1980, because most had miniscule populations at the outset. The demographics are changing, however. Our column entitled Growth Projections in Numbers and Percents represents a *low growth scenario*, when in fact the upcoming release of the 1990 census will show how conservative these numbers are. Our table shows higher percentage (factors) growth rates for the 17 munis than the 16 delegaciones, because more available land is to be found in the former, policy matters aside. Some of the increases in units will be as a result of inter-ZMCM movement, of course. Our predicted factors for growth show an across the board decline, because we believe that a point of diminishing returns for migration to the ZMCM has been obtained, and a policy of decentralization must be established for Mexico. Luis Unikel has predicted such a slowing up of growth for the ZMCM. (See, for instance, Unikel and Garza, 1976, "El desarrolo urbano de Mexico: Diagnostico e implicaciones futuras.") In any case, with this low growth scenario the total population for the 33 units would be about 17,022,484 in 1990 (we will be able to check this out very shortly). By the turn of the century our low growth estimate would obtain

19,115,680 people, and 20,786,356 by the year 2010. More important than such very tentative numerology, would be some idea of the demographic processes at work.

Given the sometimes operaitonal DDF policy on further development on open areas, and the obvious needs for planning in adjacent areas, especially in the State of Mexico, Growth will assume a given shape. We asked the lead question in terms of whether a "saturation point" had been obtained. To follow Collin's lead, is there land available? Of course habitation densities can be altered by the type of housing units, and existing developments can be altered to increase densities. Looking at delegaciones Cuauhtemoc and Miguel Hidalgo we do not expect them to grow. Ward sees them as facing "urban consolidation." The earthquake was something that will continue to impact these two areas also. Delegaciones like Coyoacan have open areas which are not likely to be altered in their function, nor is the housing style likely to be altered in the coming decades. Lands adjacent to the University could be altered in the coming decades. Lands adjacent to the University could be altered for student-faculty use, but that has not been the pattern so far. The industry in a delegacion like Azcapotzalco is not likely to go away (even though the government just closed a large Pemex refinery) so its growth will be minimal, even though many workers must commute across the city from the east. Benito Juarez started down in the 1970–1980 period, and this probably will continue. Some urban areas in el centro may face gentrification by mid-next century but there is no rush for this kind of habitat at present. For delegacion Gustavo Madero the invasion of lands may be over, but the 1990 census will no doubt show a bump in size. Ward cites Partida as seeing Milpa Alta and Tlahuac as "doubling" by the year 2000. This may happen for many of the 33 units of the ZMCM. Ward sees Tlalpan, to the south, as facing "gentrification and infilling." With only 7% of its large area into habitation, it may well increase its population. At the south end of this delegacion are of course mountains and forests, but some lands are designated as "rural" or "open." Many see real conflict over land use in areas like Xochimilco, and agricultural-conservation uses may give way to habitation.

Data for our first three columns in our table on "Growth by Units" has been derived and extrapolated from volumes 8 and 9 in the *Atlas*. We have only ourselves to blame for the growth projections, and most of the notions about process. Many macro-factors can alter the over-all as well as the unit situations. Yet many elements are likely to remain in place, especially existing developments of land. Better transportation will increase the centrifugal movement, and a change in the type of economic activity will do likewise. The processes within the munis include an absorbsion around old pueblo cores, as in Coacalco. New industry, as in Cuautitlan, will attract many people, especially workers. Further ejido lands will probably be alienated in areas like Chalco. Water shortages will slow development in munis like Tecamac despite its recent surge. These are the kinds of factors involved but the availability of land is still a prerequisite. The current author has seen land being made available by monstrous rearrangment of the topography in the northwest areas of the ZMCM. Such efforts can alter the demographic pattern as well. The ring of mountains and foothills need not slow demographic growth. It is possible that a spill-over effect may leapfrog (pardon the mixed metaphore!) to urban centers like Puebla, Queretaro, and Cuernavaca—which has already happened, of course.

Demography is concerned with the motives for migration, and with our table on the "locational process" we have tried to anticipate the choice factors of various groups and to give examples of the likely destinations. Decisions by corporations or "groupos" as well as by governments in terms of infrastructure may be crucial.

## A High Growth Scenario

> Metropolitan growth in Latin America, therefore is of alarming magnitude and will continue to be so in the foreseeable future. (Violich and Daughters, 1987, page 55)

The above quote is from a chapter called "Relentless Metropolitan Growth." It is aimed at all of the southern Hemisphere mega-cities, and these authors project a whopping 31,679,000 for the Mexico City "urban area" by the year 2000. This increase of 10,000,000 over their 1990 estimate of 21,228,000 is much higher than our conservative projections. They cite the Reference Bureau for their data in a publication called "World population data sheet." Another such gain would place the estimate about 90% above ours. At this point we do not know the basis for this very high projection. The internal nature of the demographic base and its location in the ZMCM, may be a more important consideration. Violich and Daughters in stressing "relentless" growth emphasize the depopulation of the hinterland, but his does not seem to be true of Mexico. If we add another 10,000,000 this total would be over 41,000,000. The projection could have been for more than this increase, however.

Richard Moore in an article on "Urbanization and Housing Policy in Mexico" (Aspe and Sigmund, 1985, p. 329) take the year 2000 figure of 30,860,700 for the MAMC and imply that a 5% growth rate per year would be possible. Moore's data is derived from Garza and Schteingart, 1978. This projection would lead (see our table in the appendix) to a whopping 50,268,824 in the year 2010. More important than simple projections is an analysis of the processes at work.

Orlandina Oliveira and Humberto Muniz Garcia have tried to deal with these processes in their article "concentration or deconcentration? Mexico City and its Region." They are concerned with the whole "central-eastern region (which) includes the Federal district and the states of Hidalgo, Mexico, Morelos, Puebla, Queretaro and Tlaxcala" (p. 37). The continued high population of this region is observed since Aztec times, and the processes continue. The region is on the way "to becoming an integrated urban system." Many favor deconcentration although Oliveira and Garcia cite Garza as warning against industrial dispersal in 1980. The issues of economic and demographic concentration are linked, of course. Should both elements go to the periphery of this region or indeed, outside of it? Mexico City has more than industry, and diversification into other services raises other subissues.

As to the processes at work, increases due to migration were more important from 1940 to 1950, but natural increases were more important from then on (Oliveira and Garcia, p. 43). Fertility started downward in the mid 1970's for the region and the country as a whole. Even with reductions in both natural and migratory processes, the "absolute magnitude of the flows continued to be considerable." The direction of the internal flows has been both to the north and to the central region, and is likely to continue. Up to 1985 (see p. 43) Mexico City got the highest percent of new immigrants in the central region, with Toluca next. More females also have gone in these directions, meaning, perhaps, more future potential for natural increases.

Oliveira and Garcia note changes in the labor market that continue to favor the Federal district and the State of Mexico. The tertiary labor force is declining in these same areas. "Specialization and modernizations" are not clear as processes in these areas, but changes are to be expected in the labor force. Still these authors expect "inertia" to continue in the metropolitan regions (p. 49). Movement within the region as a whole, may be the most important fact to the year 2010.

# Chapter 4

# Several Kinds of Urban Economy and Polity

One of the most vexing problems facing Mexican urban planners and economists if the fact that Mexico City has expanded far beyond its traditional administrative boundaries. The capital was once contained within the limits of the Federal District created in 1824, shortly after Independence. But in recent decades, Mexico City has sprawled into the surrounding state of Mexico, which now accounts for almost 45 percent of the metropolitan zone's inhabitants. (Kandell, p. 552)

We have placed economic and political matters together in this chapter because they go together in reality. The above quote from Kandell's *La Capital* shows this very well. The conflict of economic interests between various political constituencies and units is complex and intense. The ZMCM is split in many ways. We will preceed by looking at a variety of economic scenarios for Mexico as a whole, even though the role of the ZMCM may not be self evident in these A-Priori scenarios. We will surface various facts about how the Federal district, etc., has done as part of the total country's economic fate. Should we assume the status-quo-ante will prevail in the future?

Next we'll look at the political makeup of various constituencies in the ZMCM who will make a difference in the next three decades. It's obvious that large, unpredictable forces will determine conditions of political economy rather than various groups of actors, but even though "things are in the saddle and are riding mankind" we might still change horses or shoot it!

## The Economy of Mexico City

Alan Riding notes that the Mexican "economic miracle" was an economic success (for some) for four decades (1985, p. 134). An average growth rate of six percent was impressive even though it was sagging even before the sharp crisis of the 1980's. Big subsidies for public works, for cheap food, and some social amenities preserved "stability," however.

Prior to 1946, growth had been "unplanned," but then the regime of Miguel Aleman shifted to "import substitution" development. The latter stressed growth in the private sector by encouraging domestic and foreign investment. Much of that investment centered on Mexico City and the Federal District. To quote Alan Riding again (p. 257):

> After the war, industrialization for "import substitution" became official policy and encouraged continuing peasant migration to the cities. As Mexico City expanded, its magnetic force grew: Both foreign and domestic investment were drawn to the largest market and migrants went where the jobs were to be found.

Riding notes that Mexico City (p. 258) "accounted for 38% of the gross domestic product, 48% of manufacturing industry, 45% of commercial activity, 52% of services, 60% of transportation, and 69% of bank assets." We want in this chapter to review the economic history of Mexico City, and then try to forecast, based on contemporary economic data, where Mexico City will be headed around the year 2010.

## An Economic History of Mexico City

Frances Berdan (in *Mexican Studies*, Vol. 3, No. 2, Summer 1987, p. 235) notes how important the role of cotton was in the economy of Aztec Mexico. Cotton is a lowland crop requiring a constant warm temperature. Much of the total production, however, was woven in urban capitals (Berdan, p. 241), and a good share of the cotton crop was consumed locally or went unrecorded for a variety of reasons. Bernardino de Sahagun's Florentine Codex notes (1950, Book, 10: 75) how raw cotton moved through such markets as Tlateloco to household weavers and spinners (Berdan, p. 247). Yucca Cape fibers were also marketed through these centers, although aimed at a less affluent consumer. Cotton in various processed forms may have been a medium of exchange. From various materials, Berdan (p. 250) offers the idea that finished cotton goods out of Tenochtitlan and Tlateloco may have been the highest level of economic and political transactions. Elaborately decorated articles of cotton clothing were a many spendored exchange medium just as they are today. These items probably were the most negotiable of foreign trade items as well. As a form of tribute from warm low land areas to highland elite areas, cotton was a fast moving commodity. Evidently, Maguey and Yucca fibers were more restricted in their movements (Berdan, p. 253).

While there were numerous types of commodities (and services?) centered out of Tenochtitlan, cotton was one of the more important. Ceramics, obsidian, cult goods, and luxury items of feathers, metals, clay and animal products were also dispersed in this early economy. Let us now turn to the economy of Mexico City and nearby environs during the period of Spanish domination. As a national economic unit it will obviously be linked to the outside world—not necessarily in a fashion to enhance itself or its hinterland.

## Mexico City and Its Economy in the 1600 to 1821 Period

Spanish domination lasted three centuries, one month and two weeks. During most of this period, Mexico City dominated its hinterland. As Fehrenbach notes (*Fire and Blood*, 1973, p. 260):

> The city of Mexico because of its population, it's position as the capital, and its role of the center of Hispanic culture, always dominated. Beyond Mexico, the European population was very largely confined to the Spanish-built towns that sprang up throughout the Maseta during the sixteenth century.

Fehrenbach notes how the economy and corresponding social structure of these towns developed (p. 261). Lower class Spanish immigrants filled a void which the Creoles could not, hence there were groups "from carpenters to grocers." These immigrants had a "petit-bourgeois mentality." They "opened shops, peddled wares and served as major-domos, and kept accounts for the haciendas." Although seen as "gloomy misers," they were the basis for much economic activity. To correct the last sentence one must be aware of how much economic activity was being sweated out of the remaining indio population slaving away on haciendas or near the towns. Fehrenbach observes (p. 264) how haciendas and grain merchants conspired to create monopolistic prices. The smuggling of illicit silver to the British, Dutch, and Chinese in exchange for "contraband" (p. 266) had the effect of stiltifying home grown industry and commerce.

All of these factors led to an incredible dichotomy between urban richness and rural decrepitude. The latter has persisted, of course, and Mexico City's splendor in a cultural-architectural sense represented a collossal, exploitive relationship. Farming and ranching in the more fertile rural areas did provide for considerable wealth being generated outside of the urban areas. Leather goods, meat, grains, vegetables, and animal gear were supplied to the mining camps and towns, for instance.

One must remember that the main economy of the capital, Mexico City, was based on taxation while tax avoidance was a national pastime. In the 1700s there were reforms that allowed for capital expenditure in Mexico City and elsewhere. Under a series of Viceroys after 1750 some of these tax monies built gardens, cleaned canals, added sanitation improvements and built palaces—like the one on Chapultepec hill. The jobs created helped to reduce poverty to some extent and must have provided an economic boost in Mexico City.

Alan Riding notes (*Distant Neighbors*, 1985, p. 31) how important silver production was to the economy, but also how new industries were established to satisfy the needs of one million criolles and 50,000 peninsulares. Slow growth in the latter populations, but faster growth in indio and poor mestizo population made for no great economic boom in Mexico City or elsewhere. For the affluent household, luxury goods were the main basis for industrial production. Food and clothing production were likely to be done in the household itself. European products were available in shops and via peddlers. Permanent and weekly markets continued down to the present time and represent a significant portion of the monetary flow.

## The Contemporary Economy of The Valley of Mexico

Nearly all leftist organizations agree that Mexico's economic crisis began, not in 1982, but a decade earlier. They point to 1970–71 as the end of the "Mexican Economic Miracle" . . . (Enrique Semo, page 25)

Enrique Semo notes the "silent crisis" that emerged fully in 1982. It involved massive unemployment, production slowdowns, crippling inflation, an unbearable national debt, capital flight and declining public and private investments (p. 24 in Carr and Montoya). The Federal district was not immune to these drastic events, but may have been better able to buffer itself in some ways. Let us review a variety of scenarios by economists or political economists and especially note their predictions for Mexico City in these futurest projections.

## Individual Economic Scenarios

We are focusing on writers from 1980 on, but this does nto mean that previous work by such writers as Clark Reynolds, Beltran de Rio, Brothers and Solis, Ayala, Gonzalez Casanova, David Baskin, C. Tello, Victor Uquidi, Wilford Sykes, and Menno Vellinga are without value as economic soothsayers. Most of these writers dealt with economic strategies or policies while hedging on which ones would actually be followed. As any academic dabbler knows, no country has been even close in determining or even anticipating its long term economic future.

John Bailey's three scenarios are obvious and probably overly simple. They are real options however, and matched by other economic pundits, so they must be taken seriously. Drift or perhaps a mixture of economic moves favoring "nationalist" or "internationalist" models is a likely "policy." The way political economies are moving in the Eastern European sector it is likely that "restructuring" will involve a mix there as well. Drift may be the wave of the future for us all!

It is instructive to quote Bailey on the problems of negative predictions (p. 178):

> Mexican government officials sometimes label as catastrofistas those doomsayers who see unacceptable futures fraught with violence or increasing misery for their country. A hard look at the future might lead some to dabble in disaster scenarios. But this sort of attitude merely contributes to self fulfilling prophecy.

Bailey's point is that there are many scenarios that can succeed, especially with a pragmatic attitude toward "restructuring." Bailey seems to favor "new policies to promote foreign investment" (p. 178). He fully realizes the burden of external *and* internal debt, and stresses the probable consequences of certain choices. "Greater overt tensions" would be a likely consequence of the opening-up option, and this would be added to tensions generated by growing social inequalities in the past few decades (see p. 180). Would the middle-class put up with this same reversal?

If higher growth rates are to be Mexico's salvation, then this would be associated with more insecurity, greater environmental degradation, and perhaps more coercion. Bailey puts the least faith in state-led growth and puts forward a list of obstacles to this scenario. Although the intelligentsia and some of the business community still favor state-led growth, Bailey says that because of a need for missing state con-

# ECONOMIC PROJECTION

| Econonmist, etc. | (generally) Types of Scenarios | Consequences for Mexico City |
|---|---|---|
| *John Bailey* "Governing Mexico: The Politics of Economic Transformation," 1988 | Three Broad Routes 1. The nationalist school 2. Drift 3. Economic opening— internationalization | — More power concen- trated in Mexico City? |
| *Jeffrey Bortz* "Wages and Economic Crisis" in Carr and Montoya, 1986 * see also "Industrial Wages in Mexico City" 1939-1975) | Compares bourgeois and Marxist theories of the crisis. (Equilibrium with "cy- cles") versus (the Law of Surplus Value and the tendency toward falling profits.) | A contraction in wages or an increase in efficiency as solutions would drive the working classes in Mexico City beyond PRI and toward an alternate economy? |
| *Robert Looney* Economic Policy-Making in Mexico, 1985. Chapter on "The Policy-making Dilemma." | Policy Options: 1. Variable inflation, slow growth, stop & go fluctuations 2. Declining inflation, increased unemploy- ment and moderate growth 3. Moderate growth and stable inflation | — The three options all eventually destabilized — The government should opt for *either* nationalist or integrationist models, (pro-Gatt) — Mexico City will remain patriotic, hence muddle through |
| *Judith Teichman* Policy Making in Mexico: from Boom to Crisis, 1988, Boston, Allen & Unwin | A "political economist" and "dependendista" she stresses the fate of periph- eral capitalism and the "relative autonomy" of a weak state. — clear directions and intentions are hard to depict | — No references to such a unit, the implication being that the action exists elsewhere and the consequences for Mexico City are aggre- gated—as for the whole nation |
| *Roberto Newell G., Luis Rubio F.*: Mexico's Dilemma: The Political Origins of Economic Crisis | Political consensus pre- ceeds growth, a "modus vivendi" is needed. | The captial and PRI are at odds via PAN or the FRENTE. M.C. is to be *neutralized.* |

trolled financing it could not occur. If it did occur, it would be very inflationary. It would also decrease competitive forms of democracy because of a need for a reinvigorated centralization. Massive social mobilization would be needed (p. 186). One aspect of this kind of mobilization may have great importance for Mexico City, namely the building of infrastructure (and housing, water, education and health) in medium sized cities. This could "relieve pressures on Mexico's three larger cities." It is possible that the other two development scenarios would not push decentralization.

What of the implications of the other scenarios for Mexico City? Robert Looney's volume, *Economic Policy Making in Mexico*, covers the period into the 1982 crises. Our table notes three policy options, but he covers a wide range of specific policy areas, as inflation, an oil-based economy, and various "stabilization" programs. Various control simulations and forecasted values are presented (see chapter 14, etc.) in order to look around the corner for a point at which "stabilization" is to be achieved. Stabilization may be a synonym for paying off its external debt on very unfavorable terms. The 15 billion dollars that Mexico received for oil in 1983 would merely go to pay interest (p. 261).

Looney's only references to the fate of Mexico City in these stabilization efforts relate to the decentralization of industry—away from Mexico City (p. 26). Also, a restructuring of banking in the country and Mexico City would probably play down the role of the capital (p. 66). Noting the National Industrial Development Plan (1977), Looney observed how "the metropolitan area of Mexico City had been declared an area of controlled growth" (p. 87). Such fond hopes for "control" and decentralization are possible and desirable outcomes, but they mean more than just "relieving the pressure on Mexico City and the major secondary cities . . . " (Bailey, 1988, p. 185).

Much of the analysis noted here so far focuses on the national unit. Our approach to Mexico City stresses its broader environment in the world economy, and Judith Teichman's *Policy Making in Mexico: From Boom to Crisis*, (1988, Allen & Unwin). In Teichman's analysis, units less than the great triad of foreign and domestic capitalists and the barely autonomous state are hardly noticeable. Units like PEMEX achieved power by going along with outside interests or playing various roles for the Mexican state. Hence, Pemex to the "quasi-populists" was overly expansionistic and a vulnerable target when oil prices dropped in the early 1980's. These kinds of "para states" may have some autonomy, but often are in a zero-sum power game situation. Cities play no consolidated roles in these type of macro games, they are not even a unit of analysis; mere epiphenomenon.

## Speaking of Macro-Phenomenon Versus Epi-Phenomenon

Also, adjustments for extreme values associated with unusual and unpredictable events are made. This process of adjustment for extremes is made by calculating the standard deviations. (Jeffrey Jarrett, *Business forecasting Methods*, 1991, page 121.)

Quantitative wizards, as above, will always have a simple method for dealing with the unexpected phenomenon, outside the range of expected events. What would these macro, unexpected events by like for Mexico and Mexico City? We must remember our time frame when we discuss forecasting at all; namely we are talking here about gross qualities of the economic, social, cultural, and political systems. Large scale events that would impact the unit of our analysis in an economic sense would include a victory in the 1994 and subsequent national elections by the frente of C. Cardenas whose platform includes debt renegotiation on a substantial basis, returning privatized enterprizes to the public sector, creating more meaningful employment for millions, and, generally enhancing the public sector. Unilaterally cancelling the international debt, would create quite an economic set of waves! Another mega-event would be a 50% increase or decrease in the price of a barrel of oil. Spyros G. Makridakis in his volume *Forecasting, Planning and Strategy for the 21st Century* (1990, p. 75), has a chapter on "Identifying Megapatterns: Trends versus Cycles") in which he notes that the price per barrel of oil has fluctuated in constant dollars from 1860 to the late 1980s from $4 to $34, with the period from 1880 to 1970 being relatively constant between $5 and $10. However, the late 1970s and early 1980s seen a major price hike, a fact not lost on many policy makers!

Other megapatterns, as Makridakis calls them could include a, so-called, "free trade agreement," the end of the "parastatal culture" in Mexico, real economic regionalism, or a totally unanticipated new gestalt of economic relationships. Looking ahead 2 or 3 decades is relatively short range prediction, but applecarts have been overturned many times when one looks back that range of time. In the 1960s, for instance, the Mexican Miracle was in full bloom. In the early 1970s Echeverrias "reforms" were like a large fireworks display. The roller-coaster ride after that could not have been predicted! Someone who predicted these events, would have had to have had a random delivery nural, brain system! Perhaps there is less continuity in dynamic, economic systems than in any other, given the nature of venture capitalism bringing about its own temporary closing down. Perhaps, we should reread our Shumpater, about such cycles and their spastic qualities. Are we dealing with Kondratieff, 70 year cycles? Expansions and down-swings, no doubt, will be part of our legacy; but aren't we interested in something else? Perhaps, a more "mature" economy might be forth-coming? What about more re-distribution? Can there be fewer "Un-wanted fluctuations"? As Makridakis observes, (1990, p. 77) there are such disasters as Chernobyl and Bhopal, even though other major eco-nomic disasters have been avoided. It seems that human economies have an enertia factor, in the long run. But, what wit (no doubt an econo-mist!) was it, who noted that in the long-run, we are certainly, all dead. As this author notes, long term prediction involves three tasks, going back in history as far as possible, separating cycles from trends(?), and then in a "transparent and rational" manner determining how long the trend will continue! Such is the stuff of "Mumbo-jumbo"!

Economics does not have to remain guided by an "invisible hand," it can be guided by the less than omniscient hand of politics. Before looking at the political constituencies in greater Mexico City let us look at one economist in depth and then summarize economic variables that may have a greater impact on the city.

## Heavy Thoughts From Economists: HIGH CLASS WAFFLING

The 1990's are even more uncertain largely because of external factors over which Mexico has little influence. (Looney, 1982, page 230)

Mexico City as with the country as a whole lives in a global econ-omy. We are, for ever told, that it is warming up. Robert Looney in 1982 assumed "It is reasonable to assume" that "Mexico would find it expedient to consolidate . . . " The world glut of oil was the downsiz-ing clue, and the gulf warfare additionally told the world that expensive oil or relief from debt was not in the cards! Looney notes that Mexico's expansion on the slippery wings of oil has made them vulnerable at the same time (Circa, 1981). They could open the taps for domestic produc-tion but like Iraq in the post war period, would not be given a license to relieve themselves internationally. Looney's list of "possible strate-gies" includes "a policy of deversified industrialization"; possibly more government employment and expansion of the service sector. Mexico City has benefited much from previous industrialization, especially from the importsubstitution phase. Looney believes that the Mexican economy is policy-driven, and the "longer-termed strategy of economic development most likely over the next two decades in light of existing problems will be a continuation of the patterns established in the National Industrial development plan" (p. 195). Econometric forecasting is policy derived, if we wish to believe so! The use of "traditional monetary tools" may have a desired effect and Looney admits the choice is between "the better of two evils" selling off oil reserves or "public financing through foreign debt" (p. 197). The horns of all economic dilemmas, it seems, are pointed at vital areas in the living organism. What Looney seems of most help is the recognition of the conservativism based on "colonial memories of fast exploitation of non-renewable mineral resources for export." The National wish for modernization and development, now only a reality for urban dwellers, can be caught in this dilemma. The planners in Mexico know full well that a 30 to 40 year ratio of production to proven reserves of oil is the real time frame in which the Mexican economy exists. Nationism may be part of the decision Matrix, but the "family jewels" can only be sold once.

## If we were really into prediction. . . .

There is a great need to revise the country's system of planning (quoting Lopez Portillo) in order to fill the current gap in decision making that exists not only between the various ministries in Mexico City but also between the decision makers in the capital and those in the provinces. (Looney, 1982, page 241)

In a book entitled "Development Alternatives of Mexico: Beyond the 1980s" Robert Looney tries to predict a decade ahead (see chapter seven). Forecasting procedures involved setting up a "numerical solution" which took into consideration "structural equation(s) that depict the basic economic forces at work" and then identifying the exogenous (U.S. and world economy) variables that Mexico must live within. There is a neat dichotomy between internal (endogenous) and external (exogenous) variables, and also between possible policy variables and those which are immutable, it seems. We could perhaps, find a "numberifcal solution" to Mexico City's economic future in Looney's prognostications. He highlights "performance deficiencies" (deficits), major policy variables (government investment), and a balance in the dollar-peso ratio. The over-all "Desarrollo Estabilizator" is important for economic growth or decline of the country or its subunits.

Economists seem full of truisms. Investments must match priorities, or else it will not match them! If you handle economic instruments poorly, then you will drop them or to quote Looney (p. 197) "optimiza-tion of the capital growth stock is synonymous with maximizing the rate of growth of real gross domestic product." Yet there exist indepen-dent variables, whose impact or causal efficiency are "real" and must be reckoned with. The exogenous variables Looney chooses to deal with are the projected U.S.-Mexican exchange rates and the export value of oil and industrial products. Our chapter on urban theory recog-nized that Mexico exists within what Wallerstein has called "world system." Mexico City whether metropolis or dependent satellite or a combination of the two has its fate linked to these "exogenous" fac-tors. We need to identify both internal and external variables that will impact Mexico City in the next two decades. Looney, on a very reason-able basis, projects his basic variables with numerically stated values a full decade ahead (p. 223). From Looney's lists of variables we have selected the following which would most directly affect Mexico City. The assumption behind these choices is that Mexico City has a continu-ing economic product and role—with some changes envisioned.

Looney's 1990–1995 forecast stressed (p. 224) consumption factors, a deceleration of inflation (due to a decline in oil production), stable expansion (at 6.5%) and the size of the government deficit. Are these predictable given the uncertainty of the world economy, Circa 1992? Are they likely to go together as a case of economic consistency? (Few thought that stagflation was a set of compatible happenings!) We know that U.S. President Bush's ventures in gulf warfare and "peace mak-ing" are aimed at controlling the price of crude (at a low, but not too low level) will affect Mexico's economic future. The "oil syndrome," with flat out expansion, will not likely reoccur. Yet Mexico (and Mexico City's) diversification should provide some relief in any world market situation. Also we might argue with Looney that "a prudent oil policy" is likely into the future (see p. 229). Looney notes some independence for Mexico's economic fate (p. 229). Even as an economist Looney notes a loss of confidence (backlash) by outside investors if there was a conservative attempt to bolster the PRI (or an unthinkable victory by the left?) Would a narrowing of the gap in per capita incomes between Mexico and the U.S. mean less migration abroad—but continue high to Mexico's urban centers or northern border? These are all good ques-tions with respect to our problems of prediction. Now to note the vari-ables most likely to impact Mexico City.

# ECONOMIC VARIABLES WITH HIGH IMPACT ON MEXICO CITY

| VARIABLE | TYPE OF IMPACT ON M.C.? | EXOGENOUS OR ENDOGENOUS * | POLICY * MANIPULABLE? | IMPACT IN NEXT 20 YEARS |
|---|---|---|---|---|
| CITY'S SHARE OF EXPORT ECONOMY | IF OIL, THEN GIDDY INFLATION? EXPORT SUBSTITUTION HAS MADE A DIFFERENCE? | EX/END | ? | CONSERVATIVE ON EXPORTS, NAT. ECONOMY? (AUTARCKY) |
| CITY'S SHARE OF FEDERAL BUDGET | 79% OF CITY'S BUDGET FROM FEDERAL GOV. IN '82. | ENDOGENOUS | YES, VERY | D.D.F. CAN'T TAX ITSELF; MAY WITH HOME RULE. |
| ECON. SPILL-OVER FROM ADJACENT STATES (MEXICO, MORELOS) | PRIMATE CITY "SYNDROME" & CONURBATION WILL CONTINUE | ENDOGENOUS | 70% IN PLACE | EQUALIZATION WITH PER CAPITA INCOME WITH U.S. WILL DRAW MORE ACTIVITY HERE? |
| LOCAL TAX POWERS | REAL ESTATE RATES SUFFER? HOME RULE WILL CHANGE THINGS. | ENDOGENOUS | CONTRADICTION WILL BE RESOLVED | |
| REGIONALIZATION OF INDUST. PRODUCTION | WILL MAQUILADORES PERSIST? | END/EXOG | OF COURSE | OFF-SHORE PRODUCTION WILL BE STOPPED BY POPULIST U.S. GOV.? (G.N.P. VS G.D.P.?) |
| BLOOD DRAWN BY NATIONAL DEBT | DRASTIC, BUT MORE ON RURAL MODERNIZATION? | EXOGENOUS | YES, BY EASING AUSTERITY | MUST BE A DEAL WITH INTER-NATIONAL LENDERS |
| SPECIFIC BUILDING OF INFRASTRUCTURE | SEE GARZA, ET AL. ON METRO EXPANSION, ETC. | ENDOGENOUS | YES | USER TAXES MAY HELP |
| TYPES OF PRODUCTION | SERVICE/INDUSTRY/ AGRI-CULTURE/PRIMARY RESOURCES | EXOG/END | PARTIALLY | ECONOMIC MODERNIZATION WILL HEAVILY IMPACT M.C. |
| SALARIES/WAGES OF TYPES OF WORKERS | CHANGING RAPIDLY, AS WITH PREVIOUS VARIABLE | ENDOGENOUS | PARTIALLY | " " |
| VELOCITY OF INFORMAL ECONOMY | SUSTAINS "MARGINALS" & UNDERWRITES LABOR MARKET. | ENDOGENOUS | YES, WITH A JOBS POLICY | ALWAYS HAS EXISTED, POLICY MAY INCREASE BY REGRESSIVE APPROACHES. |
| TYPE OF CONSUMER SPENDING/ SAVINGS | CAPITAL VS. BASIC VS. LUXERY? | ENDOGENOUS | TAX POLICY, YES | TAX POLICY MUST BE INCREA-singly directive |
| INFLATION/INVESTMENT PROPENSITY | CONFIDENCE VARIES | END/EXOG. | YES, ESPECIALLY | CORRUPTION IN STOCK MARKET, MONEY MANIPULATION |

## Several Kinds of Polity For Mexico City

In Mexico City the power structure that has evolved is one of control, not one of development. (Peter Ward, "Defending the high ground, 1989, page 320.)

Mass insurrection or even mass civil disobedience . . . would, in the context of teeming metropolises like Mexico City, most hurt the protestors. (Alan Knight, "Comment," 1989, page 461.)

From top to bottom Mexico City and the ZMCM seem to be managed, so where would change occur? We will try to examine the propensity for change in one direction or another in various groups. Aziz Nassif in the volume on "Mexico's alternative political futures" stresses the regional level of political action as the place where change might take place:

Political conflicts occur at the regional level because opposition parties and groups still lack the means to mount a national challenge to the PRI, (page 95).

Let us then look at the regional groups in the Mexico City urban area. Our table on political efficacy by groups in Mexico City shows the constituencies we will be covering in most of the rest of this chapter. Let us briefly discuss our efficacy or viability index shown in this table in order to assess their most probable role.

Our viability index (adding all of the measures of strength or subtracting them from a top score) shows business to be equal to the party itself (PRI or the "regime"). Students, workers and the "poor" in so far as they are separate constituencies have much lower scores with the media-communicators being in between but probably pivotal in terms of their real, efficacious function.

There have been many other more or less subjective rankings of political constituencies in Mexico (Lopez 1989, Maxfield 1989, Ward 1990).

The combination of groups that may produce particular changes is, indeed, problematic. If the combination works itself out through an "electoral apertura" as in the 1994 election it probably will be achieved on a regional basis. A forthcoming book, *Hope and Frustration*, edited by Carlos B. Gill addresses itself to the effects of various groups from right to left in the upcoming election. We will want to include these interviews with members of the opposition in our prog-

nostification (published by Scholarly Resources, Wilmington De-
leware).

## Alternative Political Futures For Mexico

Indeed, throughtout its modern history Mexico has firmly resisted the dic-
tates (and pretentions) of social science prognostication. (Cornelius, et al.,
page 2, 1989.)

Cornelius, Gentleman and Smith in their overview to the paneled
volume on "Mexico's alternative political futures" stress constant
change, which is accelerating, which represents qualitative change and
offers real options. They offer caution about political prediction. Their
basic model relates the interaction of opposition mobilization and regime modernization. Their overall volume summarizes a 1988 work-
shop on the political processes in current Mexico. Our concern is with
how this national portrait relates to the capital and its alternative political futures. Students of Mexico as a national unit would best consult
this volume for the main ingredients to the Mexican political pie. We
see this volume as establishing "plausible ranges" for change in the
near future for Mexico and its capital (see p. 2). This tactic we have
called the A-Priori approach and it is more modest than prediction by
extrapolation, comparison or delphi techniques (pooling of expert opinion on a panel basis). Probably aspects of all four of these will always
be involved.

What one notices when one reads this whole volume are the stunning
political events that have occurred. Cornelius, et al., (Chapter One) believes that the process was "previously predictable" but that these
events may signal significant transformation. The student revolt of 1968
and its brutal outcome, the 1985 earthquake, the rise and fall of the oil
boom, the nationalization of the banks, the unexpected near victory of
the frente in 1988—all seem to portend substantial systems change. In
our discussion of predictive methods in chapter three we note in addi-
tion to plausible ranges of alternatives (A-Priori) three other basic techniques. Other ways of predicting continuities and discontinuities have
been around for decades and have separate logics. The notion is that
trends are mostly hidden and that events suddenly signify them or represent their emergence (like a thunderstorm cell emerging or a critical
mass being obtained). Though more like tea leaf reading, the latter involve much speculation based on a dramatic interpretation of dramatic

events. An assassination will always be examined for its portents even though it might be mostly "outside of history" as far as its antecedents are concerned. Theories can "key up" methods so that they can perceive the signs of transformation. For instance, given its theoretical cues a theory like Marxism can better utilize extrapolation, comparison ona a systematic basis, and a-priori ranges to predict historical transformation. On the other hand, the "surprises" in history might be better understood. The level of chaos or indeterminancy in history is probably smaller than we might believe. And, prediction is possible even where political events seem in retrospect not too likely to have occurred.

## Our Plan for This Section

Mexico City's political destiny is likely to be in the hands of various contituencies supporting the regime or its potential opposition. Cooptation, elections, or societal warfare are ways that political systems can change or accommodate. In this chapter let us look for the political potentials of various Mexico City groups to effect change in certain directions. The plan is to discuss students, the poor, workers, the middle-classes, bureaucrats, the intelligentia, and the business elite as possible agents of change. The bureaucrats will be seen as traditional, technocratic or quasi-ideological. The possible coalescence of these groups already has occurred in the Federal District but to little avail, so it is obvious that other ingredients are needed in order to have significant systems change. Our analysis probably should not ignore the agrarian sector or non-urban populist movements which may play an important role in various coalitions. Almost any combination of groups may come to represent the cutting edge of political-economic change. The Frente has been analyzed in order to understand its 1988 dynamics and the possibilities for 1994. There may be strange bed-fellows. Bartra (1989, p. 68) notes the paradoxical link of rural identifications (matrias) with urban, patriotic authoritarianism. National segments of diverse sorts may reinforce various political structures and processes, and Bartra sees a "post modern-conservativism" as coming out of this emerging amalgam. The new combinations may well help escape the sarape of apathy which previously covered rural Mexico; they may also domesticate (housebreak) new desires for change into a new period of quiescence. Alberto Aziz Nassif sees much activity in the regions where an "electoral window of opportunity" defies the older concept of unity and problem solving in the center. Not only the central region is getting its act together!

## An Overview of Political Changes

The 1988 election served as a stage for new, or at least rare phenomenon within the Mexican electoral system. (Molinar Horcasitas, ''The Future of the Election System,'' page 271.)

Many see the end of the previous political ''PACT.'' The old nationalist ''myth'' now only causes Malaise (Bartra, 1989). A coyontura (special moment, joint or break) has occurred. A previously predictable system has become otherwise (Cornelius, et al., 1989). A previously ''hegemonic'' party is losing it (Nassif, 1989). The P.R.T., P.M.S. on the left and P.A.N. on the right are totally anti- system not just discontented (Molinar Horcasitas, 1989). Yet there is an indifference to the political process despite the economic crisis (Guillien Lopez, 1989). There is revolt against fraud, even against a ''tutelage'' oriented state (Nassif, 1989). Business groups, stunned by Portillos bank nationalization, are becoming more politically active (Maxfield, 1989, p. 221). The political left has been dealt ''a serious blow,'' except for small victories in Oaxaca and Chihuahua as the body politic moves to the right. Neocardenismo is dominant in the Valley of Mexico, and challanging elsewhere. Popular movemens with general goals that attempt to overcome built-in divisions have developed outside the formal political system (as Conamup and Anocp—with its anti- austerity aims). Such are the results of ''an increasingly exclusionary system'' where the formal system marginalizes and ignores groups that used to be absorbed (Foweraker, 1989, p. 112). We want to know what the role of Mexico City is with respect to these changes. Before examining the role of constituent groups lets try to trace the outlines of this emerging urban political system.

The recent shootings of PRI politicos and the intrigue surrounding them have threatened ''political stability.'' The dramatic decline in the peso and the Mexican stock market may have been of more consequence. There are all sorts of acqusations about who did what to whom. As Ernesto Zedillos Sexenio works its way along we may see amazing changes in Mexico's political-economy. NAFTA-TLC will have (has had) great changes as well.

# POLITICAL EFFICACY BY GROUPS

| "INFLUENTIALS" (MEDIA, ETC.) | PARTY PROS & TECHNICOS | BUSINESS SECTOR | WORKERS | STUDENTS | THE "POOR" | CHARACTERISTIC ⟵ GROUP ↓ |
|---|---|---|---|---|---|---|
| 3 | 1 | 2 | 3 | 4 | 4 | LONG TERM GOVERNMENT SUPPORT (1=MORE SO, 5=LESS) |
| 1 | 2 | 1 | 3 | 4 | 5 | POSSESSES OWN RESOURCES (1 TO 5) |
| 3 | 2 | 3 | 3 | 3 | 4 | SEEN AS LEGITIMATE IN TOTAL PICTURE (1 TO 5) |
| 3 | 1 | 2 | 2 | 4 | 3 | ABLE TO MOBILIZE THE "TROOPS" (1 TO 5) |
| 3 | 4 | 1 | 5 | 5 | 5 | SUPPORT FROM OUTSIDE MEXICO FROM LIKE MINDED (1 TO 5) |
| 4 | 1 | 3 | 3 | 3 | 3 | STRENGTH AT THE POLLS (1 TO 5) |
| 2 | 1 | 2 | 3 | 3 | 4 | CLOUT WITHIN THE INSTITUTIONAL STRUCTURE (1 TO 5) |
| 19 | 12 | 14 | 22 | 26 | 28 | VIABILITY INDEX SCORE |

To Wit:

- The political changes in Mexico can be seen as regionally situated, including the Federal district (Nassif, 1989, p. 96).
- "Support for opposition parties throughout the country, including the PAN, concentrated in the urban middle-classes, and especially their younger generation" (G. Lopez, 1987, is cited).
- The mobilization of opposition parties in urban areas will lead to the contesting of faulty electorial process (as Foweraker notes of municipal elections in the State of Mexico, 1989, p. 120).
- The political left will make more gains in the Valley of Mexico (as well as other proletarianized areas; Northwest, oil states, etc.).
- A movement in PRI toward "democratization" will probably come down to the inclusion of the urban middle classes (as in Mexico City) in order to steal the thunder of the N.D.F.
- Issues such as the environment can unite various constituencies in the Valley of Mexico, at least temporarily.
- The lack of political commitment in terms of urban planning, ecological concerns, basic services, will probably continue (Ward, 1990, p. 234).
- Mass "counter participation" may force greater democratization (Ward, 1990, p. 236).
- Coercion is possible if groups like the urban poor, disaffected students or workers can't be coopted or put into "reform" structures.
- "The urban poor are becoming a social community of shared concerns . . . the movements of the poor could create models for a distinctly Mexican democracy . . . "(Kathleen Logan, 1989, p. 117).

## Mexico City's Alternative Political Futures: The Role of Various Constituencies

Few places in the democratic world have less local democracy than Mexico City. My sense is that alternative claims to the high ground may be beginning to break through those defenses. (Peter Ward, 1989, page 308 in Cornelius, et al.'s *Mexico's Alternative Political Futures*.)

Despite an absence of local democracy, as Peter Ward points out, citizens of this great metropolis played a role in the 1988 presidential elections. The majority of the delegaciones of the city, and indeed of the Federal district, supported the Frente of Cuanhtemoc Cardenas (see p. 313). As Ward observes, "Cardenas was especially strong in the low income, irregular settlement areas of Nezahualcoyotl, Ecatepec and Chalco" (p. 312). The "Colonias Populares" have given up on PRI, it seems. And, it is obvious from the 1988 vote that upper income groups in the Federal district have largely (at 50%) gone over to the right wing, anti PRI, PAN party. By and large, according to Ward's data, the periphery of the city support the left. The geographic nature of senate races is such that the Frente wins few seats, however, and PRI outdistances the Frente by 24 to 3 in senate seats (p. 312).

What can we draw from this data with respect to Mexico City's upcoming political situation? Class polarization has always been present, but previously more institutionally absorbed. Many groups, left, right, and center are going to escalate their demands for an elected local congress to run the Federal District. Opposition parties on the left *and* right do not want to remain frustrated in their efforts to bring power to their own constituents. Ward notes how city hall deflects the demands for home rule by offering other structures of representation. The local delegados are postured as adequate sources of representation and desires for an elected mayor and other officers are put off—at least so far.

Also, as we cited, Peter Ward in the introduction, there is "change to effect no change." The priorities of Mexico City governance have been to "halt further deterioration in living conditions" (p. 320). The latter is an admirable task, but then reduces efforts toward democratization or decentralization. The P.R.I. government may be shooting itself in the foot if these priorities were reversed and people did not perceive some improvements. Ward sees the unitizing of city hall with a popular mandate behind it as achieving a "development-based strategy." This may be idealistic and naive, because resources are an additional issue. The social class arrangement that is crystallizing may not allow for any working unity either. People with money, who are potential tax payers, may also flee, as has been the case in Mexico and elsewhere. As Ward notes, (p. 321), "A drastic revision of local taxation will be required by any newly mandated local authority." As a last remark, Ward surmises that whatever the changes, they still may be too slow to matter.

Let us try to envision how the macro-political environment may affect Mexico City's political destinies. We may have to delve into the nation's political economy (if not the global situation) to forecast these scenarios. There must also be more to local political outcomes than PRI's need for control in the Federal district. Our specific line of approach will be to look at different constituencies, students, the poor, workers as organized groups, the middle class, the various elites, and special interest groups (as religious or environmental communities).

# The Political Orientation of Mexico City's Poor

. . . yet with the exception of some disturbances linked to increased bus fares in Netzahualcoytl in 1981, Mexico City's slum belt has witnessed no riots or looting sprees. (Alan Riding, *Distant Neighbors*, 1985, page 265.)

Even if we should falter in our attempt to define the poor, its structural position and political response potential, it is likely that the Interior Ministry with its political control functions (vested in the Federal Security Directorate) has a good sense of its potential for manipulation or of opposition.

Mexico's poor were, of course, partly responsible for the first major political revolution in the twentieth century. Also, "machetismo" or the burning of the hacienda and its occupants has a long history in Mexico. And, although some political students of Mexico's poor, both rural and urban, see them as passive, distrustful, self-absorbed and basically out-of-the-action, they ultimately will have to be dealt with. In this section we will review the studies of how Mexico's underclasses, especially urban ones have been perceived. We will also try to graph their political responses as past and current "crisis" conditions impact them.

We agree with James Cockcroft when he notes that:

Generalizations about the political and ideological formation of the immiserated are difficult. They are located at the bottom of the class structure and yet in proximity to more class conscious or politically motivated proletarian or petty-bourgeois elements. (In Nora Hamilton's *Modern Mexico: state, economic, and social conflict*, page 251.)

Cockcroft argues that the sub-proletarians are "immiserated" and should not be viewed as "marginal." The poor in Mexico City are integrated as a reserve army of labor as a market for monopoly capitalism, as self- exploiting, small merchants in the thousands of one room stores (miscelaneas) and also as dosmestic servants.

Arizpe's study of the exploited Indian women, the "Marias," represents another such population. What is needed is a more accurate class analysis according to Cockcroft in his article on "Immiseration, not Marginalization." In dealing with the political potential of the poor he suggests that:

There is a growing recognition that progressive political parties, movements, and individuals suffer a long, uneven history of now underestimat-

# ROLE OF POOR: RESPONSE POTENTIAL

| Nature of Group | Status in Political Economy | Possible Response Scenarios |
|---|---|---|
| Recent one-way migrants (Turner's "Bridgeheaders") | — Very low income<br>— Closest to "marginal"<br>— No local participation<br>— True squatters | — Learning "means," including the politically feasible<br>— Part of "conservative poor," have challenged spontaneously |
| Well-integrated (Scroungers) *informal* economic system | — No longer "marginal"<br>— Hooked via "self-exploitation"<br>— Only community influences<br>— Very low income | — Accepts "self-help"<br>— Can join demonstrations (low key levels) |
| Somewhat integrated in the formal economic system (Turner's consolidators) or the "Self-exploiters" | — Has job in the formal system<br>— Obligations hook them<br>— Politically efficacious? | — Can effect system via work or residence community<br>— May lose from an uprising<br>— Accepts tokenism |
| Circular migrants, keep ties to hinterland The "Invisibles" | — May be invisible to census or institutions<br>— Part of family have roots on both ends<br>— Dilemma weakens identification at either end | — Not capable of revolt until they settle down?<br>— May respond along with community of origin as these interact in city |
| Intergrated in formal system in way which compromises reponse potential (The Symbiotics) | — Position linked to upper middle class via occupation & response<br>— The "snobbish-butler-syndrome" is likely | — Probably identifies upward rather than with own class<br>— Has too much to lose? |
| Well integrated in formal economic system (Turner's "Status Seekers") | — Nearly middle income<br>— Votes/participates<br>— Can comman partial response from "authorities" | — Has a variety of responses<br>— If union oriented, will follow—maybe even as break-away. |

ing, now overestimating working people of talking down to them when not romanticizing them and of generally failing to grasp the changing dynamics of their lives. . . . (In Hamilton, page 256)

Judith Adler Hellman in reviewing Cockcroft's book *Mexico: Class Formation, Capital Accumulation and the State* notes the latter writer as using the term "repeasantization" of rural wage workers *and* urban migrants. The effects of inflation, declining wages, degradation of work conditions and under-employment in the past two decades have led to this state of affairs. All thoughts of equity and redistribution went out the window after the oil bust, devaluation, capital flight and monstrous debt serving. We must be careful about which group we are talking about, because the "poor" come in many shapes and forms. In a political system based on patronage as opposed to meritocracy, where higher education is for those already favored, where "penny capitalism" is a form of self-exploitation, and where the poor are mere pawns at the bottom of some Camarilla then there are only desparate acts and thoughts.

With a cleaner vision of what group we are talking about as the "poor" we would probably include the statuses of recent migrants to Mexico City, more indigenous than mestizo, or rural hinterland rather than urban background, and the victim of poor social services and amenities in the past. We are not talking about the "working class" at this point. The latter group has at least benefitted from the state's thrust for industrial growth at almost any price. The poor, of course, work, but are sub-employed; or because they often hustle after several kinds of gainful activities, they may be "over-employed." They also may participate in to a greater extent in the "informal economy" which parallels the "real" one. When the poor "work" they are also more subject to layers of "bosses, owners, allowers, facilitators reaching to the top of Mexican society and beyond." To sell colas, gum, or newspapers they work for the biggest of firms. To sweep the sidewalks they work in the shadow realms of someone else's affluence. In the finest of kitchens and gardens they toil. They make the finest craft articles for the homes of the prosperous. They live on the tops of some of the finest buildings as caretakers or watchpersons. The poor, wherever they live or work, are in "Las Cividades perdidas."

The major question is one concerned with the political response of this group, however defined in the social structure of Mexico. Cockcroft notes that the poor or immiserated have been mobilized for political change in Algeria, Iran, Vietnam, Angola, Zimbabwe, Nicaragua, Chile,

El Salvador, Cuba and elsewhere (p. 253). Mexico City's union of popular colonies emerged in the 1970's and linked with over arching organizations and with groups like students, peasants and housewives. Such alliances drew repression and violence in many instances, and Cockcroft notes how parallel organizations, cooptation, and assassination were used (Hamilton, p. 254). In the last election the poor, fully employed or otherwise, seem to have voted for the Frente in appreciable numbers. Aggregate voting data only give us vague clues as to what the extent of participation really was. But the bet is that the poor can be mobilized in at least this fashion. Mexico and many other countries are struggling toward what weakly could be called "political modernization." We will conclude this section assuming that the "poor" will play a role in Mexico's and Mexico City's various political futures.

It would seem that moves to a nationalist country-wide thrust and a home rule attainment for Mexico City would be most likely. The poor may be manipulated to maintain the status quo also, but the resources to coopt and channel their response are currently lacking.

## Students as Political Actors in Mexico City

The attack (killing several hundred students at Tlatelolco on October 2, 1968) had the desired effect of preventing even the smallest political disturbance during the Mexico City Olympic games . . . But it also created a constituency for the political opposition that 20 years later nearly achieved its goal of dismantling the one party "democracy" . . . (Tuesday, Oct. 4, 1988, *Star and Tribune* from "Newsday")

The above quote goes on to note that: "The massacre at Tlatelolco ended the student movement in Mexico City." Obviously, 20 years later the 100,000 estimated turnout to commemorate the attacks on students is impressive commentary on the persistance of this event's political impact. In this section we'll review briefly the history of university students' involvement in politics both on and off campus in Mexico City. We will also try to assess general interests, including ideological ones of this group.

A good single source on student politics in Mexico is Donald Mabry's *The Mexican University and the State: Student Conflicts 1910–1971* (1982). Mabry prefaces his book by saying:

The National Autonomous University of Mexico (UNAM) is not only the principal educational and cultural institution of that nation, but also one of the chief oppositionalist centers to the National government. (Page IX)

This author observes that: "Thus, student politics are part of national politics" (p. X). Mabry does note their occasional excitableness as well as their innocence. Both student and government misperceptions of reality, according to Mabry, had led to the bloody conflict between 1968 and 1971. Students thought that their "just" cause would win, and that university autonomy meant popular sovereignty (Mabry, p. 249), also they believed that a hundred thousand students marching through the capital's streets would not unleash government retaliation. The latter involved the acknowledgement of responsibility of the violence as equivalent to allowing students and their allies to run the government—or at least to allow the perception of that outcome. Let us look briefly at the history of UNAM and IPN (the National Polytechnical Institute) as well as the remainder of higher education in the Mexico City area. These institutions provide some or much of the adult, political socialization of these groups.

UNAM as an elite school has often been an enemy of whatever government was in power (Mabry, p. 262). Mabry notes (p. 14) that: "the national university has claimed and achieved the role of critic not only of ideas, but of the state." The fact that many government-state leaders have in the past been recruited from UNAM, and then have had to defend that state policies from these criticisms has led to a paradox. We must note that the environment on campus has been described as a highly politicized one. Intellectual demands for autonomy and co-governance (Gobierno) go back at least to the University of Cordoba in Argentina in 1918; these precedents must be considered (Mabry, p. 16). The chronology of conflict Mabry details involves some of the following. After its installation in 1910, (UNAM), the would-be student goals of autonomy and co-governance led to a strike in 1929. Shortly after, students achieved "autonomy" laws for the University in 1929 and 1933. The fate of UNAM in the 1933–35 period, as a bastion of traditionalism was tested (Mabry, p. 123). Left-wing hostility meant that UNAM would be caught in the middle of the education-for-socialism controversy. As Mabry notes, the political climate of the 1930's was such that "The University would have few open political friends" (p. 125).

It's ironic that the government tried to force the university to the left in the 1930's and is now driven mad in the 1960 to 1990 period when much of higher education is aggitatingly to the left of the government. Various recent governments and presidents have tried a variety of tactics to redress this situation. Unfortunately, some of its tactics (as violence) have boomeranged.

# STUDENT INFLUENCE
# POLITICAL-ECONOMIC PROCESS, 1990–2010

(1 to 5; 1 = HIGH)

| | On Campus | Mass Mobilization | Via Electorate | Institutional Members |
|---|---|---|---|---|
| **As Student Participants (Based on the Campus)** | **1** | **2** | **5** | **4** |
| **Off Campus** | **—** | **4** | **5** | **4** |
| **As Members of General Labor Force** | **—** | **4** | **3** <br> increasing | **3** |
| **As Recruits into Mid-Official-dom (or as "Intellectuals")** | **—** | **4** | **3** <br> increasing since 1990 | **2** |
| **In High Places (Any Cases?)** | **?** | **4** | **2** | **3** |

We will not repeat the excellent history by Mabry of UNAM and student-government conflicts. There are also histories of UNAM which document these circumstances, as Jesus Silva Herzog's *Una historia de la universidad de Mexico: y Sus Problemas*. A 1969 book by Ramon Ramierez and Alma Chapoy lays out the academic structure of UNAM. (*Estructura de la UNAM*) Mabry's book deals with the political realities more so than other works, he being a political scientist. He notes the slow path to "reapproachment" in the 1935 to 1944 period. A "long peace" characterized the 1945–1961 period, even though there were conflicts in the larger society. In the later 1950's, the students were agitated not by university policies, but by the conditions that affected them as citizens. Bus fares were a precipitating issue in 1958 and represent an on-going set of interests for commuting students. The new metro line to the university may have helped somewhat. In the 1960's another set of problems emerged. Less than one-third of the students had jobs. The campus, including classes and extra-curricular activities were swamped by sheer numbers. As Mabry notes, faculty fragmentation and student alienation were a consequence of this "Giantism." "Sheer inertia" and "personal fiefdoms" were other outcomes (Mabry, p. 219). Issues of quality and academic performance did grab student attention, but Cuba's revolution may have had more in setting student agendas (Mabry, p. 222). Students were aware of their small chances of graduating with a profesional degree, at the same time that international activities kept their political juices surging. Strikes in hinterland universities were also very common in the late 1960's, and soldiers were used with some bloodshed in Morelia and Tabasco. Confusing the political process were the activities of pseudo-students and youth gangs or "perras," and there was uncontrollable crime on or near the campus at UNAM. Buses, as convenient targets and sore spots, became objects in the student-government conflicts. The military use of bazooka to blow down a student barricade heightened the 1968 conflict (The "Bazukazo event").

The government's activities after the Tlatelolco massacre did little to reduce tensions. President Luis Echeverria, who had been implicated in the 1968 massacre as Interior minister, had tried to visit UNAM campus in 1975, but was essentially driven off campus. Even when offering an "Apatura democratica" or democratic opening, and giving government posts to student leaders this left-*sounding* president was not well received. In fact, the Metropolitan Autonomous University set up in 1974 was meant to be a rival for UNAM, and be a safer place to recruit from than say the somewhat Marxist-oriented social science departments at UNAM.

Our main goal here is to describe the political life of this great city. Students will become leaders of this country and city, especially students from elite schools like UNAM, El colegio de Mexico, and I.P.N. These students and their faculties are an elite group, although not always appreciated on that basis. Yet as Alan Riding observes:

> Intellectuals are perhaps the most privileged elite in Mexico. Academics, writers, painters, and musicians of minimal renown inherit the right—even the duty—to participate in politics, give opinions on subjects far removed from their areas of talents, sit in judgement on the regime, even to denounce the system. (*Distant Neighbors*, 1985, page 295)

A nearly "incestuous" relationship emerges as the government pampers some of these groups. Lorenzo Meyer, writing on the "historical roots of the authoritarian state in Mexico'' notes the cooptation of these middle and upper class groups.

An example of this process is the way in which the:

> intelligentia—a possible source of conflict in any authoritarian regime—was neutralized after the governments of the Revolution made their peace with the universities in the 1940's. From its support of the Marxist ''Mexico School of Painting'' to its support of the universities, the State has provided a living for thousands of intellectuals, and its embassies are full of writers and social scientists. (*Authoritarianism in Mexico*, Reyna and Weinerts, page 16)

Of course almost all governments hire such people in various capacities. Even witch hunting, right-wing Fascist and burning populist-left regimes will eventually recruit them, and with similar outcomes. As Alan Riding notes, students as future intellectuals want to influence the government if not public opinion, especially in this situation of centralized power. To be a ''Cultural Cauchillo'' (Riding, p. 297) is a heady experience. To be asked to ''advise'' the president of the nation is mind-blowing, and Presidents Echeverria and Portillo played this tactic to the hilt. Partial government support of left-leaning media like *Uno Mas Uno* and *La Jornada* can also be a control function to be sure.

## The Business Population in Mexico City

> Nevertheless, flexibility and compromise have generally characterized relations between the business community because they have shared some basic goals for Mexican society. Most important, they share an interest in self-preservation; this is why their competition for power has been kept within limits. (Levy & Szekely, 1983, page 65)

If this reticence for direct power characterizes the business sector (''community?'') then relationships would be greatly different. The prevailing impression in Mexico City, in its El Centro, residential areas, its broad avenues and its industrial parks is that business is dominant. The media also reflect this dominance.

The economy of Mexico and certainly Mexico City ''has remained essentially capitalist'' (Levy and Szekely). Even with public ownership and an active public sector, the state has *not* competed with business men and industrialists. The private sector has much influence. When Pablo Gonzales Casanova wrote *Democracy in Mexico* in 1963 he stated (p. 159) that "Mexico is pre-capitalist." This is a different question than what role will (does) the business community have—especially in the capital city. For Gonzalez Casanova:

> The political problem of the direction of the development of capitalism in Mexico is a problem of the conflict among different groups of the bourgeoisie to determine the direction of that development (Casanova, 1963, page 173).

Given the controversies amongst all groups (right to left) about the nature of the role of the business-industrial community, we will step lightly here. P.G.C. says that the distinction between a "national and a commercial bourgeoisie is not valid" (p. 173). More important would be a distinction between the public-sector bourgeoisie and a private sector one in political terms. One group is seen as more in favor of development, limiting greed and further liberalization. We merely acknowledge differences within the bourgeoisie.

## Business Groups as Elites

There is no shortage of studies of the elite in Mexico. Menno Vellinga has studied the Burguesia in Monterrey (1979). Jorge Alonso in 1976 wrote about "La dialectica: clases-elites en Mexico." Alonso Aguilar's book entitled "La Burguesia, la oligarquia y el Estado Mexico." Enrique Alduncin Abitia (in 1988) has focused on the "expectations of business leaders" with respect to investment opportunities. The Monterrey business community has been a focus more often, perhaps, because of its integrated qualities (Jorge Balan, 1973). National elites have been examined by Roderic Camp, although he does not seem to sense where power really dwells (see *Who's Who in Mexico*, 1988).

The 1970's were a period in which elite studies were popular in many countries, the U.S. of A. and in Europe. The explosive 60's had given way to the analytical 70's. Ricardo Cinta (1977) looked at the "estructura de clases, elite del poder y pluralismo politico" (*Revista Mexicana de Sociologia*, UNAM). Mexico City's political constituencies are not usually singled out in the past, but given PRI's loss of the Federal district in the 1988 presidential election, this may change (as with Peter Ward's analysis).

# ROLE OF BUSINESS ELITE

## (BASED ON KANDELL, FERHENBACH, LEVY, SZEKEZY, CASANOVA, NEEDLER, HAMILTON;) CAMP, AND CYPHER.

| PERIOD (& EXAMPLE) | NATURE OF BUSINESS ELITE | RELATIONSHIP TO DECISION MAKING | "CLOUT" 1 to 10, 10 is highe |
|---|---|---|---|
| PRE-REVOLUTION INVESTMENT (JOCKY CLUB GANG) | MANY FOREIGNERS (2/3 OF INVESTMENT-KANDELL, P. 376). DOMESTIC B.M. RAN HACIENDAS ON ABSENTEE BASIS | CALLED THEMSELVES "CIENTIFICOS" & CONCENTRATED WEALTH & POWER(KANDELL P 373). | 8 |
| 1910-1934 (ALBERTO PANI, B.M.-ADVISOR) | RAILROADS & ELECTRICITY CONCENTRATED THEM IN M.C.:(KANDELL, P. 370). SEPARATE ELITE IN MONTERREY, GROUPS ELSEWHERE. | GOT PRES. TO CONTROL LABOR VIA CROM (KANDELL, P 447). CALLES GOV. ENDED REFORM IN FAVOR OF BUS. AFTER 1928. CONCANACO-CONCAMIN BORN(L&S, P 62). | 7 |
| CARDENAS YEARS (GRUPOS IN MONTERREY, AS GARZA SADA FAMILY) | FOREIGN B.M. WERE SUSPECT. (DOMESTIC B.M. COOLED HEELS IN OUTER OFFICES) | GIVING GREATER OPPORTUNITES TO MIDDLE RANKS- SHIFTED POWER TO BUS./BUREAUCRATIC SECTORS AFTER 1938(FEHRENBACH, P 603). | 5 |
| 1940-1958 (AMER. CHAMB. OF COMM. IN MEX.) | LAUNCHED "MEXICAN MIRACLE" FROM M.C. IMPORT SUBSTITUTION MADE THEM VERY RICH. | "ALEMAN LOOKED OUTSIDE THE PRI TO THE BUS. COMMUNITY"(KANDELL, P 493). BIG CITY IND. & GOV. SPENDING IN M.C. WAS INSPIRED BY THEM. ALEMAN CONT. DOMANINANCE OF BUS. ORIENTED MESTIZO(FEHRENBACH, P 612). | 9 |
| 1958-1970 | UNCOMPETITIVE BECAUSE OF IMPORT SUB. POLICY, FAILED TO EXPORT. | PROFITS GOT TO 41% OF NATIONAL INCOME VS 25% FOR ALL WAGES(FEHRENBACH, P 642). | 9 |
| ECHEVERRIA YEARS (LA DOCENA TRAGICA) | PRES. ATTACKED INEFFICIENCY, LETHERGY. LABOR SUPPORTED VS BUS. IN 1973). | GOV.'S SHARE OF ECON. DOUBLED(KANDELL, P 542) (AFTER PORTI LLO TO 70%). NEVER WERE RELATIONS SO STRAINED AS DURING ECHEVERRIA RE IME(L&S, P64) | 4 |
| 1972-1994 (ALFA GROUP'S DECLINE) | C.C.E. FORMED TO BLESS PRIVATE PROP. RE GIONALIZED. | PANS NEW CRIOLOS DOMINATE IN THE NORTH CAPITAL FLIGHT WORKED AS A POLITICAL TECHNIQUE. (CYPHER, PAGE 115) | 7 |
| 1994-2010 PROJECTED | NO RETURN TO LARGE PUBLIC SECTOR = LARGER ROLE FOR PRIVATE SECTOR? PRIVITIZATION STRESSED BY CASAR & PERES, AND VILLARREAL | MIDDLE CLASS & TECNICOS MAY RIVAL EFFECTIVELY "FLEXIBILITY AND COMPROMISE WILL PERSIST" (L & S, P.65) B.M. WILL GAIN CONTROL IN SOME STATES. | 7 |

# The role of business in the next two decades in Mexico City

> We will have to reach some sort of agreement as to what it means to say
> that the state is exhausted and must step aside in favor of the private sector
> (era, 1989, MAP, page 238).

While the socialist bloc seems to have been devoured by its antithesis, and others to the west are crowing over a strident (if not rancid smelling) capitalism, almost everyone in the summer of 1993 wonders about the economic process and its viability. Is recession permanent?

If you tighten the screws will capital flee? Is not public investment as good as private forms? Is there any intelligent economic life on earth? Will the Chinese system of taking in one-another's laundry work elsewhere? Can't an oil based economy work better than one based on gold?

Since Schumpater and Weber (and countless other "Smithians") the entrepreneur has trumpeted their function. In Mexico this function was obscured and placated for decades, almost to the point of denying its other consequences. In the age of Reagan, Bush, Thatcher and Yeltsin there may have been a reversal of fortunes for this group. But not to worry!

As we are in the business of forecasting, including about groups, let us put a test to the continuing viability of this "business community" by comparison to other constituencies. The results of our "viability index" for groups with potential political efficacy shows them as very strong.

In dealing with "political institutions and actors" in Mexico Levy and Szekely in 1983 discussed the business community (p. 62) and this follows in the next few paragraphs. While the political role of business in Mexico and its capital may be obscured in the general media, it can be observed through a variety of windows. When U.S. President Reagan appointed Ambassador Gavin to Mexico there was a nervous watch of this diplomat with respect to his dealings with the military and this same business community, however diverse it is.

Levy and Szekely observe the following: There has been much government support for business for many decades. The private sector was encouraged to form its own organizations (Concanaco and Concamin) soon after the revolution. The growth of the private sector under these circumstances has encouraged more concentration of capital. While not being homogeneous, as we noted above, and that the regime has exploited differences, it still has many common interests. Capital can flee the country; it can create a crisis; and it can stall economic development. Business does, indeed, have veto power and more than that.

## Decision Making Affecting M.C.'s Economy

Three aspects in particular have been emphasized in the critique of foreign investment: The loss of national control over economic policy . . . the long-run negative impact on the balance of payments . . . and the adverse effects of income distribution . . . (Paul Sigmund, *The political economy of income distribution in Mexico*, page 247).

In our previous table we stressed economic variables as if they existed outside of a political-social matrix. Countries on the periphery can attempt to regain national control or try to set conditions on foreign ownership. Of course, there are domestic sources of decision making which we will elude to in the last part of this chapter.

Specifically how have these two sources (foreign and domestic) of decision-making impacted Mexico City? One may be sure that the type of screening device that Sigmund observes (p. 248) will involve the interaction of foreign and domestic sources. Investment screening legislation that induced the 51% Mexican ownership condition shifted income to a small number of Mexican private industrialists, but it may have had other impacts, as on the level of employment. It may also have impacted the distribution of economic activities within the country. The 1973 law to promote Mexican investment and to regulate foreign investment had 17 "considerations" (Sigmund, p. 251–52) included ones which would produce jobs in other parts of the country—that is outside of Mexico City. Many of these considerations were ignored, as for instance Chrysler insisted and got 100% ownership by using a withdrawal tactic. Some compatability with national and foreign goals did allow for industry to be moved outside of Mexico City, as the border industrialization efforts. National priorities such as decentralization was an announced national priority as was export promotion.

Sigmund sites several examples of decentralization, as with the speedy okehs given to the relocation of a medical supplies company outside of Mexico City (Becton Dickenson); allowing a Texas Instruments plant to quickly be set up in Aquascalientes; and an "oil drill head plant in Vera Cruz" (p. 254). In fact 30% of the exemptions from Mexicanization considerations "were located in priority regions that

needed economic development'' (p. 255). A Pepsi-Cola expansion was
an example of such decision making. Still the urban-rural disparity will
persist.

Citing his own I.L.O. study in 1974, W. Van Ginnenken, notes such
disparities ("Mexican Income Distribution Within and Between Rural
and Urban Areas," 1974). Social security, housing and education expenditures were "twice to four times the national averages" in urban
areas (p. 142 in "Socio-economic groups and income distribution in
Mexico," 1980). Decision making about the decentralization of foreign
enterprizes (not surprising when it does occur!) or of national eco-
nomic/political units will slowly help reduce the disparities, but the
decisions (70%!) will still swell Mexico City and its environs. Much
of Van Ginnenken's chapter on "Socio-economic groups in Mexican
Society" notes the continuing problem:

> As for regional distribution of private and public investments, it was
> shown in chapter three that investments are too concentrated in Mexico
> City and some other large cities. A more equal distribution of investments
> over regions would divert the under-employed day-laborers from the large
> cities to smaller cities (page 145).

The latter is, of course, the crux of the problem. It does seem that
some decisions are being made to impact the imbalance, but the process
is slow and must involve a compatability of motives.

Angel Bassols Batalla's 1979 book *Mexico: Formacion de Regiones
Economicas, Influencias Factores, y Sistemas* has 1970 data showing
the massiveness of central dominance (as diagram opposite page 494).
It does not seem possible that significant change will occur by the year
2010. Other regional studies as by Menno Vellinga of economic development and social class in Monterrey do show a different pattern as to
dispersal, but not as to the inequality generated by economic enterprize
in Mexico (1979, Van Gorcum, Assen). The "Unitary Ideology" of
entrepreneurs and management is noted in this study (p. 103). This
powerful "enclave" was challenged in the Echeverria period when the
pro-business governor was replaced (see p. 188) moved to other areas
of Mexico and "have made them the natural spokesmen for many Mexican businessmen." We wanted to stress the role of decisions in this
section, and will return to the topic as we discuss the political role of
the business elite. Decision making theory (as to sources, not the logic
of the process) do lead one off into areas where we are not privy to all
of the events or relationships, but as Charles W. Mills notes in a book

35 years ago, the outcome of decision often reveals the nature of the process leading to it.

It is true that local elites are chipping away on the Federal district's hegemony. A recent seminar held in Tijuana on a "free trade zone" for the border goes along with the Maquiladore program. By 1993 this region may generate its own dynamic for the next quarter century. It is doubtful that the center can hold given these regional-centrifugal forces. What is the actual past national role of business in decision making is not really clear based on the variety of ways in which coordination was achieved. The pattern in the Federal District has been speculated upon, but out in the hinterland it has been even more camera obscura. Some relationships in the latter sphere have been noted, as between Portillo and the Alfa group. What seems to be coming more clear is the relative size of the groups involved.

Pablo Gonzalez Casanova in 1970 discussed "the factors of power" and decision making. Citing a 1960 study by Jose Luis Cecena of the largest 100 enterprizes, foreign participants garnered 50.27% of the total income, the independent private sector got 13.52%, and government enterprises received 36.21% of this total for the top 100 firms, (see p. 49). Various forms of coordination and consultation were observed. We have already noted the role of CONCAMIN and CONCANACO and the mostly common strategy that they utilize. Largely by criticizing executive policy (quietly!) they make their impact. The role of enterprise, however, was seen as "minimal." Private investments, as various economists have noted, are "a dependent variable of public investment." Also as Casanova noted (p. 55) "State intervention is highly dependent on foreign financing" (up to 47%). All of this data reveals the puzzle of state autonomy versus other forces. Casanova in 1970 in his "Marxist analysis" (Chapter 10) seen Mexico as "pre-capitalist" and (therefore) also pre-democratic. Business is seen as taking advantage of existing political forms, but "does not have a pure political expression" what ever that means (p. 163). The bourgeoisie is in fact seen as leading an "anti-imperialist national revolution." At least some of this differentiated group is seen as doing so.

Coming into the 1990s this entrepreneurial group may be perceived differently, and also their relationship to decision making. James M. Cypher's 1990 study of *State and Capital in Mexico: Development Policy Since 1940* uses a study of the largest firms (private national, transnational, and parastate) and their share of sales from 1973 to 1981. (Latter study was by Eduardo Jacobs, see p. 101). The top 23 groups in the private, national sector now had 48% of the sales, out of the top

100; transnational firms were at 25.2% and parastate firms at 16.8%. A time of "ascendency" for these "interlocking national economic groups" clearly had occurred. Noting Carlos Tellos' 1979 study, Cypher said that the "business elite had paralyzed the government" in 1973 because of Echeverria's foreign and domestic policies (as with "no more large scale benefits from the state" p. 102).

We find a wide range of opinion about the decision making role of business in Mexico and Mexico City. In discussing private-public relations Roderick A. Camp (*Entrepreneurs and Politics in 20th Century Mexico*, Oxford, 1989) notes a variety of business leaders with respect to the political function (see p. 251). The range is from "conservatives" to "activists." Camp observes that as the private sector become stronger, it becomes more questioning of the state's role in development. The "disciple" questions the "mentor," although the state can still take advantage of the heterogeniety of the private sector. The final issue concerning the strength (clout, for someone from Chicago!) may come down on the degree to which this sector is able to act in a unified manner on basic policy matters as opposed to being subject to divide and conquer.

We have not missed the obvious pattern of "distorted development" which David Barkin is writing about at the present time (Westview, 1990). Barkin observes that much public investment has made this emerging pattern the way it is now. He also observes the low, actual private investment in increased productivity. Also observed is the increased polarization, and such tragedies as the increased need to buy food abroad with declining revenues. Barkin has a remedy for the 1990s, this being a return to a "war-time economy" (see Chapter 7). By stimulating food production and replacing imports, a reversal may be achieved. One suspects that the business sector and the transnationals would favor this strategy as it would both stabilize the political scene and provide for more freeing up of national capital—and perhaps continue "distorted development."

## Summary of Basis for Political Change in the ZMCM

A strong case could be made that those interested in public policy formation in Mexico would do well to concentrate upon decision making processes within the PRI-government apparatus and/or the political culture of the political-administrative elite itself. (*"Political culture in Mexico: continuities and revisionist interpretations" by Craig and Cornelius, 1989, page 379.*)

The above quote would have us focus on the policy making elites in order to foresee the future for Mexico and the ZMCM. Our section of this chapter on the political action in Mexico City has focused on the general political efficacy of groups, and would not seem to greatly dispute this appraisal. The political establishment (what ever its constituent membership by the year 2010) and the business "sector" seem to have equal efficacy based on our analysis. Our lead quote stresses the autonomy of the state apparatus, while writers like Nora Hamilton (along with Timothy Harding, 1986, p. 67) notes the limits of state autonomy. The former writer gives a bottom line (p. 98) that:

> It is clear, however, that those controlling the Mexican state today no longer have the option of effectively defending the interests of underprivileged groups against those of dominant groups and classes.

This was written before the near turn-over election of 1988. One would be hard put to project the basically centrism of the Frente's accomplishment in the Federal district, and the P.A.N. continued veto of PRI in central and northern areas into a systems change senario. Regional outcomes involving minor changes seem more likely. We do not want our predictions to be hedged in by a kind of political fatalism however. The latter have been well represented in the past by students of political culture. The Almond and Verba kind of analysis of Mexico, which over-emphasized an urban sample—including Mexico City, stressed the frozen nature of this country's politics. The passivity, authoritarian qualities, and apathy of the general public was emphasized, as were the cynicism and regressive aspects of psychological character.

The latter indeed would prohibit change from the bottom. As Craig and Cornelius point out, however, the 1968 data gathered on Mexico (even with its Mexico City overloading) ignored social class relationships (p. 335), failed to note regional differences (p. 337), and failed to note "deviant" forms of political response (p. 239). The latter forms included protest participation, anti-systems movements, land invasions and political violence which may change the system. The 1968 data were based on materials which would not likely reflect sources of change ("field observations, clinical data, newspaper reportage and elite interviews, conducted primarily in Mexico City"). This individual or on the other hand systems-wide focus may have missed the structural sources of change.

Craig and Cornelius note all of the major "attitude and behavior" studies from 1959 to 1976 (p. 343). These authors dispute the "know-nothing," apathetic quality of respondants in Mexico City (p. 353). The mediated participation of politics "through patron-clientistic networks is, of course, a dual process of response and control; but it is not complete passivity. The sense of efficacy needed for political change is linked to past successes—not to eternal damnation via childhood socialization (p. 363). Education and class mobility also impact the sense of political efficacy and these are occurring in the ZMCM and elsewhere. So where does change come from.

Craig and Cornelius say that they do not believe that, as the radicals apparently do, the sources of change are "structurally determined" (p. 381). They believe that "certain highly stable attitudes, values and beliefs" lead to the acceptance of the political-economy and its spin offs. Despite Cuban and Peruvian cases to the contrary, the status quo will be maintained. Yet these authors end by noting the "complex and interactive" nature of the issue, and by perceiving possibilities for an "opening up" in separate regions; the latter could include the ZMCM!

## Where is the NAFTC-T.L.C. Activity Going— To Mexico City?

"And Maquiladora statistics show that there is movement away from traditional areas in the north." ("War: From Chihuahua to Chiapas, States Fight For Foreign Investment," *Mexico Insight*, October 23, 1994, page 24.)

So where are NAFTA-TLC projects going? There is super competition for foreign investment or what Brendan Case calls the "free trade pie." Case observes that (page 25) U.S. (and other) corporations what to be near, but not necessarily in Mexico City or even the Federal District. The first example used by Case was a clothing manufacturer which passed up Puebla for a more accepting Tlaxcala. All kinds of deals are made with the advantage being with outside corporations. Cheap land, low wages, free technical training (Queretaro) and exemption from taxes are some of the inducements. Industrial parks and joint ventures are becoming as common as inexpensive bus rides.

The point is one of growing and ever-more sophisticated competition. Mexico City will attract its share of certain kinds of enterprises— perhaps financial services more than assembly plants. It may not involve a distribution of high versus low tech or from components as opposed to scratch. The days of hazardous industries in the Federal

District seem to have come to an end with the series of disasters such as the Pemex plant. The growth of an urban ecological consciousness would prohibit a whole range of industries, but one must remember that even an electronics outfit like in silicon valley has its spill-over. By virtue of being a capital and a site where the gringo C.E.O.s would respite, Mexico City will benefit from NAFTA-TLC.

Much development from NAFTA-TLC will be far from Mexico City. Case notes the development in the Yucatan, but then there are amenities there as well. The laws have, of course, been changed to favor noncentral areas. A real move to decentralization may occur with NAFTA-TLC. Cancun or Merida can be decent places for foreign investment. Low wages are more likely in the hinterland as well, not to mention freedom to avoid ecological concerns of more central areas. The amenities of many peripheral areas are yet to be discovered. It is true that the Federal government can reach out to enforce environmental labor or even financial arrangements. (See Sam Quinones, ''Flawed Diamond,'' *Mexico Insight*, Oct. 23, 1994, page 30—on an Acapulco project slowed down).

The entrance into world of Mexican corporative activity can be easily based on the incorporation law of 1934 (or as amended in 1992). An S.A. or Sociedad Anonima de Capital Variable or a S. de R.L. (Limited Liability Corporation) have low thresholds for entrance as long as you are exporting. Doing business in Mexico is another matter, especially in competitive areas like the major cities—one suspects. Auditors are demanded to enable monitoring on behalf of shareholders as an additional, necessary, complication. Lawyers who understand the law and the politics are also a necessary element. With the S.A. arrangement for mega businesses and the S. de R.L. for small enterprises the path opens up. To see how complicated matters can get one should get hold of a journal like *Consultorio Fiscal* (as numero 106, 16 de Enero de 1994) where there are 150 pages of Leys and exceptions. The thing to watch for is when new rules kick in, as in the year 2004.

The main exports from Mexico to the U.S. are autos, electronic goods, machinery parts, plastics and glass. (Roberto Salinas-Leon, ''The Fruits of Free Trade,'' in *Mexico Insight*, November 6, 1994, page 32). Autos, glass, and electronics are not products of Mexico City, but stem from Puebla, Monterrey and the border areas. The extent to which the other exports come from the Federal District is not known at this time. The handling of the 15 billion dollar investment in Mexico probably has sweetened Mexico City's share of NAFTA-TLC, however—at least for financial institutions and their managers. Many of these most frequent exports are as a result of joint ventures.

The net contribution to the Federal District of NAFTA-TLC may be the opening of Mexico City to U.S. marketeers. Besides Walmart and Sam's club and expensive imports there is a flood of other kinds of merchandising as catalog shopping. Sears has been in Mexico for a decade, doing this, but J.C. Penney's is now flooding the country with catalogues. As is Nieman Marcus! You even can find competition between U.S. corporations, which is not really that surprising. Digital Equipment Corporation ran "earth shaking ads" against Hewlett Packard on the air and in print. (See Sam Quinone's article "New Wave" in *Mexico Insight*, November 6, 1994, page 20). Just as various Mexican states are competing for investment funds, foreign corporations are fighting over markets. The NAFTA-TLC agreements is not one in favor of flat out competition among any parties in the 3 countries. For instance, foreign banks can not be more than 8% aggregate share in Mexico (15% down the line). According to Brendan Case (*Mexico Insight*, "Bankers Limited," page 11, November 6, 1994), "NAFTA allows for lower participation." There must be areas where the flat out, pedal to the metal versions of competition are encouraged as well. We are dealing with smart nationalism in each of the 3 countries!

Sometimes glitches occur without adequate explanation. The NAFTA-TLC agreement on paper may not describe what actually exists. Take for instance the late 1994 disappearance of U.S. breakfast foods from grocery shelves in Mexico City. The shelves are empty at Comercio Mexicana and Aurrera because customs won't let them in. Trade deficit control or "end-of-the-sexenio blues"? (see Mark Stevenson in *Mexico Insight*, November 6, 1994, "End of the Sexenio Blues," page 14). And remember, even when a deal is cut and the product is on the way, there are the "coyotes"—the Pirahna—like intermediaries who take their toll.

*Chapter 5*

# Features of Mexico City that Should be Dealt With:

## A. Public services and housing

### Human Services And The Quality Of Life In Mexico City

> Greater affluence transforms social behavior. The dramatic expansion of the middle classes, above all since 1970, has led a growing number of urban Mexicans to adobt a more liberal lifestyle. (From chapter on the "Safety Net," by Alan Riding, 1985, page 248.)

In this chapter let us look at the relative contributions of the distribution of income and the net of human services offered to the citizens of Mexico City and also the nation as a whole. We will try to project the human service benefits from the past decades into the nearby future. Will there continue to be such great disparities? Will the "welfare system" continue to "paper over the cracks" as Peter Ward assumes? What is the nature of progress in this area? Surely the middle class knows its way to the water holes of affluence, do we ever doubt this tale of the social classes in the modern world? First let us look at the projection of incomes for the people of the nation and of the ZMCM. Then, let us review the human development, social policy contributions, which are considerable for *some*. Our concern may not be acceptable to everyone, because we assume that the *actual* level of living of people is the most basic issue. Business and governance survive or fail in an absolute sense on this matter. One need not take a "Freedmanesque" position or Marxist-Latin-American-revisionist position. How will the various peoples of the ZMCM do in the next three decades? What is

# HISTORIC EXPANSION PUBLIC SERVICE

| Program | Years of Initial implementation | Target populations | Likelihood of expansion | Comments |
|---|---|---|---|---|
| Casadel pueblos (education for masses) | 1920-30 | rural, urban poor | reached many, small expenditures | lowest participation in Chiapas, oaxaca versus D.D.F. and nuevo leon |
| I.M.S.S. Social security-health | 1940's | urban workers | slow, keeps spending low | goal never was redistribution |
| I.S.S.S.T.E. | 1950's | public service workers | what the traffic will bear | most government workers in Mexico City |
| Profit sharing | 1960's | urban workers | token? only if multi-nationals utilize? | does effect Mexico City workers more than others |
| Tax reform | 1978 | econ.active pop. | change in marginal rates important | some equity and increase |
| Child care | 1960's-80 | urban workers? | yes, with 2 bread-winners | daycare in 1980 |
| Restructuring of higher education | 1970's | middle class | aid to states reducing. geog. concentration | UNAM agreed to slower growth |
| S.A.M. & CONASUPO | 19760's-70's | rural & urban poor | suspended in 1980's geographic problems | did they miss their target? |
| Housing | 1970's | 8.9 million deficit | 800,000 shortfall in Mexico City | Gov. urged private market to cover it--or PRONASOL.? |
| COPLAMAR | 1977 | depressed zones & marginal groups | only 1.7% GDP in 1980. 70% of total pop.? | huge reserves? |
| Family safety net | 1970-80 | needy? | | more for middle groups? |

controvertial about our position is that the very nature of personal improvement, is such that it precludes further development along the choice lines of individuals, and, especially for the classes immediately below them (meaning, that their futures are of course dependent upon them in crucial ways). We intend that this chapter will focus on the nitty-gritty of social life.

Aspe and Beristain (in the *Political Economy of Income Distribution in Mexico*, 1984, p. 24) note the main objectives of government activity from 1934 to 1976. "Wage growth" was a central goal in two early periods, as was an "increase in employment." Income redistribution among workers and social groups was a central goal in the 1941–46 period and again between 1959 and 1976. "Improvement of the Standard of Living" was seen as an important objective from 1947 to 1976, through five or more sexenios. We should be concerned how this latter objective was implemented, although we are not one of those social policy types who neglect basic incomes! These authors also give a breakdown by presidents from 1934 to 1982 for % of public expenditure for education, health, and social welfare. These figures are separated as to total expenditures and "investment" monies.

Our focus as to human services and welfare is of course, on Mexico City at this point. Aspe and Sigmund (who are central to social statistics in Mexico) see 50% of the country's poor as being in CIUDADES PERDIDAS in the three largest cities (Mexico City, Guadalajara and Monterrey). Naturally poverty then is found proportionately elsewhere and has to be dealt with by uniform national policies and economic processes. The latter may not be likely however. Urban areas have a tendency to appropriate national resources, disproportionately not to numbers, but to regions.

The poor are pictured (p. 4) as significantly under twelve years of age, more often connnected with agriculture (but having representation in all employment categories), and are people who must spend much (70%) of the income on food in order to survive.

The policy implications of these and similar facts seem clear. Youth can not be dealt with by immediate employment policies, but education, health care and food policies are more relevant. The poor are able to spend only 1.2% of their income on education, and 45% have not finished primary schooling. Agriculture for many is also a trap in terms of levels of living. Working in the "modern" sector does not solve all problems either, where the high costs of urban living with its attendant pollution, crime, stress, etc., make for lower actual levels of living.

The authors are utilizing data from a 1977 Household Survey of income and expenditure (p. 4). Social justice, these authors note, has not been achieved, but neither abandoned. We are interested in the likely scenarios for the next generation. There are many slips between cup and lip! Namely that we document the shortcomings, and the mechanisms for remedy remain inadequate. The remainder of this chapter will be an attempt to spell out various scenarios for the welfare function in the next few decades.

Austerity has cut welfare expenditures since the early 1980's. Privatization, cutting subsidies (as on food stuffs) skimping on education and social security outlays have shrunk the total scene. Declines in public employment have been considerable. What probably has happened is that, overall, the increase in expenditure has slowed, with shifts to reprioritized hot spots. If our methods of prediction were to extrapolate from such post expenditure data of the kind James Wilkie collected up to the 1970's we would find a ragged but generally upward course through the 1970's.

Aspe and Beristain's data from *Cuenia Publica* can be used to augment the earlier studies for a considerable time series. We know that there are "lies, damned lies, and statistics," and the motivation to stress only the positive aspects makes much data suspect. The typical explanation of low levels of living also leaves much to be desired. Carlos Salinas de Gortari (now Mexico's president) notes in this same volume that Mexico's rural population is now 33% of the total, but up absolutely and still only generates 11% of the G.D.P. (p. 524). What seems to be description becomes a kind of explanation: to wit, the poor generate less wealth. But the poor are also descriptively suffering from rural locations which "complicates their access to the country's social services and development programs." Obviously urban poverty with easier access then needs a different explanation. This picture was published in 1984, and stresses as an end product, "support for the system." Leopold Solis writing in the same volume (p. 481) observes that "poverty (is) to be a phenomenon that is mainly rural" but the cost of expanding a rural or urban share is "enormous." "Modernization" is to be the saving procedure, and indeed Conasupo did make a different for awhile.

Our table below shows the types of historical programs (Promises?) to elevate the total population and achieve other goals as well. Many of these programs were implemented to a greater extent in Mexico City although some of the earliest were aimed at rural constituencies (as the Casa del Pueblos and the land programs). Aspe and Beristain note the hyperconcentration of health services in the Federal district (p. 315) where there are only 474 inhabitants per medical personnel (versus 5612 in Oaxaca). A "growing decentralization" may be found in secondary and higher education however (p. 324). More specific imbalances are noted however. Too much liberal arts training, not enough preventative medicine, and a scarcity of paramedic personnel are found especially in rural areas.

Urban absorbtion of human services will remain high although decentralization is occurring. The statistics documenting this imbalance will, of course, have an impact on policy! Our table is an attempt to predict the specific areas in which this will occur. Let us focus on housing as one of the most likely areas of contention after a modicum of educaitonal, nutritional and health access are achieved. Peter Ward's two major works stress the "reproduction of social inequality." A number of points are made by Ward about housing in Mexico City.

Housing is exploitive because of the low cost. Cheap (illegal) land and sweat equity ease the pressure for increases in real wages (1990, p. 189). Self building is self exploitation and this distorted the labor market as well. The nature of the housing and rehousing (as after the 1985 earthquake) process benefits the politicians who can manipulate it in a variety of ways. Self-help as an ideology reproduces inequality, and leads to the adoption of petite bourgeois values (1990, p. 192). State control is linked to the "stratification of housing provision." The size of the cake never gets larger, only the pieces of resources get smaller (Ward, p. 192). The more radical citizens would then be "renters, harrassed squatters and displaced downtown tenants" (p. 193).

Without going over Ward's whole thesis let us try to access the outcome of this for our predictions. Housing services (loans, land availability, title assistance, self help, provision of utilities and amenities, etc.) will only slowly expand to match the political pressure. Ward notes that the government response could be quick however, as in the State of Mexico when a payment strike by residents to companies brought "remedial" action (Ward, p. 151). We have in fact, two different scenarios—one of foot dragging forever, and the other of quickly responding. The latter may not lead to a permanent remedy, however. The model really is one of balancing one group's claims against anothers (Campesinos versus squatters?).

Ward's main concerns seem to center on the issue of the "consolidator" who builds on land (illegally) on the urban periphery and finally benefits from their "sweat equity" (Ward, pgs. 52, 186, 191). The ability to generate an "investment surplus" was related to the level of the final product and this was, evidently, related to real wages and costs of

# FUTURE OF PUBLIC SERVICE
## (1985–90 DATA FROM WARD, RIDING, NORD, ASPE)

| AREA | Type of Change | Mex. City's share of the total 1985 | 2010 |
|---|---|---|---|
| Education<br>- general<br>- higher | Average schooling in 1985=5 years, goal should be 12 by 2010.<br>Middle classes keep pressure on for more college education. | -1970=lowest # of illiterates(Aspe, 1984, page 275)<br>-41% of total, (Ward, 1985, page 54) | 30%? |
| Health<br>- public<br>- clinical | Regressions will spotlight need for resurgence.<br>Pressure for high tech medicine from middle groups. | Fed.Dist. 50% more doctors than nee Barry, '92, page235.<br>-44% of total hospital budget (Ward, p.54) | |
| Income Distribution | From top 30% getting 73% (Ward) to bottom half getting 40% of income (transfers)? (Gini coefficients from .476 to .569) | -37.4% of gross internal product (Ward, page 54) -will still grow? | 40%? |
| Water, Fire, Trans., Sewer, Garbage | Transportation up 2000-2005.(metro expansion)<br>More services for "lost cities." | See chapter VI on infrastructure States given more of Federal budget, Municipalities more so | |
| Housing, planning | More consolidation, gentrification; more employer linked housing? Teeth in plans? | -57.5% of public, low cost housing (Ward, page 54) | 40%? |
| Age Groups | In 1985-56% under 20 = will be aging in 2010 to 45. | Young & old do better in M.C., pressures under PRONASOL may change this | 50% |
| Social Security Pensions | More of surplus will have to be spent because of aging population.(Middle groups have gained at expense of marginalized--E. L. Thalman, 1984, p.399) | -IMSS serves whole population -proportional if follow,I! Model | |
| Nutrition | Conasupo must compete better with private sector. (Food stamps, target group subsidies, would be most cost effective-Nora Lustig, 1984, page 465.)<br>Programs criticized for too many vitamin pills. | Barry(1992) notes PRONASOL's concern for nutrition, appropriate) rural. M.C. has abundant markets. | |

building materials (p. 191). Recent trends (likely to continue?) seen a double crunch on wages and costs, thus, deminishing the investment surplus.

Our ability to predict the well-being of citizens of the ZMCM especially of the lower middle classes, seems dependent upon these macroforces of real wages and the costs of resources. Can we assume more of the same decline? Are these the halcyon days? Our predictions must be based on more specific factors than the current crunch. To do this we will look area by area at human services in terms of those factors. We hope to go beyond an overall pessimism or optimism. First as to education at all levels.

## Educational Projections

Aspe and Beristain discuss the meeting of educational demand in Mexico ("Distribution of Education and health opportunities and services," 1984, p. 271). Their table on schooling by states shows the period from 1960 to 1970 with the national totals improving from the percent of no instruction from 43.6% to 34.8%. The Federal District had of course the lowest number without any instruction (from 21.7% to 16.7%). The worst states were Chiapas, Guerrero, and Oaxaca. As to higher education the Federal District went from 3.6% in 1960 to 4.8% in 1970. Now 20 years later trying to predict the next 3 decades, can we assume continued progress for Mexico or Mexico City? The policy change toward slowing UNAM's growth and also the funding of State Universities will transform the relative statistics and the total educational involvement. The pressure of the various constituencies from consolidators to middle class will increase educational expenditure—now one of the lowest in the Americas.

Hadley Cantril in the 1950's did a world survey of common human needs, and the demand for education was near the top along with health and security for their children. The pressure will be on, and minimal education is not as expensive as clinical medicine or effective mass transportation. The formula we could use for prediction would include pressure (or fittingness) for improvement (1 to 5); cost of the service (5 for public health as inexpensive, 1 for housing); and timeliness (1 to 5). The latter element refers to a range of matters that include urgency (public health in the 1920's or workers pensions in the 1940 period of industrialization); visibility (the pollution issue was not seen as life-threatening in the 1950 by many); and remediable (in the 1990's pollution abatement technology was more available).

To use this formula on education in the 1920–40 period the pressure for elementary education would be high (+5); the cost was moderate (+3); and the timeliness was high (+5) due to "urgency" and visibility as to importance—even with disagreements about its functions or "socialist" content. In the 1960's to 70's the formula for technical or other types of higher education would loom larger, even though the types made available may seem to lack balance (too much in the elite subject areas?). The pressure for higher education (including liberal arts and technical in the 1960's and beyond period) will continue for the next three decades (+5). The costs will be a drawback, but "cost efficiency" will ameliorate the drawbacks, hence +4. As to our third element, timeliness in the sense that higher education has the appropriate remedies, a +5 is guaged.

## Housing and Other Amenities in Mexico City

> There is no doubt that in most respects, low-income residents enjoy considerable advantages compared to their counterparts in rural areas. (Gilbert & Ward, *Housing, the State of the Poor*, 1985, page 56.)

From affluent housing in the Pedegral-San Angel-Coyoacan area through upper midele class Satellite city abodes down to the "irregular" colonias populares, the range is, of course, incredible. Our concern in this section is with the housing and amenities of the less affluent, although we will discuss this in relationship to what the other sectors seek and obtain. Many students of housing and land in Mexico City are in print already and focus on problems of the poor. These include Gilbert and Ward, our main source, and other scholars such as Edith Jimenez, Wayne Cornelius, and Rene Coulomb.

We are especially concerned with issues centered on the very appearance of such irregular housing *on a vast scale* in Mexico City and its down the road consequences. Ward and Gilbert note three reasons for the "vast scale" of this sector in Mexico City (1955, p. 87).

Summarized these include:

1) A demand for housing workers where huge side profits could be made.
2) The existance of land not too many interests covet or can lay their hands on.

3) Real estate practices of manipulative sorts.

Although we can overemphasize issues of private greed and public corruption they may go a long way to explain the facilitation role of such an otherwise natural looking process. Our effort probably should not be to explain the overdetermined events, but to prognosticate its down-the-road consequences. Let us conceptualize, piggy-backing on the above, alternative futures in the amenity-housing area. The assumptions we are proceeding on include:

a) that a capitalist-export oriented urban economy will persist with a need for workers on a very *particular* basis.
b) the locational outcomes of such poor communities have only, minimally, been offset by "planning" and a sprinkling of amenities—the structural problems remain.
c) real estate practices can be modified, but not totally restrained.

And, with respect to the newest trends, things are in the saddle and riding mankind; and they are global in scope. Systems analysis has moved to a global level and Mexico City is a dependent satellite to remote metropolis power. Being the largest urban population will not reduce the problems of the cost of building materials, energy, interest, or of labor. The external forces include the way in which Mexico's foreign debt must be paid, the value of its petroleum and other exported products, the costs of needed technology from abroad and the demands of remote banking gnomes.

More specifically on Mexico's economic predicament we can review the Inter-American Development Bank's assessment. In their 1989 special edition on "Savings investment and growth" the construction sector is the gloomiest by far from 1985 to 1988 (p. 380). This construction sector would include housing, of course. Overall, the main policy objective was to stabilize prices. Optimism was registered with respect to manufacturing exports, especially autos—but these are not made in Mexico City. Imports went up sharply because of the "pent-up demand" (p. 381). Unfortunately for construction, the real interest rate rose to "an unprecendented level of nearly thirty percent." The results of this were to reduce all construction, at least in the near future.

In construction the high real interest rates, the reduction of investment spending by the public sector and the sharp decrease in credit during the first half of the year resulted in a drop of about five percent in overall activity. (Page 382)

Not even the generally affluent are going to borrow money at a 30% interest rate to build a home. Actually the poor get no credit so it is not a big issue. Public housing starts, even with post-earthquake pressures, are also minimal. The demands for conformity to the foreign banks are reinforced by many factors, not the least of which is that any real growth is predicted on external resources. (IADB, 1989, p. 384, says $7 billion are needed annually to attain a 4.5% growth rate.)

With respect to the total construction sector much of the investment will be in infrastructure. Transportation, utilities supports to export-oriented industries will be the lion's share of new construction.

The poor have always relied on self-help for construction. Legalization of land titles is one aspect they have turned to government for, and down the line they have received utilities and other services. Richard Moore in a 1984 study "Urbanization and Housing Policy in Mexico" (in Aspe and Sigmund) note such activities of the poor in Netzahualcoyotl (p. 340). Of 90,338 units ⅔ are owner occupied. Ninety percent are of inferior construction (plaster board, adobe or packed dirt). Thirteen percent are in a state of deterioration, and 20% are basically "families without housing." While considerable variety in housing and land use is noted, assistance still needs to be targeted. The very poor are seen as "price rather than location oriented" (p. 341). Policies that focus on regularization and the securing of land tenure have been in effect for over two decades, and we would assume that they will continue.

In 1970 the largest problem was having any kind of housing. Moore seen 102,374 families as needing housing (not meaning that they were on the streets, but being in houses already occupied), (p. 337). In the Federal district the number was 129,681 families. It was true that the larger proportion of these families had an "effective demand" (they earned at least 85% of the going minimum wage). Where are we at in 1993?

# B.  Mexico City's Environment:
# When Will the Air be Clear?

## Mexico City's Environment

With a population ever more knowledgeable about the state of its environment, it is certain that demands for more and better information

# SOCIAL PROBLEMS
# CHANGES 1990–2020

| "PROBLEM" | CHANGES, TRENDS. ETC. | MITIGATING CONDITIONS? |
|---|---|---|
| CRIME & DELINQUENCY | -PATTERN OF FACILITATION ALWAYS CHANGING <br> -YOUTH MORE ALIENATED? | -INCREASED CITIZEN PARTICI- PATION <br> -CHANGE IN U.S. DRUG USE ALLOWS CHANGING MEXICAN PRIORITIES |
| EDUCATIONAL SHORTFALL | -SHORTFALL STILL NOT REDUCED? <br> -NAFTA STRESSES TECHNICAL TRAINING | -BETTER TEACHER'S SALARIES <br> -1970s REVOLUTION REMEMBERED <br> -MARKET EXPANSION MAY IM- PROVE MIDDLE LEVELS |
| JOBLESSNESS | -PERSISTANT LAG IN MINIMUM WAGES. & BENEFITS <br> -INFORMAL SECTOR STILL LARGE <br> -"OPEN ECONOMY" PROTECTS FEW | -PRIVITIZATION AND NAFTA HAVE HAD MAJOR IMPACT <br> -UNIONS RECOUPING ON WORKER RIGHTS |
| REMEDOABLE ILLNESSES | -CONTINUED UNDERREPORTING <br> -STILL TOO MANY PROFESSION- ALS IN THE CITY, RURAL AREAS SLOW | -AIDS FACED UP TO? <br> -GROSSER ASPECTS .OF ENVIRON- ment & NUTRITION IMPROVED <br> -MORE EFFICIENT ACTION ON EPIDEMICS? |
| POLLUTION | -CONTINUED RESPIRATORY PROBS <br> -ENVIRONMENTAL DEGRADATION CONTINUES. a "CIRCLE OF POISON" | --AUTOS & FACTORIES TAMED? <br> -CALAMITIES GALVANIZED POLICY CHANGES |
| POVERTY | -PRONASOL WILL HAVE TO BE REINVENTED <br> -NEWER JOBS MODELED ON EX PLOITED MAQUILADORES? | -INFORMAL ECONOMY MAY BE AN INSTITUTIONALIZED LADDER <br> -YOUTH MOVES TO BETTER AREAS WILL CONTINUE |
| APATHY AND NON- PARTICIPATION | -"DEMOCRATIC" FORMS WILL CONTINUE TO EVOLVE | -CHILANGO IDENTITY WILL BE SEEN AS MORE POSITIVE IN REGIONAL COMPETITION |

about the air quality are certain to grow. But information is expensive, and unless priorities shift or the government receives outside aid, it is doubtful that offices such as SEDUE will be able to provide as much of it as people would like. (*Mexico Journal*, Dec. 18, 1989, page 24, "Counting the Particles.")

The above quote shows the contrary factors that will decide Mexico City's alternative futures with respect to environmental concerns: More public awareness and demands versus government prioritizing and limited funds. One must also assume the existence of powerful interests in favor of maintaining the status quo. The situation in Mexico City has gone far enough as of 1988 to try to affect auto-truck emissions, for instance. The Transport Program 1988–2000 stopped trucks from passing through Mexico City enroute to adjacent areas. "Alternative routes" from Queretaro to Puebla were mandated, and so forth. Other suggestions were bus only lanes, luxury colectivos in wealthy areas, direct colectivos to places like the airport, bike lanes (good luck in Mexico City's traffic) and other traffic reduction measures. One in particular, which was implemented, had to do with "a day without a car," (*Mexico Journal*, Dec. 18, 1989, p. 10) where people with certain license plates found themselves ticketed if they drove on the wrong day. Whether symbolic or not, this will not clear the air, so it must have other purposes. Evidently, (Lazaroff, 1989, p. 10) some pollutants declined marginally and others (lead) did not. The new "Oxygenated" gasoline actually raised some pollutants.

Our task in this chapter is not to deal with monitoring or informing issues, because these seem to be moving incrementally toward their optimal deployment. Rather, the potential for change will be examined on a two decade time frame. Key elements (auto emision, control of industrial polluters, technical breakthroughs, improved use of energy, etc.) will be approached so as to assess their potentials for change. The maximal improvement may be based on the public's level of tolerance. There is a bad joke about urban citizens who would not trust any air they could not see. The current author's attachment to Minnesota's relatively clean water has led him to note the greater tolerance for highly polluted water (nearly a fire danger) elsewhere. Let us proceed with our model to explore the potential for change. One's goal or hopes can not be completely utopian. The landscape paintings of Jose Maria Velasco of the Valley of Mexico in 1891 and 1905 showed no deterioration in the clarity of the air (humidity and dust excluded) and there can be days when the background, snow-capped volcanos will be visible again! Indeed, on a recent Easter weekend, when people have shut down or left the metro-area—the air was indeed clear.

# A Model of Environmental Change:

As noted above, the major change factors as far as the environment are concerned, are:

Public Tolerance
Information Levels
Technological Improvements
Affordability—generally
Level of Resistance by vested interests
Political Reform of appropriate agencies
Nature's Cooperation (i.e., no volcanism, fewer inversions, etc.)

Let us plot these factors on a "predictive scale" where a number of assumptions are made—conscious ones. These assumptions include the following:

The technological elements in producing better air, water, and an end to environmental degradation are close at hand, but do involve costs, as: improved fuels or a switch from petroleum to electricity

Information levels depend partly on technological factors (for monitoring) but more on agency responsiveness and public demand and utilization. Discrimination between 5 or 10 or 100 parts per million of a specific contaminant (lead?) will not come easily and the cause and effect relationships will be variously perceived. A focus on mortality data may be of greater value. (See "Healthiest Towns and Unhealthiest, Too," *Boston Magazine*, April 1987.) Death rates (standardized mortality ratios for a specified period might be a better form of information than levels of specific pollutants. Cancer "hot spots" might also be noted, as with bladder, kidney, or lung cancer; and these would constitute the type of information which would help mobilize people.

We would hypothesize that the level of public tolerance for pollution would decline in relation to certain types of "mobilizing information." Information that could only vaguely by used in a cause and effect fashion might lead to confusion and apathy. Actually, Sedues' 500 point scale with verbal designations at various points may be more likely to affect public tolerance levels than "parts per million."

Mother Nature ranges from beneign to beastly as we all know, and remains unpredictable. The unkindest cuts for Mexico City are earthquakes, possible volcanism, ordinary thermal inversions, or winds that blow filth around. Floods from unusual rains could transform parts of Mexico City into a sewer as well. The buffering of nature has occurred by great effort, and this will continue, especially when many of these other factors come into line. It is well known that the 1985 Mexico City earthquake (as the more recent one in the San Francisco Bay area) have raised many issues of preparedness.

Affordability being placed number 5 on our 1 to 7 scale refers to the costs of technological improvement and to its likelihood of being a high priority. The competing problems of potable water, a declining infrastructure, sinking buildings, lack of affordable housing, and a transportation nightmare keep the costs of a clean up in a problematic state—especially with the current cut of public expenditures. The *Mexico Journal* notes a windfall of fines from the "leave your car at home policy"—which could be earmarked for environmental concern. Each new regime offers the possibilities of political reform, and a victory by the "Frente" seemingly more so. Local home rule may or may not be the essential reform as all of these other 6 factors have to be dealt with. Sedue may just need more workers and monitors. More policies to reduce smoking vehicles are quite feasible, and do not need radical reforms. Getting people to stop littering may be as simple as a few thousand trash baskets and an ad campaign. The real rub politically will be our last category, namely to deal with vested interests in not changing as with faulty technology and passing various costs on to the public rather than improving it.

## The Perils of Naive Extrapolation Or Comparison

There is a built-in caveat with respect to arm chair, apriori speculation, this is the case with respect to explanations and certainly with attempted predictions. Even comparisons are cautiously approached, and popular logic speaks of the error of comparing apples and oranges. On the other hand there is less concern about the possible invalidity of extrapolations or of their ability to predict counter-trends. History hardly knows of a "trend" that goes with certitude to its inexorable outcome. The world's population growth and the increase in general, human affairs are closest to sure bets, but the pace and occurance of reversals seem to defy prediction. Worst of all is the fate of optimistic predictions based on continuing "trends" extending into the near future, as with the supposed impact of better technology to ameliorate pollution. Pollution, or any environmental-social issue, is not merely a technological problem! For instance, the United Nations had the monitoring capacity to compare the world's great cities as of 1980. Particulate matter, sulfur dioxide and carbon monoxide could be compared, but as of 1988, Mexico choose not to participate. (*New York Times*, August 6, 1989, page 19.) It was true that 30 of the 50 cities monitored by the Global Enviormental Monitoring System did exceed the original standards set by W.H.O. But

Mexico City is still seen as the worst in the world, and in such pollutants as lead, it is horrendous. So if solutions are available, why do not technological and social "trends" lead to their application?

So what is the problem?

While demographic extrapolation involves a kind of belief in natural and predictable forces, which may or may not be warranted, cleaning the environment does not merely involve the appropriate technology nor the alignment of favorable attitudes. Our previous table of predictions balks at weighing the obstructing role of vested interests. Clearly when the staff of one of the first air monitoring units in Mexico City resigned in wholesale fashion over such interest group manipulation, then we have a manifest problem.

One can project the long term "trend" of big industries as one of having their own way! The idea of a countervailing political force has a bit of magical thought associated with it. The photo chemical smog in the valley of Mexico does not hit the powerful, well-to-do who live above the polluted bowl of the central city. It is also true that the prevailing winds blow-ill for the people in southern parts of the city— some of whom are affluent and politically active. Many people caught in this incredible pollution, may loose their sense of political efficacy. Along with transportation sources the industrial complexes to the north of the city must be tamed, not just the most obvious polluters such as chrome or petro-chemical plants. The terrible explosions in Mexico City and in Guadalajara may heighten the resolve on the part of publics and elites. Change will come as a result of technological evolution as well as a result of increased political will. The Metropolitan Air Quality Index (IMECA) shows that Satelite City and Lomas areas to the west as being much better off thant he almost equally affluent areas of Coyoacan and the Pedregal to the far south. Probably the increasing participation of social elites in the cleanup efforts will bring about more commitment to the solutions. But what are the real dangers in the kind of extrapolation used earlier in this section?

Naive extrapolation (or any type of analysis, as comparisons, etc.) fails to relate what it observes to a range of theories or attempts at explanation. Ward and Gilbert (in *Housing, the State and the Poor*, 1985, page 241) note that whether the phenomenon at hand has to do with land, housing, clean air or water or any other amenity, it is obvious that these special benefits are not immediately available. Contrasting liberal-managerial, Marxist instrumental, and structural approaches they say that none of the three are entirely satisfactory. There is too much variation, apparently, in the various situations observed especially as to how the poor get their due. We can believe that threats of instability, problems of capital formation and the furthering of the state's interests must be involved. We will not review Ward and Gilbert's analysis, but can suspect that similar elements are involved in environmental improvement. Clearly bureaucrats have some autonomy; states often facilitate elite-private interests, and the impact on the work force and its political efficacy are often the modus operandi for action.

Sophisticated analysis, of what ever type, is aware of elements that have potential and possible causal impact. Environmental improvement will probably follow from the coincidence of many of the above; namely a win-win interest game, an absence of major sources of instability, relative state autonomy, and the cessation of open class conflict.

More often than not when an actual environmental issue emerges, some other game obscures the "solution." For instance, the issue of needed open land (a "Zona del Ajusco) according to Stephen P. Mumme ("The evolution of Mexican Environmental Policy," LASA, 1984, page 24) pitted "largely middle class environmental activists against urban squatter communities." How exacerbating was this conflict is not known, but it is likely to occur—especially as a diversion.

More basic conflicts may involve the macro-economics of the urban scene. A recent conference at Loyola Institute for Latin American legal studies dealing with the subject of the Latin American Free Trade agreements impact upon the environment featured Cuantemoc Cardenas on the need for a social charter that would coincide with old and new predicaments. The pressure for increased National product under such agreements will produce a more hazardous, dirty environment under the present pattern of rule. The present legal machinery and levels of enforcement will not head-off environmental destruction on a terrible scale. There will be no viable social charter in the near future! Ecological concerns, may however, be included in the planning process.

We realize that naivete may enter the use of any theory or method. A Delphi panel may use extrapolation, comparison, of personally derived instruments with smarts or without them. Predictions beyond zero-order levels, however, are possible. The linkage to the world community may be the ultimate factor in the cleaning-up of Mexico's environment, and adjustments can be made in this relationship. Let us close here on a note of realism from Ward and Gilbert: (page 250)

It cannot be assumed that more sophisticated and rigorous planning necessarily helps the poor. In the urban environments of most Latin American

countries there are too many already powerful, vested interests already to
benefit most from a better organized urban fabric.

# C.  Mexico City as a Mega-Culture . . .

## Mexico City as a Super Center of Culture

Those who are intensely proud of the cultural heritage of Tenochititlan
would also remember the mistreatment of commoners, the infanticide,
cannibalism, slavery, bloody festivals and vicious tribute. The Huitzilo-
pochtli cult was especially used to terrorize people into contributions
(see Kandell, 1988, p. 62). We know how the Spanish state church and
general culture used Mexico City's hegemony to pound the country into
its mold. Kandell observes correctly that the colonial centuries did not
have one consistent cultural voice or impact as with the split between
regular and secular clergy (p. 226). The turbulent centuries of independence seen a confused cultural projection from the nation's capital.

Self-conscious efforts to make Mexico City the hub of national culture probably picked up again after 1850, but were perversely of a pari-
sian character (Kandell, p. 340). A "Royal European atmosphere" was
to be created (p. 342) for the capital. There was only contempt for what
was Mexican. Diaz after 1876 had another cultural role for the capital.
After first fighting the highwaymen, the "cesspool of crime" itself,
Mexico City, was to be cleansed—at least in affluent areas. Mexico's
more independent newspapers (*El Democrata*) criticized these clean up
efforts. But the Porfiriato was a high point for creole influence, and, of
course, was death to Indian culture at the same time. It was a jingoistic
culture in the extreme, and traditional Mexican people were actually
kept out of the central zones. Kandell traced the "geography of wealth
in Porfirian Mexico City" (p. 377) to the Jockey Club. "Literacy lectures and debates on positivism" (p. 378) were issued from this cultural
center. Near by the Reforma was dressed up to look like the Champs-
Elysees. The Francophilia was not entirely shared by the new middle
classes and their tastes ran to music halls and low comedy rather than
lectures and opera. Kandell notes the themes of romance and money
problems. Bullfights were the height of culture for the middle-to-lower
classes. The city as a whole did prosper under Diaz but the crowning
cultural event was yet to come.

To offset challenges there was to be a splenderous celebration in Sep-

# CULTURAL RESOURCE POTENTIAL

| CULTURAL FORM | CURRENT ROLE AS TO: PRODUCING AN URBAN CULTURE | PRODUCING A NATIONAL CULTURE | POTENTIALS TO 2010 |
|---|---|---|---|
| UNIVERSITY BASED OFFERINGS | UNAM, El Colegio de Mexico, produce constant supply Intellectuals "Play the Politics of Culture" (Riding) | Occasional touring groups Book publishing important, competes with State Universities | Financing fluctuates, state universities have great regional potential |
| GOV'T SPONSORED MEDIA | Most significant involvement may be via advertisement of public service messages. Private stations must take 12.5% of content from state (not always available or utilized) | Films represented most active area (1960's?) State television a "poor competitor" (E. Mahan) Its "ambivalent" (Channel 11 & 13) | Financing fluctuates, did provide stability Interested in a "national integration of values" (Schnitman) |
| PRIVATE, ELITE CULTURAL INSTITUTIONS | Tamayo Museum National Institute of Fine Arts (gov't supported) National Institute for Anthropology & History | Worked to move intellectuals away from Stalinism | Must focus on a national synthesis Not be divisive in self-interests |
| SPONTANEOUS POPULAR SOURCES | Guadalajara's mariachi took root in Mexico City | Radio spread popular corridos & musica ranchera Caribbean sales now more popular than Mexican music | Popular culture moves on waves of its own (?) No prediction forth coming |
| POPULAR MAGAZINES | Provenemex, televisa = major owners; "women's" magazines are popular, comics, photonovels = big business | Gov't banned some comics & photo-novels in 1980's; (hinterlands reaction to "pornography?") | Printed media will continue—has a permanent part-time audience |
| SERIOUS MAGAZINES | Excelsiors Plural, Proceso, Nexos, Vuelta are some of most import | Michoacan and other states do well on their own | |
| CINEMA | Subsidization is down | Gov't sponsored films did glorify Mexico's past; Charro films were clearly Mexican | |
| RADIO—TV | Televisa monopoly, radio ownership less concentrated, dependent on ads | Televisa = "most powerful cultural entrepreneur in Mexico" (E. Mahan) | Channel 13 as yet can't compete with televisa (Riding) |
| NEWSPAPERS | From fly sheets to La Jornada, a good range-hyperactive (economic) competition—23 dailies (Robert Pierce, p. 105) | Excelsior is close to national paper. Cultural supplements help | |
| RECORDED MUSIC | | | |
| TRANSNATIONAL SOURCES | 39% of T.V. content imported in 1970—Tunstall, 1977, p. 278 11th largest foreign market for Hollywood films Morelos satellite system | Media imperialism may be declining, allowing more national content Middle class likes U.S. style music (Riding, p. 311) Has nationalist motives vs. dependent development | Must find an alternative to cablevision S.A. which brings American networks into Mexican homes (Riding p. 313) |

tember of 1910. Although the centennial celebration did not achieve its ends for Diaz or for Mexico City as cultural fountainhead for the nation, it did focus the country on the issues of what Mexico and Mexico City had become. A new cultural ambiance would be coming from Mexico City; rather than Francophilia, European elite culture and parades of Rurales, it would now show case revolutionaries or at least the depth of the emerging conflict. It is true that Mexico City's culture was only thinly realized in the hinterland. Mexico City had spurned native and Mestizo culture. News of Madero's assassination were much more influential on country than the city's pitiful representation of national culture. The capital was totally discredited by events and its own nature in the decade of the 1910's.

The attempt to recoup the capital and "forge the fatherland" would lead to a new cultural change for Mexico City. Jose Vasconcelos, Obregon's secretary of education, would now subsidize Mexican culture, music, and other arts. Mural painting on behalf of nationhood would be enlisted. The San Carlos Academy of Fine Arts would not be cradle of this new cultural form, it was still doing its European thing. Other combinations of cultural threads would come together in the new Mexican socialism. It was at least a cultural image of what Mexico wanted to be (Kandell, p. 450). The Fresco techniques did require group efforts, and this did impact the character of the new cultural form. The bohemian freedom of the syndicate did allow the aboriginal cultural theme to emerge. Mariachi songs, pulque, and strong language became their style, and a change in national culture was afoot. Of course, most of it was lavished on Mexico City, but the revolutionary rhetoric did spill over to the hinterland. The cultural transformation that did occur, however, was that pre-Columbian peoples and their survivors were now to be seen as a cultural treasure. Anticlericalism, proworker sentiments, and secular learning were part of this cultural message—not always to be appreciated in the next decade.

## Mexico City Versus the Nation

> He (Cardenas) was the first Mexican president to attempt to narrow the political chasm between Mexico City and the provinces. (Kandell)

In the 1930's Mexico City would become a different kind of center for the nation. The new cinema and the beginnings of radio would bring a new popular culture to the hinterland. The newspaper circulation remained local, but copies could be bought in outlying towns along transportation routes.

One must remember that Mexico's next two largest cities, Guadalajara and Monterrey have been a bit standoffish with respect to culture and power issues. Alan Riding has written (*Distant Neighbors*, 1984) about "the other Mexicos." Although "millions of capitalinos maintain nostalgic ties to some distant home" (p. 276) there is also a perspective "of suffocating control and indiscriminate imposition by Mexico City" in the hinterland. Perhaps it is the elites of these other large cities who are so wary about Mexico City's influence in various spheres? Riding does note the obvious differences between "the mestizo and colonial center, the modern Americanized north and the old Indian south" (p. 278). In any instance, the cultural resources of Mexico City may not be all Mexico's cup of tea! The dynamic, outward-looking-north and the resistant south both may "regard Chilangos as interfering foreigners" (p. 290).

We want to assess Mexico City's cultural resources especially as they might aid in the production of national culture. In doing this we will be reliant on Elizabeth Mahan's article "Cultural Industries in Mexico: preliminary observations," Alan Riding's chapter "Culture for some and for many," and our own observations going back to the late 1960's. Our table summarizes Mexico City's cultural resources and tries to assess their national role, now and two decades from now.

Alan Riding notes the propensity of the Mexican intellectual (most who are in Mexico City) to play the "politics of culture" (p. 295). Popular culture, so called, has been left to commercial interests, but as we shall see, not without serious reservations. Televisia is seen as "involving the greatest cession of power by the state since the revolution" (p. 295). The main complaint is that Televisia is "denationalizing the country by presenting the American way of life as a new ideal reachable through obsessive consumption" (p. 313). Having Mexico City as a cultural fountainhead probably has never been high on the agenda of other Mexicans. There may even be a feeling of "internal media imperialism" to go along with the fear of external varieties. Historically the cultural e xport from Mexico City as Carlos Fuentes (quoted in Riding, p. 296) went from one dogma to another, namely Catholicism to Marxism! One must remember that Mexico City's influence has historically gone from Aztec bloodiness, to four centuries of European imposition with the crowning Francophilia under Diaz. Only with the departure of revolutionary art did this previous veneer give way to Mexican themes, prehispanic and contemporary. Riding notes the syncretism that has taken place in most cultural areas, except for classical music where an attempt to "incorporate a native force" led to a reaction against "folkloric content. . . . in music, dance and opera" (Riding, p. 303). The muralists, who were accused of establishing a "cactus curtain" had their influence from the capital, but the provinces would produce its own art style in the more surreal, abstract works of Tamayo, Merida and Toledo. Riding notes the great gap between high-brow culture and the "mediocrity of mass entertainment" (p. 307) and attributes it to the average level of education at five years. The impact of U.S. media imperialism is also stressed. More burdensome is government censorship as in the 1950's when the government subsidized film industry censored almost any political content for "fear of political and moral subversion" (Riding, p. 309). The strongest criticism by Riding, however, is reserved for Televisa which "has become the country's Ministry of Culture, its Ministry of Education and its Ministry of Information" (p. 311).

In dealing with the Mexican media one must also remember that great profits are involved. The spinoffs from Hollywood are one thing, but telenovelas were the basis for the Spanish Internation Networks (SIN) which took its programming successfully abroad. It would be hard to say that U.S. content was dominating the Mexican scene, when they are great exporters themselves, but such may be the case. Clearly, cablevision is a conduit for almost total U.S. broadcasting (see table below). U.S. movies stand out on Televisa and even S.E.P. sponsored Channel 11 has as its highpoint an old U.S. "classic" (as Bob Hope in his portrayal of Casanova). We do not have data on the rediffusion of Mexico City's newspaper or electronic media. Way back in the early 1970's the message of cultural Channel 11 was rediffused by 10 medium-wave, 10 short wave and 3 FM transmitters (Robert Pierce, 1979, p. 111). The government was evidently buying up commercial radio stations and concealing their ownership at this point in time. We do not know what the surge of privitized actions did in the 1980's however. Pierce in 1979 notes the chain of 28 educaitonal and cultural channels, under the control of Mexico City's Channel 11 (p. 111). One interesting side light about Mexico City's capacity to serve the country was the near blackout of diffusion after the September 1985 earthquake which did impact the city's media for a short period.

*The Almanoque de Mexico* in its "Arte y Cultura" section has a list of newspapers, magazines, and radio and T.V. stations by state. Although circulation data is not given, it does show linkage with Mexico City and hinterland regions. Given what Robert Pierce says about government ownership practices, as in radio, we do not know all of the linkages from the capital. Televisia's channels are well represented as far as T.V. is concerned and Channel 13 is also. The most frequent channel represented outside of Mexico City is Channel 2, which may be Televisia's flagship channel. Our table below shows the typical content from the various channels, and also the amount of non-Mexican content in such media systems as Cablevision.

Much of the history of attempts to balance Mexico's media content over the years is written about in Fatima Fernandez Christier's article "El Derecho a la Informacion y los Medio de Disuion Masiua" in *Mexico Hoy*, 1979, p. 329. Balancing "la libertad de expression" with the mass availability of information has been no small problem. It is not just one of Mexico City versus the hinterland, obviously. Basic problems of political reform are involved. We will finish this chapter by trying to speculate where these problems of mass information and political reform will be in two decades.

## Cultural Potential of Mexico City in the Next Two Decades

Our table covers a range of university, government, private elite, private media, transnational and spontaneous sources for cultural materials. The supply of pesos drives the machinery of most of them. (Popular culture does have some "democratic" roots.) Under current role for producing an "urban culture" examples are given. Only under private T.V., large newspaper activities and "transnational" sources were some estimates of size noted. Televisia, Excelsior and Cablevision are very large, and will continue to be so in the future one suspects. Tunstall's *The Media are American* reflects a decade old assessment about T.V. content and the "movies." Many see "media imperialism" as declining, but new technology may alter this. Many nationalistic Mexicans dearly want to alter this invasion, but may retreat to their own cultural digging as they have done elsewhere.

As to the production of a national culture, the hegemony of Mexico City in political and economic matters would argue for an imposing role. Much resistance from the "other Mexico's" has been the case historically as we have tried to note in this chapter. This closeness of Mexico's north to Yankee influences and the rugged, if not splendid, isolation of the south have reduced the capital's import. As state universities evolve their own case of culture producers they will augment or even rival those of UNAM one would suppose. This is already happening and is being goven various support. Government activities in film radio, T.V., and publishing may well increase, but will fluctuate as money, policy and political expendiency allow. Private, elite institutions have their own web to spin, but may have to go along with "national destiny," like all other agencies.

By definition, spontaneous sources of popular culture and knowledge will remain unpredictable as to source, content and influences. These forms may come from almost anywhere given their syncristic nature. Jeremy Tunstall (1977, p. 274) discusses "local, authentic" media hybreds, and spontaneous cultural elements which will arrive as they always have. People remain inventive in the presence or absence of structured formal cultural forms. It may be that music, folk arts, games, social forms, verbal bantering are what emerges. These may be a reaction to national or international stimulus, but once established they will inspire atttempts to capture them for commercial, artistic, or political gain. These spontaneous forms, with their grass roots origins, may be supported so as to rival the currently institutionalized forms. We must not forget neo-traditional varieties either. Mexico's "national culture" will probably remain pluralistic, given current diversity.

And what of the next two or three decades?

## Mexico City's Cultural Resources in the Year 2010

There is a very large amount of cultural product being made available every week in Mexico. Much of it comes from the capital, intended for local, national and even international consumption. These cultural materials range in information content. It ranges in "authenticity," and in the satisfactions it obtains. The massiveness of the mass media may be its salient characteristic, here or anywhere—as quantity replaces quality in the eyes of many observers. The basis for a national culture must be centered on Mexico City even though we have noted the variation in the national landscape. Decentralization as to some aspects of national culture is continuing to take place.

However, Mexico City's cultural products are now serving a latino population north of the Rio Bravo and spinoffs of printed and electronic cultural products are distributed to other parts of the Americas. The future would seem to be one of enhancement in this direction. Our table shows specific predictions of the role and potential of various cultural sources. Then we will use a diagram to predict at least the direction of "possible media forms and their accommodations."

## Possible Media Forms and Accommodations

Despite the complexity and variety of mass media systems experts often urge the adoption of a simplistic scheme of classification—a bipolar view with the "free" U.S. system at the desirable end of a continuum, and totalitarian systems at the other end. (Alan Wells, *Mass Communications: A World View*, Ed.)

Our triangular figure was suggested by Alan Wells attempts to deal with the complexity of media situations. Instead of public, commercial and political control our triangle has government-public sponsored, commercially sponsored and non-Mexican (multi-national?) media. Admittedly these are not different types in the same sense as Well's 3 types, but they allow for a dimensional space in which certain relationships can be noted, including the possible directions of change and accommodation. Government sponsorship in one form or another in Mexico takes many forms, some of which we may never be fully aware of. Although Televisia seems very independent, there seem also to be symbolic ties to the government. U.S. films are used in many places and Tunstall notes that 39% of T.V. content (not just utilized by Cablevision) was imported in 1977 (p. 278, in *The Media Are American*). We are not striving for simplicity in this diagram, but instead trying to show how future accommodations might be in the process of "becoming."

Elite, popular and specialized media were noted by Wells and probably all 3 could be placed in this diagram. Our chapter concerns the whole of cultural influence, not just one of the above. Indeed each of these sponsors government-public, commercial and foreign probably are involved with all 3 "levels." Elite media one might predict are most nationally specific while popular media, especially as to its forms (story telling, self-improvement, sports, etc.) might be the most universal. We are probably not too conscious of how the types change over times or interact with one another. Elite media (printed, electronic and participatory) in Mexico and elsewhere probably disdain the popular, although over time the distinction blurs (see Herbert Gans writings on U.S. popular culture, 1974, for instance). Specialized media (as with "educational" content) often find their own separate channels and evolve along their own dimensions. The higher costs of some types of productions

# CHANGES IN MEDIA

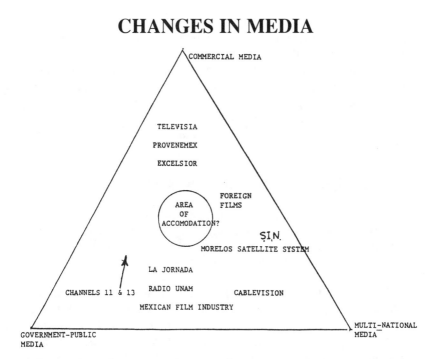

may have something to do with possible accommodations down the line. (Lavish films, cultural productions like orchestras whose product is broadcast, and educational series would be more expensive than photonovelas, soap operas, quiz shows, or comic books one might expect.)

We know that the Mexican government has financed much public and some commercial production. The efforts in the 1960's to sponsor the film industry are well documented. The effort to buy up radio and T.V. stations outside of Mexico City are noted without much detail, however. The rough details on the dumping of foreign production have been noted by Jeremy Tunstall in *The Media are American*, (1977), in his chapter on "The other America" (especially pages 182–184). The Azcarraga-O'Farril partnership involved Televisia, major newspapers (*Novedades* and *The News*), stadiums and hotels, heavy industry, and "main Spanish-language television group within the U.S." (p. 183). Border stations funneled U.S. advertising dollars as an example of the symbiosis. American magazines were also translated in Mexico for other Latin countries. Huge interactive deals crossed the border in both directions and one might wonder if a bipolar model might not be better for Mexico.

Tunstall notes how Mexican nationals may view these mutual movements of T.V., movies and advertisements as somehow in "balance." What may balance the relationship is not quantity, or peso-dollar exchange, but that Mexico has become a spin-off "media imperialist." Even the Mexican government could be seen as a "peripheral elite" carrying out a strange policy for remote metro-elites in New York City. It would seem that almost all aspects run together more than our model suggests, and the future decades would mean even more of the same.

## Technological Change and Our A-Priori Boundaries

Revolutions affect society, and the Information Revolution is no exception: It will change relative wealth, experience, mental skills, amount of free time, entertainment, consumption habits, and almost all aspects of our personal, family and business lives. (Makridakis, 1990, page 268.)

We have not discussed the role of technological change much in this volume. It will obviously impact the way culture is transmitted, and other areas like environmental clean-up will also have their time tables altered by it. The above author notes the following technological trends: Diminution, digitalization, computerization, globalization, instantization, customization, automation, robotization, and, as far as this chapter is most concerned, leisurization. It also may bring various elements together in new ways. Consider the Morelos satellite.

Bella Mody and Jorge Borrego have written about "Mexico's Morelos Satellite: Reaching for Autonomy." (In Sussman and Lent's *Transnational Communications: Wiring the Third World*, 1991, p. 150.) They want to analyze technology in a form of "Contextual Analysis" in which "political, economic, and sociocultural forces" rather than the advantages or cost efficiencies of the technology itself are determinant. We would hope to do the same for the topic. These authors discuss the high priority given to the project, the possible motives for the actors involved, it's probable impact on communications, and some of the puzzling aspects of its utilization so far. "Corporative/bureaucratic self-interest" was seen as being centrally involved. So was the motive to capture the space slot in a finite set of orbits. The possible interactions between the Secretariat of Communication and transportation (SCT) and Televisa were observed. The question of why only 32% of the capacity was utilized was discussed, when the original estimate was for 75 to 80%. The users so far are noted in this quote:

Primary users have been the telephone company, Televisa, IMEVISION (INSTITUTO Mexicano de la Television), state network, three radio net works, and corporate data networks (e.g., Chrysler, Ford, Televisa). A tel-emedicine application is the sole health service use made of Morelos. Secondary education (telesecundaria) applications have not materialized (page 156).

Noting an overloaded terrestrial system (p. 157), and the need to incorporate "33% of the population out of reach of microwave telecommunication" there are obvious motivations for the system. Avoiding the "Americanization of Mexican values" is another. "Cultural preservation and national identity" will inspire any such expenditures, and there is also the motive to keep the private company, Televisa, from dominating the scene (which the latter is quite conscious of). While the topic of under-utilization has many interesting aspects, probably the recessionary atmosphere has most to do with this lack of social utilization. Let us discuss instead the impact on Mexico City in this new media-cultural environment.

Mody and Borrego note so many rumors of collusion between corporations, governments and agencies that the issues of media centralization in Mexico City were seldom broached. However, the satellite and its backup, Morelos II, will give great room for regionalization of Mexican media. These authors observe that: "State governments assumed regional uses of television would reflect and maintain those cultures," (p. 159). These author's table 7.1 shows these subnational uses. Much of these author's discussion in contextual terms notes the wider impact of "dependent state capitalism," and we do not disagree with their analysis. Regionalization may be just a cultural sop also, and not reflect the larger issues of political-economy. The authors note other issues than those of under-utilization, as for instance, the speed of development of the system where the technology was transfered intact, and the Mexican scientists were reduced to "learning no more than systems operations and maintenance." All in all, the authors conclude: "This is consistent with Cardozo's conception of the role of the state in dependent societies: Development is conditioned by the needs of foreign capital rather than underserved national groups," (p. 163). In any case, the possibilities of escape from media imperialism in any form, including the varieties from the capital, are at hand. New kinds of cooperation with respect to cultural production are also to be found.

## Chapter 6

# Geography, Infrastructure, and the Future

## Geography, Infrastructure, and Mexico City's Future

This approach (Central Place Theory) adds up-to an aid program for infrastructure very similar to the kind commonly promoted by the international aid establishment. While such programs can improve the quality of life in less urbanized areas, however, insofar as they reinforce the local marketplace they reproduce all of the inequalities of the marketplace. Some believe that building up the towns and cities amounts to a sort of internal colonialism (Gonzalez Casanova, 1970). (From Thomas Angotti's paper presented to the 1992 LASA Meeting, "The unhappy marriage of dependent urbanization and metropolitan planning in Latin America," page 13.)

After collecting as many historic maps of Mexico City as time, money and initiative allowed, the question for the current project is how they can tell us where this metropolis is headed. Angotti sees two trends in the paper cited above: One involves "the continuing unplanned growth of Metropolitan areas" and the other is "toward more balanced development," (p. 18). Cautiously he notes: "It remains to be seen which of these two trends will predominate in the years ahead." We have relegated our collection of maps to an appendices of this volume, even though any theory about what kind of trend will prevail may well find its confirmation on an ex post facto search of these same maps.

While Angotti sees an escape from the automobile bias of previous, recent infrastructure investments back to the bicycle (for Cuba), we do not foresee this for the ZMCM. A way of predicting with these maps would be to see how previous infrastructure investments shaped the future, along with other influences. As well we could possibly see how infrastructural decisions *FOLLOWED* and supported popular relocation decisions. What are these infrastructural decisions that could be per-

ceived in historical and contemporary maps? Major travel routes
(blessed with concrete), dams, canals, monumental buildings, and utilities are examples of "infrastructure" that would show up in maps or
historic accounts of administration. Popular settlements, legal or otherwise, would represent the counter-component to the system as would
industries, firms, and various functional utilizations of enhanced space.
Typically the two components develop together, with one or the other
taking the lead at various times. The ZMCM's history would and will
have examples of both sequences. Our main predictive effort here will
be to see how the "Fifth Ring" of development preceeds, as the almost
inevitable expansion of the total area takes place. Planning is one way
by which infrastructure can preceed the later development of "functions" whether public or private, but his may not approximate the scenario that will take place in the next few decades. Reasonable planning
may cut down on the infrastructural developments of the ZMCM in
such a fashion as to achieve deconcentration, but let us project a scenario of mixed public planning along with a range of private decisions—where some are more efficacious than others. Let us first review
an attempt at prediction of another metro area future, this being the
world class city of Toronto in a recent (1991) work by Ross Newkirk.
We will examine the type of factors which this author focuses upon.
This author sees the need for an historic approach and in that, at least,
we have common ground.

## One Attempt at a Framework for Prediction

> The absence of a capability to work effectively with concepts describing
> alternative long-term futures has contributed to the fact that some planners
> and policy makers have tended to leave the future to itself as they concen-
> trate upon the more immediate issues of growth management—that is,
> responding to current pressures rather than trying to influence long term
> outcomes. (Ross Newkirk, "Mapping Metro Area Futures: A case study
> from Toronto," Chapter 10 in *Spatial Analysis and Spatial Policy Using
> Geographic Information*, page 204.)

Many, very compulsive, data based, technical approaches (GIS) have
failed to predict urban expansion patterns, according to Ross Newkirk.
Short term approaches have dominated activity patterns of the profes-
sionals involved. Newkirk sees the need for an historical approach in
his notion of a "trend based simulation." Traditional modeling approaches are seen as inadequate, despite the mathematical frenzy, be-

cause they cannot match the qualities of the real world. Specifically "these models do not deal explicitly with the impact of decisions—either past, present or future." They do not handle long term capital based decisions any better than governmental public ones. The local context is vaguely perceived in these attempts, especially local infrastructural expenditures and their possible implications. The model that must replace earlier ones should be more comprehensive as well, and there must be greater attention to the mode of "tensions" being generated in the total urban environment, or at least in the interactive simulation models themselves. The geographic information systems (GIS's) are to be used beyond the mere descriptive levels as model- based analysis is utilized "interactively." Research must get real! Supposedly the scenario-based model will generate these tensions which will be further analyzed to see which of the alternative futures seems most likely. Let us summarize what Newkirk says are the problems with previous approaches in terms of the problems of prediction, and what he (and the WATGUM, Waterloo Generic Urban Model) see as an improvement.

Mostly a lack of results shortens the life of any model! Those models which search for an elusive "equilibrium" are also unproductive, it seems. It seems that decisions and decision making are ignored as well, especially having to do with capital stock or the outcomes of productive processes (p. 210). The new idea is to "simulate various alternative decisions taken at arbitrary future dates." This author is as fond of focusing on decision making as any sociologist who worked in the 1960–1970 period, but there are other elements for analysis. The natural environment in the ZMCM is much to be reckoned with. We will look at the events whcih have shaped Mexico City and local environs, both natural and human-made, in order to get a more comprehensive view, of the kind which Newkirk asks for. Finally we will look at three areas of importance in the growth (or decline) of any urban area. Afterall the first great urban center, Teotihuacan, rapidly self-destructed after 650 A.D., as resource gaps destabilized it (supposedly!). Our appendix on the nature of pre-European settlement may be of some help in our model building. Although we are focusing upon expansion of the heavily used parts of the metro area, we are well aware of the needs for revitalization and reconstruction as well. We are equally aware of the needs for deconcentration, and hope to take a clinical, as opposed to a booster view of urban expansion.

Newkirk offers three "competing urban structure concepts" which are labeled "spread, central and nodal." The first is a projection of the current trends (for Toronto) of low density spread at the periphery and continuing office concentration down town. The "central" version sees development as continuing to be augmented in the existing areas but slowing beyond present boundaries (p. 217). Nodal development is somehow intermediate, but growth will be enhanced in a compact form using up less of the "underdeveloped land relative to the spread concept." It seems that other "concepts" than these 3 could be obtaineed, but the analysis of these could be of more value than their exhaustiveness. Mexico City's future would seem to be unlike any of the specific concepts, and least likely the "central" notion. Each of the three were evaluated on the basis of potential transit efficiency, usage of existing infrastructure, and preservation of community values. These kinds of factors should be analyzed for the ZMCM at some point.

Toronto may be a worthwhile comparison for Mexico City because it likewise is growing rapidly; it is a key economic resource for its region and country; it is using up its most easily developed lands; and it must expand its infrastructure in an efficient manner in order to prepare for its almost inevitable growth (the latter es pecially being transportation, sanitary facilities, utilities, and general services). Newkirk's analysis assumes growth, but with three sub-scenarios about its distribution. His concerns about specific aspects of these growth scenarios approximates our ultimate concerns for the consequences of various possible outcomes. How will urban lives be impacted under various outcomes? Newkirk notes how *all* "concepts" or outcomes will strain some of the resources and infrastructure, and result in augmented costs (as collection of waste in the Greater Toronto Area). Transportation and pollution control costs will go up with any scenario of change, whereas pressure on open land would be likely with the "spread" option. Newkirk has concerns that are specifically administrative rather than with the problematics of potential urban form and function.

## Relationships Between the Development of Infrastructure and Spatial Expansion

> Today, what we call the urban infrastructure provides the technological "sinews" of the modern metropolitan area: Its road, bridge, and transit networks; its waste and sewer lines and waste disposal facilities and its power and communication systems. (Tarr & Dupuy, *Technology and the Rise of the Networked City in Europe and America*, 1988, page XIII.)

In the preface to this set of articles the editors note the complex nature of infrastructure, including what is publically and privately constructed. Technology is stressed as a force for meeting or savaging human needs. The timing of the installation of infrastructure (historically in France) was such that it was "unevenly inserted" (p. XIV). It was also a "piecemeal, decentralized approach." Several examples of infrastructure being developed *after* the decision to settle into a functional niche are noted. (See the article: "Sewerage and the development of the networked city in the U.S.—1850–1930," by Joel Tarr, p. 169.) Sometimes builders provided streets and sewers ahead of time and sometimes they came afterward, paid for at public expense.

Our main interest in infrastructure has to do with its power to shape the future of the ZMCM relative to other factors (environment, the nature of the political economy, for instance). In the case of Mexico City the infrastructure supporting residential enhancement has come, if at all, after the fact (as with mass transit, utilities, etc.). On the other hand, the infrastructure for major processes of political economy has utually been on a prior or simultaneous basis. The drainage and water problems of Mexico City clearly preceeded all other forms and functions going back to Prince Netzahualcoyotl. Causeways, dikes, aquafers, major avenues, and civic gathering points have all preceeded other developments. Later the railroads and highway upgrading would preceed expansion of other functional units. What is the power of prior infrastructure to determine various outcomes? Can important socio-economic forms emerge without prior types of infrastructure? (As the prairie farm pattern did with only the railroads in the mid-west of the U.S. from 1880 to 1930.) Can urban forms proceed without elaborate forms of infrastructure? Are the forms of infrastructure now in place sufficient to determine the future of the ZMCM in significant ways? Our appendix "C" has copies of historic maps of Mexico City. Can recognizable forms of infrastructure on these historical maps predict the subsequent development of firms, homes, and various public functions? The answer in the case of roads, canals, and railroads is obvious, but partly because these features of infrastructure already accommodate to the environments—which also must mold the outcomes. Most features on historic maps represent some kind of infrastructure investments and following them over time will see obvious convergence to more or less anticipated forms. These prior investments are indeed the skeleton on which the urban flesh is grown. Let us look at the time series of infrastructure investments that these maps reflect. Our answer about the efficacy of prior infrastructure investments will, no doubt, be that it is considerable. In the conclusion of this chapter, we will offer a tripartite model involving distance factors, resource factors, and preference factors as a more complete set of possible predictive elements. Let us try to develop a model to help explain the nature and sequence of subsequent urban expansion of the city of Mexico. Good roadways will become axial zones of enhancement, a civic gathering place will attract those functions capable of bellying up to them. The utilization of infrastructure will follow existing social cleavages. The hierarchy of uses follows the qualities of the social order. (Peter Ward discusses the "reproduction of inequality" in the housing developments of Mexico City of the late 20th century.) The obvious power-class dynamic of establishing prior versus later infrastructure for one's residential, economic, or political functions if obvious. Having worked in city planning, the present author can remember the highly subsidized provision of infrastructure for entrepreneurs while the previous owners were hardly compensated at fair market value. Our next step will be to look at selected maps of Mexico City to try to establish the actual relationships—which might represent an almsot chicken and egg type dilemma of sequences in some cases. The type of map to be inspected is critical, and the different types portray a range of infrastructural characteristics. If the map is one of highways, railroads, drainage features, and so on, then it is totally one of "infrastructure." Most of the maps to be inspected are general ones involving the prominant features and uses highlighted by the dominate transportation system. Historic cities will vary in their emphasis on types of infrastructure.

We might expect Royal cities of Mexica and Spanish derivation to differ from later varieties in some important ways, especially with business-industrial or revolutionary-political orientations. It will become obvious that many historical groups will have their way with the city's spatial arrangements and permanent features. Industrialists, the defense minded, the ostentatious state shapers, the marketeers, the boosters of plazismo, and occasionally the general land-use planners (as those in the DDF over the preservation of open lands) will leave their characteristic marks. We will have to learn to read maps in a new way, perhaps. Maps being the stylized, culturally filtered, politically sanctioned documents that they are, with their unknown criteria for selectivity may give us only puzzles instead of data. Even a sequence of aerial photos may obscure any processes we might be concerned with. The historic strategies of dominance by urban groups over their respective hinterlands can be infered with some accuracy from an inspection of the machinery of exploitation shown in routes, wharfs, and control centers. What else can we infer from these depictions of past urban systems? Do previous "irregular settlements" show up in these maps, or did the ancient chamber of commerce types hide them? Cultural histories must supplement any interpretations of historic maps.

We should not loose track of our purposes having to do with the prediction of Mexico City's form two decades from now. Planners should be interested in the notion of infrastructural determinism being examined. But, suppose they built infrastructure and nobody came? What if they lavished on one kind of infrastructure and it almost obliterated alternative forms, as what the U.S. highway system pegged on Detroit's product did to mass public transportation. The very lavishing of construction on Mexico City surely reinforced the total insularity of the country, not to mention the primacy effect. All permanent investments in facilitating technology are time bound, not only because of growth beyond their intended scope or their life expectancy, but unintended externalities. The incredible drainage system underlying the city may be an exception in that it may last centuries and continue to perform its intended function. In an age of accelerated auto use, any "freeway" (what a terrible bit of obscuratism) may quickly be obsolete; it also can lead people and firms to relocate outward, rather than orienting toward the center. The building of two or three super ports on the coasts may lead to economic policies that bleed the country of its natural resources, if they are not value-added processed before exportation. The pouring of concrete may have unintended consequences, especially down the line. With one-sixth of the population of Mexico, but one-half of the revenues to spend, Mexico City can buy much cement from the city of Monterrey.

Let us look at the types of maps available for Mexico City and the greater ZMCM. Then let us look at the major events which have impacted the area, especially those that have augmented their infrastructure.

## Defining Mexico City

For an urban area chartered in 1522, included in a federal district in 1824, and spilling over into the state of Mexico recently, it is not an easy entity to define. Alan Gilbert and Peter Ward in their essay on housing in Mexico City and two other locations note:

> The boundaries of Mexico City require explanation. Throughout this study Mexico City refers to the contiguous built up area. (Page 285, 1985)

The built up areas do include much of the federal district and several municipalities of the State of Mexico. Some of our maps show the changes in this built-up area since the early 1500s. We hope that this lack of an exact definition will not hinder our understanding of the processes which the maps included here otherwise might reveal. A phenomenon to be "real" does not imply a static definition.


## Mexico City in Maps

Maps are super sources of stored information, and they offer a dimension that some assume to be "reality." Many kinds of data can be graphically plotted and recent atlas productions on Mexico (Pick, Butler and Lanzer, 1989) and Mexico City (Gustavo, Garza, and El Colegio de Mexico, 1987) cover our area of concern. There were earlier atlas productions on Mexico as a whole (University of Texas, 1975) showing various demographic characteristics and societal functions. Maps of many kinds exist for Mexico City, but we will focus on those closer to our socio-economic-political concerns.

Modern types of maps got their start in Europe in the thirteenth century. Observation and measurement was involved (see *The Maps Catalog*, Joel Makower, editor, 1986, Tilden Press) rather than "literary sources or mythology." The first areas well mapped were those in the nearby seas (Mediterranean and the Black Sea) based on the use of the mariner's compass. The Italians out of Florence did some of the best work, and governments snapped them up for their own varied purposes. By the time Columbus "discovered" the New World and Cortez descended upon Mexico, maps were widely used. According to *The Map Catalog*, (1986, p. 10), "The telescope, pendulum clock and logarithm tables" led to improved accuracy.

Despite the improved accuracy, the 400 year old (1569) mercator projection distorted the size of the caucasian parts of the world. (North America and Africa were depicted as the same size even though Africa is 60% larger in actuality.) We will see that maps of Mexico City reflected these early biases and myths. Later photogrammetry would transform maps as with aerial photos and their five lens cameras and radial line plotting techniques (Ibid, p. 13). Electronic imaging and digitalizaiton of map data were yet to come, as were electronic distance measuring, space based photography, remote sensing and storage-retrieval skills.

## A Brief History of Maps up to the Early 1500's

Map making well preceeds the deliniation of Mexico and Mexico City after 1520. R.A. Sketton and Leo Bagrow's *History of Cartography* note the characteristics of the maps of "Primitive and Ancient People" (Greece, Babylonia, and Egypt). Some of the latter depictions were merely "discs floating on the sea," although city plans were more detailed because that's where many of the austute lived. The Greeks added an orienting line of great importance and moved toward parallel lines to denote fixed distances (p. 33). Ptolemy had guidelines for map creation and added coordinates. The *Geographia* was produced 400 years before Mexico City's map would emerge. Early maps of Mexico City would not be state of the art, except that, like many Greek and Roman maps their main concerns were practical, or even artistic rather than a geographical accuracy.

The middle age "darkness" preceeding the "discovery" of Mexico gradually illuminated its periphery. The earliest maps here were "small and schematic," (p. 42) and only gradually became detailed. Some climatic maps and sea charts, of course, existed. It was seemingly true that "no clear cartographic development" occurred (p. 46) because of the limited purposes being served. Islamic cartography of an earlier period consisted of route maps and later of "ingenious schematic drawings" that were artistically well done (p. 55). World travel was eluded to, and there was exploration of the nearby world as with the peoples around the Mediterranean basin. The Arab maps had focused upon the Indian Ocean and sea charts were one of the most successful forms (called Charta or Tabula by the Italians). The Italian and Catalan charts often anticipated areas that were "terra, incognito" (as the tip of Africa before Barthelomy Dias and Vasco de Gama). The Genoese world map of 1457 did not anticipate the new world in any reasonable form, however.

The point of departure for Mexican maps would have been this total heritage down to the late middle ages. Maps became separate works very individual in style. Many were works of art rather than high points of accuracy. There were, of course, concerns with real distances (as to Iceland and the edge of the world) and in the early 1500's the world maps included a fragmentary image of the "new world." Maps associated with Johannes Ruysch, Bernardus Sylvanus and Sebastian Munster had skimpy versions of the North And South American landmasses on their left edges. Printed world maps were available after 1477 and, of course, Africa started to assume a reasonable shape. The "Terra Incognita'' was still out there in the hinterland, however, and it would be awhile before the new world was depicted with reasonable form (as in the A.F. Van Langeren map of 1595). Given this brief history of map making up to the early 1500's, let us now discuss what we hope to achieve from maps of Mexico City which emerge from this point in time.

## Historic Maps of Mexico City

We wish here to examine maps of Mexico City from various epochs in order to sense where this city came from and may be headed. The city's geography has been prologue, but it would have been hard to predict its current gargantuan scale. Still there are intrinsic qualities that can help us to understand the growth of this collectivity into what may be the world's largest urban place. We will try to match these intrinsic qualities with the equally important contextual elements of Mexico City within nation, hemisphere and world.

We will preceed here by examining types of maps of Mexico City and its immediate environs and noting what they may reveal about the city's growth. We will then analyze the role or function played by these maps in various periods, and then preceed to our prognostication about the city's future. Can such a future, short of catastrophic events, be in doubt as this capital of new Spain, current explosive population center, and state for global initiatives, proceeds into the 21th century? The expansion of the urban population and the augmenting of urban resources will also be the focus of an ''intensification index'' for Mexico City, the Federal district and State of Mexico. The hope with the latter will be in possible prediction about future form and functions with planned infrastructure as its harbringer.

## Major Events Shaping Mexico City and Its Face

Many man-made and natural events have determined the central features of this city besides its natural geography. As the numerous small villages competed (unconsciously?) for early primacy, the classic period produced the great Teotihuacan. One must ask why urbanism was not merely restored on the ruins of this great urban center, and the answers probably have to do with basic resources and their distribution in the valley of Mexico. The presence of the big ''T'' must have haunted every person in the area, with its size and mysteries. It must be seen as a continued stimulus for both urban living and an imperial purpose.

Because water control has been and continues to be a shaper of Mexico City and its map we will mention many instances here, as Prince Nezahaualcoytl's long reign and orderly life style which contributed a dike and an aquaduct to the pattern. The city in the 1400's is described by T.H. Fehrenback in the following way:

> Tenochtitlan was the largest and grandest of all the centers, in kind as well as degree. The built-up mud flats in Lake Texcoco had become one of the great imperial centers of the world. From the colorful, buzzing market plaza of Tlateloco on the north to the magnificent palaces at the cerimonial center to the causeways that joined at Xoloc, Mexico-Tenochtitlan surpassed in many respects its contemporary imperial sisters, such as Venice or Istanbul.

Attempts at control over the valley's environment probably were central to the dynamics of growth. This was clearly a city on its own merits before being reduced by Cortez and his "divisa et impera" strategies. After the drastic "marches and massacres," the small pox epidemic and the treachery "nothing remains but flowers and sad songs." The Mexica were subjugated and the beauty that was Tenochtitlan was usurped. Fehrenback notes how Cortez was aware of the "strategic and symbolic location" of the city (p. 189). The old buildings were torn down and swept clean with fire. Now the "most loyal city of Mexico was laid out in rectangular spanish fashion" (p. 189). The south end of the old town became the new center for the spanish city. A plaza was put where the Mexica palaces had been. A new municipal center, a church and shops were also developed where the Zocolo is today. Wide avenues went out in several directions to water's edge. White washed walls and red buildings gave a renewed presence to the city floating in the lake. The palaces of the Conquistadores were, of course, substantial.

Throughout the last half of the 1500's the city grew in relation to European visitors and peripheral valley populations being displaced by spanish herding practices. As a dispatching point for goods coming and going, Mexico City took its new dimension. The Indios who were building the new city were supposed to have lived outside of it with their clans but parts of the population did not. Half-breed legions were, thusly, created.

Fehrenback describes the spanish building fever in the following decades.

The major event of the first century (1520–1620) as far as Mexico City was concerned was this "progress toward civilization." The collapse of its alternative surprises many, although Indian cultures did survive in Mexico, the Andes and elsewhere. (Page 204)

The new events in the 1600's must be seen as natural in the form of repeated flooding, and the response to this situation. Maps in 1607, 1629, and beyond were focused on this flooding and its amelioration. There were other developments in the first two centuries for Mexico City. The Bourbon control of commerce would bring much wealth to bear on the status architecture of the city. Further Europeanization was to be its fate as well. The Alameda Park, for instance, was to be a setting for inquisition based burnings and whippings although not with the glee or frequency as in old Spain. Many new world citizens were fleeing the established horrors of the old world even at this point.

The 19th century saw a modernizing inclination for the city. Maximillion's beautification was followed by Porfirio Diaz' "francophilia" and lasting changes were made in the form of Mexico City. Whether the widening and extending of the Reforma were to match the Paris Boulevards, the ideas of Georges Eugene Hausmann were followed (see Whittick's *Encyclopedia of Urban Planning*, 1974, p. 686). The general plan (such as these have ever been) "show some influence of French concepts of the second half of the 19th century." Diagonal avenues and "domero" terraces were used along with English type gardens and parlors. Public buildings were added in the central areas. After the 1870 Revolution in Paris, the idea to widen the boulevards to allow the marshalling of troops (supposedly) this idea took hold elsewhere. To keep citizens from tossing all sorts of debris from buildings on to their "protecting" armies, wider avenues were needed. The centenary of Independence in 1910 was an attempt to showcase these accumulated improvements.

The 1910 Revolution fought mostly in the hinterland meant that Mexico City would again be a haven for refugees. The Revolutionary furor would eventually leave its mark on the decorative aspects of the city—its walls and intersections. A new nation demanded a new capital. But even more potent changes were at work in the form of industrialization and the rise of the new classes in search of status housing. Several neighborhoods, variously planned but all expensive, emerged. Whittick (p. 690) says that they were sometimes, as with Tlatelco "poorly designed and the design is questionable." At the same time the industrially related slums also emerged in Mexico City, Monterrey and elsewhere. The Unidad Independencia may have gotten better marks, but all of these developments were impacted by the thousands of factories spawned by President Aleman's surge to industrialization and import-substitution development. Where the factories were put and where the workers lived was another story to be told (see G. Garza).

The central parts of the city in the 20th century were to be impacted by private and public decision as well as acts of nature. Private decisions by multi-national corporations; public building of agency headquarters and of park structures; and the 1985 earthquake would "re-arrange the furniture" so to speak. The age of the auto would take some reconciling as well as the needs for mass, public transport. The obvious desirability of the economic kick of tourism meant other decisions about urban land use would be made. The property values in the Zona Rosa meant that swank construction would focus there as well as in outward directions. The pressure on land would mean the end of corn fields with in the city's perimeter, and would also mean that the remaining Ejidos would be eyed for other developments. Despite the limited perimeters of the valley of Mexico, urban sprawl would occur. The "parachutists," working class squatters, would fill in the gaps where ever this was allowed. New communities would abound, and old ones would get pregnant with the overflow. The massive inflow of hinterland folks, and the explosion of development elsewhere led to the expression "outside Mexico City everyplace is Cuantitian." People were experiencing urbanization in many places. The metro system on its rubber-French tires was to get them there quicker as well. And, as anyone who has ridden on this beautiful system at rush hour and at off hours knows, you get a lot of transportation for less than a nickle.

The 1980's would see the impact of austerity and President De La Madrid's "slow growth policy." It would also see a deadly "terremoto" in September of 1985, whose after-shocks would include a rush off the old tremulous lake bed. The city had already experienced its great vulnerability in the Tlalneplanta permex explosion, and a Bophaul type disaster is not out of the question in the future. There were efforts to forstall the perils of its own by products as auto-freeways were carved out of the city. Pollution control efforts got serious in the 1980's as well. The earthquake had led to the nationalization of parts of the city's core, but the tangible results of this control move were/are negligible!

Barring mother nature's cruel games, the city's future shape could be impacted by serious decentralization, more reasonable land use, further accommodations to the transportation crush, renewed housing efforts and such niceties as an environmental cleanup. The impact of eventual home rule may be physical in form as well. The total picture may or may not be a planned experience, but there are land use plans available (see Chapter VII).

## Major Events in Summary

Reactions to 1600s flooding must have been the main early factor in the transformation of the City's shape. Later the pretentious desire to elevate the city and the status of its denezins led to much ostentacious building. Indeed, three centuries of it. The elaborate baroque style with facades of light volcanic rock (tezontle), and the neo-classical structures of the 1700s must be noted at least for their visual effects. Pretentiousness was involved in the Paseo del Emperado of the 1860s and many motives came together with Haussmann's "modernization" after 1876. Drainage reached high efficiency in the early 1900s, and electric street cars and tracks would have had their impact on outward movement. The war of the Revolution did hit the city between 1910 and 1917, but seemingly did not slow in-migrants. The first U.S. type buildings started in the early 1920s, and the first skycrapers a decade later. The industrialization of the 1940s and beyond would transform more than building structures and immediate land-use types. All during this period the urban area spread to nearly 800 square miles with a population density approaching 21,000 in various areas. While the city itself may be loosing density the Federal District and the State of Mexico seem to be increasing at an increasing rate.

The physical nature of the city will continuously adjust to the lacaustine plain in the old lake bed which is sinking at a rate of 6 inches a year. The hundreds of "Ciudad Perdidas" will not really disappear from their present locales, although the upgrading will proceed. (See INVI reports.) Decentralization will mostly occur within the valley, and less so to the hinterland—one might predict. Open areas and parks such as central Alameda and the "Desert of Lions" will also persist. New housing must be obtained, but may be dealt with as a carrot to lure people outward—further than Nezahaulcoyotl this time. Now that the nearby Ejidos have been absorbed, and hillsides are being bulldozed, the view from landings and take-offs at the airport will also be transformed. The glare of sheet metal roofs on the hillsides has already declined, unless one knows where to look. We will end this section by noting that our section on change or planning maps will try to project some of these eternal varieties and to anticipate new ingredients in the physio-geography of the city. The D.D.F. in 1980 put out the "plan de desarrollo Urbano" and it is to this projection that we will ultimately proceed.

## A General View of Infrastructure Investments in Mexico City

The explanation for this similarity (between Europe and America) may be in the fact that cities, regardless of the national context, had common needs for water, transport, energy, and communication as they expanded in the 19th Century. (Tarr and Dupuy, *Technology and the Rise of the Networked City in Europe and America*, 1988, Preface, XIV.)

All cities must eventually meet basic necessities via investment in infrastructure on a public or private basis (I-Is). Water control and transport "I" were early investments in Mexico City. Specific function energy and communication infrastructure came much later, and all of these major categories are continuously changing based on needs, technology and inspiration. The Mechica effort at water control was one of the earliest new world mega achievements, rivaling the great wall of China, the early forms of monumental architecture and the massive old world irrigation projects. The Spanish crown inherited the flood control and drainage situation. Previous water control by desilting canals that serviced the chinampa system could be seen as early maintenance. Human physical labor and engineering by reckoning rather than elaborate technology were involved in dike, causeway, aquaduct, and roadway construction. The I-I in some of these cases must be seen as being contemporary in its purposes, but also having a future determining capacity. More land was finally claimed from the lake bed by these activities. Our map (page 185) shows the aquaduct, the major dikes and a grid of roadways. The original compact nature of the city was eventually surrounded by a grid of squared-off roads and environmentally induced diagonals. By the late 19th century several rail lines (The "Main line," the Inter-oceanic lines via Morelos, the Vera Cruz railway, and the Northwest oriented lines) defined a hub with Mexico City as its center. The "Gran Canal" variously impacted the living capacity of the valley. The provision of individual services to residents and firms had a considerable price tab that locked in the total pattern and limited future choices. The turn of the century seen a wide "I" network in order to serve the stable water needs of the population. As to roads, the rectangular grid was of course already bisected by the Haussmann type diagonal avenues (in order to get Maximillian to the castle or the troops to the rebellion on time?).

## Infrastructure By Periods: The Gran Tenochtitlan

The valley of Mexico has an obvious physical problem as the basis for the world's largest city. It is water logged, and must be managed. Water control, however, is a dynamic process known by many to propel urban design and development. (See Wittfogel's "Oriental despotism.") Some could argue that controlling water, both flooding and generating potable water, set in motion a dynamic of growth for Mexico City. Jonathan Kandell in his history of *La Capital* describes the period very well in terms of infrastructural necessities. Prince Netzahualcoyotl, who was Motecuhzoma's cousin was "already renowned for engineering feats in his city state," (p. 46). There had been previous attempts to control water levels and salinity, and Kandell observes the opinion of many that it was the "most sophisticated hydraulic project in pre-Columbian America." The result was a nine mile long dike built by driving huge logs in parallel rows 60 feet apart then filling in the row with rocks and gravel. There were sluice gates every so often in order to let canoes pass.

The results of the dike construction solved immediate water fluctuation problems, flooding and increased salinity by adding water from Xochimilco. It would be easy to claim capacity extending results to the dike as the ultimate results allowed for more suitable water for irrigation. The future was improved upon and the present made less soggy. The second engineering feat involved getting water supplies into the city proper. Both of these types of infrastructure preserved urban life at Tenochtitlan and extended it into the future. The existing springs on the city proper were inadequate, near by lake water was polluted so the Prince was again requested to develop "I" for the city. Another complicated task was handled by running parallel ducts about 6 feet in diameter from Chapultepec to Tenochtitlan. These were made of wood and stone, and were engineered in order to avoid obstructing lake traffic. The main result of this effort was a good water supply with the nobility and major priests being served by direct water via clay pipes. Commoners got to fill their jugs with siphones rather than with elaborate plumbing.

Even more important than dikes and aquaducts, perhaps, were the canals from whence most water was actually managed. A recent (1990) book on "Canal irrigation in prehistoric Mexico" by William Doolittle even stresses the regional quality of some of the systems. Many technological changes were involved in these infrastructure sequences. The former accomplishments no doubt benefited from prior canal construction and hydraulics. The whole chinampas complex was an evolutionary process in itself. Kandell summarizes much archaeological research in noting the efforts at Xochimilco and Chalco. The lakes were filled in with highly fertile platforms and seeded plants were placed on these platforms in the water. Twenty thousand to 30,000 acres were improved to the point that up to 6 crops per year were completed. Intercropping by running squash, beans, peppers and so on under the maize plants; efficiently using human excrement; terracing and better cultivation meant a real revolution in food production. Kandell warns us, however, that canal efforts north of the main lakes were also very productive.

> The most potable of these feats took place north of the lake system where a major river, the Cuauhtitlan was diverted off its course by dams and canals to irrigate a large farming zone. (Kandell, page 59.)

If canals are "infrastructure" then are the terraces likewise? Mostly any utilization of technology to produce permanent structures is based on a set of ideas about how to achieve certain results. The investment in the intensification discussed here supported a large urban population that would have persisted into a future sequence. In the year of the 500th anniversary of the coming of the Europeans we can well ask what would have transpired as to infrastructure evolution had not a new complex of technology and ideas not interceeded. Let us look at the Spanish contribution to the tooling-up process, especially that part that propelled the urban dynamic down the path.

## The Spanish Contribution To Urban Supporting "I"

Without exaggerating the previous wisdom about the environment and the impact on the geography of the valley, the Spanish did not add up the impact of the utilization of wood upon the valley's "balance." Infrastructure not only achieves a limited purpose but has "side effects." The buring of wood and its use in construction denuded the hill sides of the valley. The rapid spurt of rebuilding after the conquest accelerated this process of quick runoff, and nature waited its opportunity to flood the city. Wood was used not only for piling, but for scaffolding. There was an effort to dry up the lake beds, and it was temporarily successful. There eventually was no place for the inevitable rain waters to go. The dikes also fell into disrepair in the drier years and this added to the ultimate flooding.

It seems that only Enrico Martinez recognized the flooding diaster and its causes as they got more serious in the early 1600s. The partial remedy for the deforestation and erosion was an outlet for the rainy years water. An 8-mile tunnel-ditch into the Tula river was a partial answer—if followed through upon. Using 60,000 workers over 10 months a version was completed by 1608. This "desage" took almost 20% of the silver revenues. (This might be the basis for comparative pricing of any large infrastructure improvements during the colonial years.) (See Kandell, p. 199.) An early "peso overrun" resulted in a shortage of money for the drainage of Texcoco. The ultimate test came after 1629 and 6 feet of water settled into Mexico City, and only part of el centro, the "isle of curs" or stray dogs remained above water. Blaming the canal builder Martinez for his unsupported previous project was not very useful, but by 1634 the idea of a better drainage system sunk in.

Much debate centered on the question of even rebuilding on the old sites, but real estate values had become so important that the recommitment was made. The decision to pay the bill for this dewatering effort down the line was concluded. It was obvious that the forced labor system (repartimiento) and other local resources allowed for the rebuilding. Basically put, the tribute system would support it. The previous grid pattern with wide streets and open squares would be reproduced. The city was visually the same within 3 years and become the "place of the Mexicas."

## The 1700s and 1800s In Terms Of Infrastructure and City Expansion

Kandell notes how the 1700s was a period of attempts to control markets, land, and human effort. The elite spawned a strategy in order to control agriculture, and only 17 families controlled ½ of the land around Mexico City (p. 241). One family owned a flourmill that processed ⅓ of the wheat sold. The concentration of wealth thus obtained would transform the city and its hinterland into a wealth making machine for some. The uniform quality of the city with wide streets and many public places were the physical consequences of this pattern of political economy. This occasional "splendor" was to fade by 1825, especially on the east side of the city, but its size was now 2 miles from north to south and 3 miles from east to west. Water was still carried by aquadors from the public fountains. Infrastructure spread slowly for a variety of reasons, and the vecindades were festering and laden with cholera. There was money, but it was used to build and dominate ports and similar infrastructure for trade. When Maximillian and Charlotte entered Mexico on their way from Veracruz to Mexico City in the mid-1860s the former was garbage strewn, the railroads were not completed, the main road was potholed and narrow. It was no wonder that Maximillian spent money on beautifying Mexico City and in modifying some of the infrastructure. The main avenues were not widened in order to get quickly to the capital as one critic claimed, but fulfilled other motives. During much of this period the church owned central real estate and not much working capital was obtained. Maximillian, according to Kendall, planted trees, placed gas light, and collected the garbage. It remained for the reign of Porfirio Diaz to modify the infrastructure and labor emphasis of the urban area between 1876 and 1911.

The Diaz period would see railroad, port and electric increments in I-I. The surface area of Mexico City would expand five times. A model prison, Lecumberri, would be put into operation. But Kandell is correct (p. 367) in saying that a transportation explosion was central to the extension of Porfirian "order." Mexico's geography would finally be conquered by 11,000 miles of track to the extent that only 2,000 additional miles were added later. The real revolution was the trail of commercial, social, and political events after this expansion of infrastructure. Freight went up 500 times in a year and the cost was cut to ¹/₁₀th of the previous one. The lines built by the British and Yankees opened many markets for sugar, tobacco and coffee which now competed abroad. Mexico City's control was also strengthened by the speed by which troops might be marshalled. Much of the newly created wealth was rechanneled into public utilities such as electricity—the latter allowed industries to move to the cities and away from river bank sources of power. Kandell observes (p. 371): "Under Diaz the capital received more than 80% of all government investmetns in infrastructure." The latter included road surfacing, telegraphs, schools, water supply and especially a drainage system. Mexico City could become something other than a "fetid Venice." The modern drainage system was built between 1885 and 1900 at a cost of 16 million U.S. dollars. S. Pearson and Son, who had built drainage for London and New York City eventually constructed a 30-mile canal and a 6-mile tunnel which reduced the flooding and attendant spread of contaminants.

Everything was up to date in Mexico City or at least Diaz in his daily trip to the palace via the Paseo de la Reforma thought so! The remedy for remaining doubters was to be a centennial celebration whose costs would firnally surpass those other budgets such as for education of the nation. There would be new hotels, theatres, and statues. The revolution was probably not slowed in coming by these expenditures. Infrastructure investments slowed between 1910 and 1940, even though many changes took place in other societal sectors. With railroads, adequate drainage for the most part, major traffic routes and rudimentary communication in place, a new "take-off" platform was ready by 1940. Many other prerequisites were also met by this time.

## 1940–1970: The Flowering of Infrastructure Investments

Political histories stress the development of nationhood up to 1940. Economic historians may look at the internal and external market situation, especially with the on-coming war. Mexico City's infrastructure was also transformed to serve factories, commerce, and the newly affluent for their residences. Skyscrapers relied on special underground drainage technology. Much of the city was tranformed by "I" in order to serve ¼th of the nation's 120,000 factories by 1970. Public transportation, sewerage, potable water, available (working!) telephones, and adequate electricity were in place during the later part of the period for the majority of the city. The "Mexican Miracle" helped fund this explosion of "I" which was a prerequisite for a full economic modernization. Not all sectors thrived on these investments. Housing in central areas changed little. In newly developing areas people struggled to get close to the "I" changes, with occasional tragic results as around the Tlalnepantla area in 1984. Hundreds of squatters were killed as they attempted to piggyback on electric, water and transportation grids. Infrastructure in any urban area is seen as very valuable, even to the point of pirating one's way into its benefits. It is also the object of great concern for control, and when strikes at Ferrocarriles Nacionales in the 1950s threatened hegemony the workers were brutally repressed. And, this was not the only such instance where infrastructure was involved.

(See *Mask of Democracy: Labor Suppression in Mexico Today*, Dan La Botz, 1992.)

Before we project our lessons about infrastructure let us summarize our history of previous investment in the following chart which notes the forms that met contemporary needs and also those that shaped their futures.

## Prediction About the ZMCM on the Basis of Our History

Angotti says that we have two ways to go with respect to the city's growth (any Latin American mega-city). These are planned or unbalanced growth. We have tried to see how previous I-I decisions have impacted one or another historical outcomes. Some of these previous responses were to environmental predicaments that they have found themselves in—that is, flooding or earthquakes. Other infrastructure was implimented in order to bring about a more productive future, and this included railroads, better communications, electricity, and more recently an up-graded airport. The quality of life was the target of improvements, for example, in water and sewerage. Obviously, many kinds of outcomes were achieved by various I-Is. One way in which planning becomes reality is by guiding it via the control of infrastructure changes.

Newkirk says we need to simulate various scenarios via modeling in order to better plan (and predict). Specific outcomes in urban development can be anticipated by inspecting the "tensions" generated in the simulations. This approach will guide us to the solutions and these will be achieved by "some optimal sequencing of infrastructure development," (p. 209). In our history the I-Is that made settlement possible (dikes, water aquaducts, etc.) did come first. Service oriented I-Is that improve the quality of life come next, we might hope. Down the line I-Is that greatly enhance productivity are possible. Railroads and other efficient transportation, energy conduits, accessible markets, regulatory facilities, and inter-regional connectors (ports) will foreshadow future urban developments. All of these can be optional additions to the urban setting, bringing about fairly specific consequences—hence planning made real. The infrastructure additions are optional in that decisions about their realization are often in the political sphere. Running a large natural gas line north to the United States (which was subsequently turned down by the U.S. president) would have been such infrastructure that would have influenced the future in several ways. The creation of superports on east and west coasts would move exports and lessen Mexico's ties to its northern neighbor. Just as a railroad line helped to determine the fate of towns in the American west, the upgrading of transportation routes would shape the central zone of Mexico (or any area). Installing the basic utilities for an industrial zone or a worker's residential area would shape more than these targets in the longer run. And to repeat, the post smoke stack industry will need different I-Is, perhaps. Planned outcomes are possible with tighter control of infrastructure, and can impact any of the three outcome modes which are outlined by Newkirk: "Spread, central, and nodal." Upgraded highways will spread the ZMCM, all other things unchanged. Provision of good utilities anywhere will reinforce that pattern for residences or firms. Rail spurs and canals are somewhat dated infrastructure, whereas pollution abatement oriented infrastructure will have more future impact. The history of assigning one kind of infrastructure at any given point in time will totally be one of contest, more than over sexual access or normal forms of property. Collective social life of any kind springs from the nature and distribution of it. Intergovernmental cooperation on I-Is may be more important in terms of planning than the specifics of something like a sewer line.

Having a political organization or movement that stresses one kind of I-I or another can have an enormous impact on the shape of the ZMCM. There is a margin for intervention, although the evolution of culture and technology (the demand for television) may shape the response. Technology that h as the capacity to change urban scenarios can be advanced or retarded by policy as well. Focusing on the extension of the existing metro system within Mexico City as opposed to the provision of light rail (as an example) within the greater ZMCM will certainly shape the area. Doing neither of the latter, but focusing upon the outrigger communities may be doing the right thing. Perhaps, any I-I should be applied only after public impact statements are filed! The pressures have been to obscure the impact of the larger investments (nuclear generators?) and only to publically acknowledge the populist pleasing proposals. In a world of scarce pesos it is also worth while to repair the older, usable infrastructure, which should be just as worthy of photo ops as ribbon cutting or shovel turning on new I-Is. Consciousness of the past impact of infrastructure decisions and a focus upon proposals in the pipeline are all we can offer here. Lastly let us outline an alternative set of parameters that we can be aware of in the likely expansion of the ZMCM in the next three decades. The fifth ring is not likely to be the only change, and cities may be stabilizing as some observes claim (as Luis Unikel).

## An Exercise in Back Prediction: What Really Happened?

But there is also the argument that the poor do exercise real choice about where they live. They make important locational trade-offs at different "stages" of their urban and residential experience; cheap markets, sources of unskilled employment, and low-cost rental (tenement) accommodation. . . . I challanged several of these assumptions. . . . One important reason has been the gradual absorption of many formerly outlying towns into the built-up area. For example, in order of absorption from the 1920s onwards: Tacuba, Azcaptotzalco, Tacubaya, Tlalnepantla, Tepeyac, La Villa, Mixcoac, Ixtapalapa, Coyoacan, San Angel, Ecatepec, Contraras, and Tlalpan. (Ward, 1990, page 93.)

Time and energy permitting we could examine the reasons for the absorption of these communities. (See maps by Hayner, 1954 and Ward, 1990, p. 36.) Ward chalks these moves and sequence up to the "large number of land-use and service functions" that were previously found only in the old core—which the Turner thesis predicted. Currently, a similar process is supposedly at work as Tepotzotlan, Coacalco, Chiconcuac, Chalco, and Milpa Alta are absorbed, because of their own core qualities. All of these advantages and services are possible because of infrastructural additions at one point in time or another. Our three variables, distance, resources, and preference should largely cover the expansion, although one may be more important than another at times. These additions to the contiguous built-up area are probably over-determined by the factor of being adjacent and having values which people need and seek. If we were to develop an "intensification index" the elements in this expansion would be central to it. We are not going to forget real estate manipulation nor real policy implimentation in any of this either.

## Where Next, And Why?

The present effort will be to examine the prospects and basis for the territorial expansion of Mexico City, or what we will refer to as the Greater ZMCM. Our title for this effort is "The Fifth Ring." Previous expansion areas and periods could be designated in different fashions, but we are refering here to the more or less concentric urban spread from the historic cores of this great metro area. The process itself could be labeled urban sprawl or conurbacion, but it involves the intensified useage of the peripheral areas of the ZMCM. Perhaps it is a series of questions that we are addressing. What are the dominant spatial trends for this region (an equivalent term to the "Greater ZMCM" in this instance)? What is the dynamic mixture of centrifugal and centripedal movement? What is the relative role of resources, infrastructure, or improvements in determining the future pattern? Do people merely follow "work"? What are land use policies able to accomplish, or any other policy? How is distance managed by people who become part of this process? How should we phrase power and social class issues in the whole scheme of matters?

Where should we take our lessons and models from? Are there good comparison in this instance? Is an appraisal of power issues on Santiago, Chile useful in the fleshing out of our paradigm? Is extrapolation of existing "trends" of value? How about the perceptions of experts? Is an explosive set of new factors brewing up? What data would we use for any type of speculation, which is in fact what it would amount to? We can wait for the census of these areas in the year 2015! Traffic surveys are being made, and it seems true that people vote with their shoes—or wheels, or busfare. Shopping malls will follow people, and to some extent anticipate them. We hope to use the yellow pages to plot commercial decisions already made, and we hope to involve the speculations and exhortations of planners for these hinterland regions.

In short order we will examine a theory for urban growth, for regional development, and for public and private decisions that will impact our area of study. The hope is to use both shoe leather as well as archival data in "data" collection.

## A Little History

The sequence of cultures in the basin of Mexico includes 6 or 8 from pre-classic periods up to the Kulhuacan Mechica. These established only village horizons, although they were often spread throughout the valley. Prince Nezahualcoyotl helped to define the next phrase, and the first phase of urban growth. After Cortez the superimposition of the laws of the Indies, and the centuries of attempts at drainage control helped to define the second ring. Colonial rule gave way to independence, and in 1824 the Federal District started to define another peripheral zone. Later in the 19th century we could stress the impact of bourgeois activities and its focus via the Porfiriato, a fourth, concentric circle formed where the environment permitted. Individual choices were augmented by national policies which reflected the larger political-economy.

In the 1970s and 1980s another powerful movement accelerated, (partly centripedal, but in essence centrifugal). This resulted in the subject matter of this essay as a fifth ring of urban development. This "urban sprawl" seems to encompass the largest, demographic entity in the world, although it is large by any measure. "Rings" may not be the best metaphor for this metro-area development. The "Atlas de la Ciudad de Mexico" and many other renderings (as the DDF, 1990 series) stress the processes in the separate units, rather than larger dynamics—what ever their geometric shapes. Roughly there has been a centrifugal spread in the past 400 years, and much of the dynamic involved can be encompassed in this manner. Can prediction be placed into this modality? It is probably important to emphasize area, radial distance, and the general geographical-economic opportunism of the overall process. We are not offering any geo-concentric determinism, however. There is no natural history to the unfolding either. We should attempt some kind of ranking of variables as a kind of theory, or more importantly as an attempt at the operationalization of predictive qualities.

## The Fifth Ring: All The Theory We'll Need

> Human activities are distributed over the national territory in certain rhythms and patterns that are neither arbitrary nor the workings of pure chance. (*Regional Policy*, Friedmann & Alonso, page 3.)

Ultimately regional theory is involved in urban studies. In a search of theoretical volumes on urban expansion into regional hinterlands we looked for explanatory and predictive variables. Either backward explaining or foreward predicting elements were sought. We sorted out three types: *Distance maximizing*, as with elements of location theory; *Resource maximizing*, as with other elements of location and choice theory; and *Preference maximizing*, as more clearly with choice-decision theory. The following table attempts to place various multidimensional factors into these 3 categories—which are not always analytically or practically separable. (See page 128)

# VARIABLES

## DISTANCE

DESTINATION ROUTES  (QUALITY OF TRAVEL—HASSLE-FREE)

INTERVENING OPPORTUNITIES  (KIN, ERRANDS, SHOPPING, OTHER JOBS)

TRANSPORTATION TYPES  (TRAVEL INFRASTRUCTURE AVAILABLE)

DISTANCE COSTS VS. BENEFITS  (TOLLS, FARES, FUEL)

## RESOURCES

ACCESS TO SERVICES  (INFRASTRUCTURE AVAILABLE—SCHOOLS, MEDIA, ETC.)

LAND USE AGREEMENT  (TITLES TO LAND, PUBLIC LANDS)

SCALE ECONOMICS  (SUFFICIENT POPULATION, CRITICAL MASS)

REGIONAL INCOME DISTRIBUTION  (GENERAL LEVEL? POOR PEOPLE CAUSE OTHER POOR PEOPLE?)

RELEATIVE POWER DISTRIBUTION  (LOCAL CLOUT OF COMMUNITY)

PUBLIC-PRIVATE DECISIONS TO LOCATE THERE  (FIRMS, GOVERNMENT CENTERS)

AVAILABLE NATURAL RESOURCES  (WATER, CLIMATE, ETC.)

PLANNING FOR PEOPLE  (PROPENSITY FOR IMPROVEMENT)

## PREFERENCE

QUALITY OF LIFE  (LESS SMOG, CRIME, ETC.)

CONSUMER ACCESS  (PLACES TO EFFICIENTLY SPEND PESOS) (HOUSING)

CLASS BOUNDARIES  (OPENESS OF COMMUNITY)

EMPLOYMENT OPPORTUNITIES  (ALTERNATIVE WAYS TO MAKE A LIVING, AS THE INFORMAL ECONOMY)

DEMANDS FOR SPECIAL SERVICES  (INFRASTRUCTURE, AS HOSPITALS, ETC.)

PERSONAL ATTRACTION FACTORS  (CLOSE TO FAMILY, ETC.)

# GROWTH AREAS

| Growth Area | Quadrant | Distance | Resources | Preference |
|---|---|---|---|---|
| Pachuca | NE | 88 KM | Mines, Agriculture, Industries | LOW, but picturesque |
| Texcoco | NE | 30 KM | Market town for Woolens, Pottery & Glass | Downhill? LOW |
| Mex Route 85 | NE-axial | _to_ | | |
| Tecamec | NE-con-tiguous | | | |
| Chicoloapan | NE | | | |
| Queretero | NW | 222 KM | Much current Industry, Tourism | MEDIUM, still tranquil |
| Cuautitlan | NW | | | |
| Mex Route 57 | NW-axial | | | |
| Nicolas Romero | NW | | | |
| Cuernavaca | SW | 85 KM —new auto pista | Recent Industry, Tourism, Crafts | HIGH, but "losing charm" |
| Toluca | SW | 65 KM | Communications, Industry, not much Tourism | MEDIUM |
| Tres Marias | SW | 76 KM | | MEDIUM |
| Yautepec | SW | 88 KM | | |
| Mex Route 95 | SW | MC to Acapolco | Varies much | |
| Puebla | SE | 126 KM | Auto Assembly much Industry, Tourism | MEDIUM |
| S.M. Texmelucan | SE | 75 KM | | |
| Amecameca | SE | 114 KM | | |

Distance variables include exisitng (and feasible) routes, hence incorporating axial theory (routes along which expansion and interaction are likely to take place). The prior existance of outlying sub-centers (with reasonable potential, resources, and prefereable qualities) augers well for utilization and spillover. Expansion to outriggers and general regional filling-in will be continuous, but will pulse with the total shift of conurbation. Prediction as to specific regional coutcomes depends on all three sets of variables with none necessarily being preeminant. All three are perhaps necessary for given outcomes, but not individually sufficient. (Distance, low resources and so -on can be overcome.) Distance and directional variables (which way do migrants, soujourners go?) have been reasonably well studied. Resources (available land, jobs and amenities) must be present in appropriate combinations for the populations involved. Recent in-migrants obviously want jobs and amenities, but may tolerate transport costs and forego preference hierarchies to some extent. We know that the affluent moved centrifugally early in the game for preference reasons, while weighing distance and resource concerns in their own personal equations. Decentralization policies will have efficacy for certain populations, and less so for others for whom substantial relocation has no great net advantage. Preference variables might be the best focus for regional planners in order to reinforce the initial viability of deconcentration moves stressing resources—make the new place look liveable! Distance gains in moving people may have an upper limit, that is, beyond a certain point, movers might as well go to Los Angeles.

Existing urban sprawl did not preceed on a theoretically perfect, open plane. Mexico City is a bowl where mountainous peripheral terrain raises transport costs in most directions, but also focuses resources that can upgrade the routes involved. Better roads increase the supra- regional quality of enhancement, but in an age of globalization and "free trade" agreements the old boundaries are vulnerable anyway. Massive pull factors to the north, combined with the push factors of the tierra caliente, have always been involved in Mexico, but the Greater ZMCM remains as a central option. Spread within the latter is impacted about equally between our three types of variables and policy driven considerations. Regional planning in the past has recognized the preference leapfrogging involved in demographic dispersal. Good transportation, of course, facilitate this dispersal, while the other two variables (resources and preferences) are necessary ingredients. Our effort here will be to look at the ongoing growth dispersal within the enhanced ZMCM area in terms of these variables. Which ones explain movements to the

States of Morelos or Puebla or Mexico? Can we operationalize these variables with obtainable data? Can planners understand the forces at work and direct them—or minimize their negative sides? We do know that our concentric metaphor used here is of more use for a regional picture, and that the ZMCM is better seen as a scattering of sub-regional centers and varied uses. The DDF's series of delegacion maps has an excellent one showing the "Subcentro Urbano" areas as well as the "Poblado Rural Concentradors." We will describe these for the adjacent states of Morelos, Mexico and Puebla as well. We, however, will not forget the historical phases of this area and the table on the "Relationship of Core to Region" is included in order to try to see where we are headed. The description of the most recent ring as one of "Neo-Accumulation" might tend to play down these kinds of activities in other periods—but "new" turf seems to be up for grabs. We will draw upon this Table later.

In dealing with real space, as we have observed, there is a movement out from a center when conditions warrant it. There is a predictableness to this movement especially along transportation routes—the development may be said to be axial. Briefly what does this involve? The sub-theorems note that elaboration or development following these major routes (highways more than rail routes?) will take on a star shape (as geograph allows). These radial lines lead to other centers, and qualities of the center may diminish as peripheral areas are reached. Core areas tend to dominate, at least until efficiency factors reduce the core's viability or create "drag." Local, sub-sutonomy is a result of the latter, as well as with the growth of regional efficiencies. The latter seems contrary to dependency theory, and would have to be examined closely. Certainly deviations are noted in any of these models, and results will often be particularistic. The greatest efficiencies are to be had in what is already established, be it a route or a sub-center or a network circumstance. Let us next look at the likely growth areas in the adjacent quadrants given some of these preliminary theoretical notions. These centers or strips of likely growth in the next two decades will then be examined in terms of a conglomerate of terms used to analyze urban and regional phenomenon. The ZMCM should be made more understandable by such an effort. First, the likely growth areas.

## Factors Involved In The Ring of Neo-Accumulation

Cities are centers of power and privilege. In every Third World country, the urban sector accounts for a disproportionate share of consumption as

# RELATIONSHIP OF CORE TO REGION

| RING | POL·ECON | SPATIAL | CULTURAL |
|------|----------|---------|----------|
| AZTLAN-OBTAINED | CORE DRAWS IN ECON. GOODS AND HINTERLAND POPULATIONS | STRATEGIC REGIONS ARE ANNEXED | STYLE SET BY DOMINANT CORE, FEW GROUPS BY-PASSED |
| IMPERI-COLON | DRAWS IN ECONOMIC GOODS, BUT MARGINALI-ZES HINTERLAND POLITI-CALLY | AS ABOVE | DOMINANT (INTOLERANT?) CORE; MANY GROUPS (W/ OUT ECON. FUNCTION) BY-PASSED |
| PORF-EUROP | AS ABOVE - - - - - - - CORE PROSPERS GREATLY | OTHER REGIONS IGNORED UNLESS COMPETITIVE OR SYMBIOTIC | AS ABOVE |
| REV·BOURG | SOME DECENTRALIZATION AS TO ECON. & POLITICAL STILL PATERNALISTIC OR CLIENTALISTIC | STRONG CENTRIPEDAL AT FIRST, THEN SOME GROUPS GO OUTWARD | CHANGE MOSTLY FROM CENTER: FIRST IDEOLOGICAL THEN "LIFESTYLE" VIA CONSUMERISM |
| NEO·ACCUM | DECENTRALIZATION CON-TINUES, AQUISITIVE STYLE CLONED FROM CEN-TER: "NEW"(?)POLITICS | MOVE TO SUB-REGIONAL AUTONOMY(?) STRONG CENTRIFUGAL MOVEMENT | HYBREDIZATION OF STYLES POSSIBLE. (CHILANGO Vs ECLECTIC) |

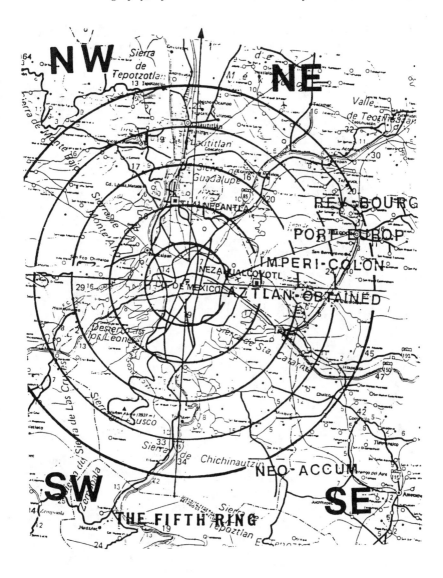

# REGIONAL EXPANSION OF MEXICO CITY INTO THE 21ST CENTURY

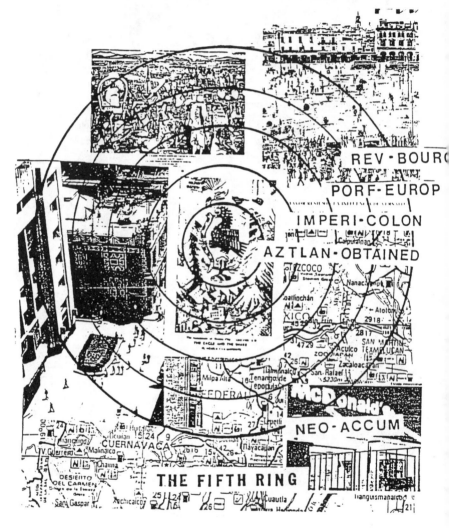

well as investment. (Josef Gugler, *The Urbanization of the Third World*, 1988, page 85.)

Expansion of all of our rings is based on further investment, this time in a broad area where transportation allows for a leap-frogging to older, peripheral areas. Do we still call this area the ZMCM, or merely conurbacion, regionalism, or urban sprawl? Prediction of the pace and direction of such entities is not new, but the application of systematic information supposedly is new. Ross Newkirk (in "Spatial Analysis and Spatial Policy Using Geographic Information Systems," edited by Les Worrall, 1991) has written about "Mapping Metropolitan Futures," this time based on a case study of Toronto. We have tried to list the factors that may be involved in the Mexico City area. It may be that the possibilities of exogenous stimulus associated with a likely NAFTA will have more to do with its occurrence, but the questions of directions and pace will remain. Governemnt policies of deconcentration will be involved, as will the "natural" patterns already in place. Advantages will build upon advantages, and once public-private investments are made the results are often over-determined.

The match of big decisions with personal ones will occur in various settings. "Growth" may occur in older, peripheral centers, along axial routes, in spill-over, contiguous expansion, and in new, planned areas. The installation of services or infrastructure will reinforce and legitimate these decisions. The process at a macro-level will involve government policies to decentralize, attempts to maximize labor or other resources, land speculation activities, mass activities as land occupations or environmental movements, contradictions in the elites (see Gugler), and long periods of recession (as in the 1980s). General Motors (the Polanco plant) decision to pull their plant out of the Federal District in the next five years was said to be because "It's the right thing to do" would be an example of a big decision. (See *The News*, March 28, 1992, page 1.) No doubt other advantages have been maximized by the move as well. Partly for ecological and for profit maximizing reasons Pena Pobre paper company pulled out in 1982. Plant closings and relocations may result in expansion of the fifth ring or beyond. The mix of firms benefited by a potential NAFTA or another agreement oriented southward are yet to be experienced. The mix of firms in such negotiations will determine the location decisions within the greater ZMCM. People movements on a distance-preference basis will make the overall metro area expansion more circular or filled out. Industrial and commercial decisions (that may make sense only in retrospect) will complete the picture of 5th ring expansion. A patina of fast food emporiums, small shops, and street vendors will complete the urban motif.

Economic activities and state expenditures will harden the pattern. Speculators, promoters and bureaucrats on the move will do likewise. The ebb and flow of land values will be impacted as early exploiters interact with traditional folks. Outcomes are problematic. Will there be "bridgeheaders"? Will there be gentrification flowing one way or another? Will state governments try to balance the growth pattern under the pressures of competition and implimentation? Will the national policy facilitate the best and help to mitigate the worst? Many, like Susan Eckstein, ("The politics of conformity in Mexico City," Chapter 16, page 294 in Josef Gugler) see the acceptance of "help" as bringing organizational restraints and also powerlessness. The planning of infrastructure will probably remain minimal, and as usual the larger things will dominate the smaller things.

# Chapter 7

# Planning for the Metro Area

## A History of Planning Regarding Mexico City

> Mexico has little experience of professional planning owing to the small number of qualified practitioners, for there have been only about 50 persons with a professional education prepared to deal with the subject. (Francisco Jose Alvarez y Lezama in Arnold Whittick's Encyclopedia of Urban Planning, 1974, page 685.)

The author of the above quote notes the absence (up to 1974) of legislation referring to urbanism and the resistance to the very notion (p. 684). Laws passed as about "general planning" have not been implemented. The near absence of schools of planning was offset only by a few courses connected with engineering or architecture programs. "Amateurs" in such groups as the "Mexican Institute of Social Planning" and the "Mexican Society of Planning" are noted.

Yet Mexico City received planning intentions from pre-Europeans as from Prince Nezahualcoyotl and his water control projects. The Spanish law of the Indies did leave its imprint, and grid or checkerboard patterns of the city were in fact planned. French and British influence would later mark the city with diagonal boulevards, terraces, parks and gardens. The last half of the 19th century saw the influence of Georges Eugene Haussmann (as in the Paseo de la Reforma) and the more oblique influence of Patrick Geddes whose views were known, and some see as the founder of city planning and environmentalism. Geddes had been in Mexico in the late 1870's (see Paddy Kitchen's *A Most Unsettling Person*, 1975). Probably the "planning" that most impacted the face of Mexico City was the flush of public works in the Diaz period with government palaces, theaters, avenues, railroads and sanitation structures in great profusion. (See our section on events that have shaped Mexico City.)

# 100 YEARS OF PLANNING EFFORT

| Person or groups | Scope of Efforts or Focus | Special Concerns | Extent of Implementation |
|---|---|---|---|
| Georges E. Haussmann 1853 | The Paseo de la Reforma, other cities | Movement of people, military (reflecting European values!) | Extended in stages |
| Carlos Contreras 1927 | Trying to bring professional urban planning to Mexico | Regional, environmental, transportation | Major thoroughfares got more academic support |
| Federal District (Planning Dept., Coplade, SCM) | Unofficial long range land use plan for Mexico City | Produce a master plan. Commercial, industrial, educational uses in relation to residential density | Slow and Problematic. Produces land use maps, little executive power? |
| SEDUE, 1983 (Previously SAHOP) | Ecological planning | Housing, economic planning | Had role after 1985 earthquake |
| Comision de Conurbacion del Centro del Pais 1982 | Flow of settlement in relation to contours. Regional scope | Along with SPP and CNA | Underestimated growth. Was it a serious attempt at city-wide planning? |
| Major groups today:<br>*SEDUE<br>*Conurbacion Commission<br>*Urban Dev. Dept. of State of Mexico & D.F. | | | Small budgets. Little sympathy for implementation |

"NO SERIOUS CONSULTATION"
WARD, page 129

SOME SEE THE RADICAL SCHOOL OF ARCHITECTURE AT UNAM AS A NEW WAVE?

## PLANOS DE LA
## CIUDAD DE MEXICO

INSTITUTO DE INVESTIGACIONES ESTETICAS
UNIVERSIDAD NACIONAL AUTONOMA DE
MEXICO
DEPARTAMENTO DEL DISTRITO FEDERAL

---

# PLANOS DE LA
# CIUDAD DE MEXICO

## SIGLOS XVI y XVII

ESTUDIO HISTORICO, URBANISTICO Y BIBLIOGRAFICO

POR

### MANUEL TOUSSAINT
### FEDERICO GOMEZ DE OROZCO
### JUSTINO FERNANDEZ

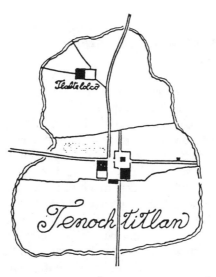

XVIº Congreso Internacional de
Planificación y de la Habitación
MEXICO                              MCMXC

In the 20th century Alvarez y Lezama notes the role of individuals, influenced by their activities abroad, who inspired planning and zoning laws in the Federal district (Carlos Contreras in the 1930's), and also helped organize "planning committees" who worked on Mexico City from 1938 to 1947 (p. 688). The latter were largely ignored. There were various "congresses" and conferences, but the governments involvement seemed to be with visible details rather than the analysis and pursuit of a general plan. Problems are met only in the breach, not to be anticipated. Housing projects would (as Tlateloloco) alter the landscape of the 1940's and 1950's.

Leading a group of planners, Carlos Contreras put out a journal of "planificacion" in September of 1927. Besides focusing on the region in which Mexico City resided there were separate articles on planned thoroughfares, traffic problems, and the role of their organization (Association Nacional para la Planificacion de la Republica Mexicana). The backgrounds of their membership and a bibliography were included in this journal. The latter were very international in scope and had British, French, Irish and U.S. sources. The Chicago planning (Bernham, Wacker, etc.) was especially evident, but the overall effort was to give legitimacy to the proclamation involved in this journal, *Planification*.

## Governmental Units and Planning

Apart from the valiant efforts of planners working outside of the structure of efficacy (if governments may be so described) there are the governmental units themselves. Robert C. Fried describes the process ("Mexico City" in *Great Cities of the World*, 1972, p. 653). Both Mexico City and other municipalities were allowed to keep their councils or ayuntamientos. There was, however, a shifting of authority back and forth between state and local government. The size of the Federal district has increased, and represents much of the settled area. An organic law of December, 1928, attempted to get Federal supremacy in the D.D.F. As of 1968 the bureau of public works handles city planning, suburban works, streets and supervision of building.

Policy in the district is not made the same as in the U.S., Europe or the Soviet pattern; rather the President of the Republic and the governor of the Federal district act unilaterally (Fried, p. 666). But, presidents are also mindful that one-seventh of the population and much of the dominant party's support comes from the Federal district. Thus with projects such as Ciudad Universitaria, the first expressway, Viaducto Aleman, and major improvements in water or hydroelectricity (Lerma), the president will make it a photo-opportunity.

Fried notes how governor Urchurtu (1952–1966) of the district made many planned changes. Besides cleaning up, literally, and also working on corruption many public facilities were developed. A ring road (Anillo Periferico), the expansion of Chapultepec Park, the development of new markets, schools, water structures, hospitals and new sports centers were part of this picture. The down-town was "beautified," but at the same time squatter settlements were starved. The latter may have led to Uruchurtu's downfall or it may have been the larger issue of the next president-to-be, where he would have had an inside track after the 1968 Olympiad. Many people in Mexico City and surrounding areas had been by-passed in the "planning" involved here. In any case an increasing part of the built-up area of Mexico City now lies outside of the district. This "conurbation" process has spread into the State of Mexico, of course. New industrial developments of the last two decades and many residential developments have moved to the northwest into the State of Mexico. Problems of regulation, water control, pollution, unchecked growth have not been improved by this conurbationistic cancer (my term).

Fried deals at length with planning for the Federal district (p. 679). Early on the "Traza de Cortes" of one square mile had been divided into lots for the conquerors. The plan of 1524 would leave its mark, and Fried believed it "was the first and last effort to plan the city's development." Perhaps in terms of total impact Fried is correct, but there have been many efforts since that point. Comprehensive plans he believes were offered in the 1930's, but forgotten after WWII. Governor Uruchurtu was seen as hostile to such plans. It seems that the revelation of intentions was not consistent with private moves in secrecy. Even efforts at national economic planning did not necessitate urban planning in any detail. Still Fried believes that the central areas and upper class housing in suburbs did well. Neither did tourists suffer from a possible lack of comprehensive planning. One third of the populace were stuck with their unbeautiful colonias proletarias. Squatters had "do-it-yourself suburbs," a term Fried attributes to Berhard Frieden. Recent arrivals hanging on by their fingernails hoped to regularize their uncertain land titles and acquire urban services. The aspiring middle class could look forward to some government assistance on housing.

As to the future, Fried saw the ban on further subdivisions as exerting some restraint on "overgrowth." The maintenance of superior metropolitan services meant that hinterland amenities would be less attractive. Fried stresses the relative power and autonomy of local, state and federal units in approaching any process, including urban planning. The recent (1988) election victory of the PRI opposition in the Federal district may count for something down the line.

## Other Views of Planning for Mexico City

Peter Ward in two books (*Housing, the State and the Poor*, 1985, and *Mexico City: The Production and Reproduction of an Urban Environment*, 1991) seems to be a "realist" about the potential for planning in Mexico City. He sees "real commitment of governments to community participation" (or to provide funds for urban projects) as "extremely limited" (p. 201, 1985). Contrasting liberal, instrumentalist, and structuralist views of the state he asks whether an accurate view of housing or planning can emerge unless we have an adequate view of state functioning. Clearly the municipal powers have not used land use planning in such a fashion as to benefit the poor and their housing whereas the opposite is true for real estate and industrial interests (p. 59). Land use planning in Latin America generally favors high income users (p. 70). Land use planning is used to legitimate government actions and upper income investments (p. 72). And for Ward these actions have an international context although did not choose to stress them in this 1985 study (p. 240). Still planning authorities are seen as trying to integrate as many low-income communities as possible (p. 245). The outcome of planning might be more residential segregation, however, and even when the poor are included in the plan the hook-up costs may exclude them in the near future. Being included in the planning process may not solve all problems.

Ward's 23-page chapter in his 1991 book is full of reasons why planning on behalf of people has *not* occurred in Mexico City. Basically a lack of "political" commitment to improve life chances and living conditions" is involved (p. 114). Planners also "occupied no political space, whatsoever" (p. 114). Now, however, there is "a growing consensus that planning is desirable" (p. 115). Planning when it occurs is likely to be an "ideological tool" although three recent presidents (Echeverria, Portillo and, perhaps, Salinas) have supported economic and physical planning (p. 115). Ward's focus is on the fate of the 1980 Federal district plan.

What Ward lays out is an alphabet soup of development oriented agencies, COPRODES, SAHOP, CONAPO, SEDUE, AURIS, CMA and COPLADE were some of these agencies between 1971 and 1989. Their tasks included the decentralization of industry, the reduction of population concentration, and the fostering of economic growth. Planning legislation from 1928 to 1984 was aimed at establishing zoning, dealing with specific problems such as housing and creating specific agencies and administrative procedures. Although Ward professes that planning hardly exists, he does see a move away from mere decoration of the physical environment. A master plan to regulate population, attempts to rationalize traffic flow, the creation of buffer zones (open areas) and, as of late, efforts to improve the environment have been some of the thrusts (p. 125).

Specific problems in the planning activity itself, according to Ward, include: "a multiplicity of agencies with overlapping and/or competing responsibilities" (p. 127), political weakness, a lack of clarity as to purpose, and bureaucratic factionalism. Lack of public participation is an obvious shortcoming, public referendas are seen as threatening governments, and protest groups have remained "isolated" (p. 133).

In terms of the goals of our book to anticipate the outcomes in the next two decades we will note Ward's prognostications. Under the topic of "planning for whose interest?," Ward notes a probable inability to prevent illegal expansion into buffer areas (p. 135). Planning will continue to justify government (and private?) decisions already made. Planning will also continue helping some at the expense of others, as with highway and metro extensions. Land speculators may be constrained by planning, but some will see their acquisitions increase in value. Some (the middle class?) may gain from the zoning-out of undesirable land uses. Perhaps some of the poor will benefit if they are lucky to find their residences included in expansion of the service nets. Some will also face eviction from areas the plan considers "illegal." Greater legitimacy must be seen as a future gain as well as greater control. Ward is a fervent believer in active citizen participation which he believes will supply needed continuity across sexenios (p. 137). Without a single case of a launched referendum, it is an unlikely occurrence.

Ward's volume also has a brief chapter devoted to "future development during the 1990's" (chapter 8, p. 233). He assumes that past patterns of response may well allow some hesitant predications about future directions. He also assumes that "the crisis is on-going" (p. 234) even though centuries of work on water and drainage may be paying off. Ward seems to be saying that some of the "crisis" is manufactured. If urban oriented academics can not decide about limiting the growth of cities or letting them grow flat-out in order to achieve "economies of scale," then how can we arrive at a consensus about the nature of the "crisis."

Ward separates himself from "contemporary Marxists" who posit increased deterioration in living conditions (p. 234). He argues that Mexican resourcefulness will stave off the dysfunctions (whose source he does not specifically indicate). The burden of problem solving will follow the burden of increased population and this is likely to be in the State of Mexico. He admits to having not looked at that specific area (p. 235) "where the battle over future city growth will be won or lost." Ward does not justify his own "optimism" very well, because there are few signs of planning for growth in the latter place. Also: "Initiatives in urban development amounted to superficial 'bread and festival'-type actions (mini-urbanismo) which presently, are not good enough" (p. 235). The present author did work in an urban planning office early in his career. As a draftsman I did all of the early graphics for grant applications. The city planning commission had a "plan" for Minneapolis, but it was to preserve or slightly modify existing zoning. The work was not future oriented in any real sense. On the other hand, our housing and redevelopment agency did plan for communities and for renewal of a portion of the loop (El Centro!). There was also a free wheeling "long range capital improvements committee" for the greater metro area which did assess priorities to a great variety of developments. Thus, total plans, slight changes and area developments had an actual, responsible agency—although one could discuss the frustrations, conflicts and venality endlessly. The point here is that overlapping agencies, despite the confusion, may represent more input from more interests.

## D.D.F. Plans

The most complete history of the planning process for Mexico City is Jaun R. Gil Elizondo's "Planeacion del desarrollo urbano de la ciudad de Mexico." He starts reciting the "evolucion" of this process with the D.D.F.'s 1928 organic law. This law was somewhat in effect up until 1940. A committee was established that passed along regulations, many of which survived the processes of political economy. The second article in this law relates Mexico City to the total Mexican plan—no small accomplishment.

In 1936 a second law was passed which created an auxiliary organization that evidently linked Mexico City to national planning. Supporting financial-economic plans were to be prepared, and these were heady times in terms of possibilities for national development. Indeed the 1940–1970 period stressed planning for accelerated change. It was clear that industrialization would be a major factor in change and in causing deterioration. Population increase was inevitable and, hence, the need for space, services and general order to the scheme. Further plans for railroad and canal access were made. By 1953 an obvious need for more coordination led to a ''reform'' of the 1936 laws. The topics of housing, commerce, communication, sports, health and recreation and basic necessities were emphasized.

In the country as a whole the emphasis in the 1960's and early '70's was on balancing the forces of very rapid growth. Obviously the previous structure of relationships would persist, a 1975 Ley de desarrollo urbano del Distrito Federal shows some effort toward decentralization. The area had been divided into 16 deligacions and the 1975 Law tried to get responses in the areas of transportation, space, water and general living problems in urban areas. Reorganization seemed to be a way to mobilize communication and authority. The big effort seemed to be on ''desconcentracion'' at least as to administration. The structures created included the ''secretaria de asentamientos humanos y obras publicas,'' and the goals were to rationalize planning and control the major forces at work. By 1982 the structures created (comision de conurbacion del centro) focused on the sprawl being introduced and the future that would surely arise out of this. As planning proclamations came out of this decade the words ''control'' and ''democratic'' would appear. Late in the decade of the 1980's ''environmental protection'' would be on the masthead of legislation and organizations. All of these were credible goals and motivations. The later goals involved reserving territory as yet undeveloped (68483 ha or 45.6% of the land) for ecological conservation. It is not that we are long on plans and agencies and short on implementation, it is that we are getting better and better at ''tooling up!'' There were to be serious efforts at decentralization and environmental restoration. No one doubted the more immediate planning goals involving potable water, drainage of residual water, transportation control, more housing, and installations to upgrade education, health or recreation. One could pass by such activities every day.

Planning strategies as well as objectives were delineated. The picture in the year 2000 or 2010 may be unrealistic, but it was clearly stated. A 2.2% increase to 12.7 million people in the district has probably already been surpassed (see page 404, article by Hugo Garcia Perez). The amount of green space to be preserved might be more accurately forecast, but predictions about service levels (hospitals, schools) more problematic. In the latter case one must remember that "new" areas of the valley opened to development might well be better financed from the public end, because that's the way things work.

## Alternative Outcomes for Mexico City Planning to Consider

Picking winners is supposedly based on form—previous performance— and it is here that the historian may be of some limited service. Of course form is sometimes turned upside down, history is full of surprises. (Knight, p. 454)

Apart from the history of planning in this great urban center, there is history itself. Some would like the former to guide or at least constrain the latter. As to the latter a range of outcomes are possible. Let us consider this range and then speculate on the feasible role of "planning" for each of them.

Our table attempts to delineate the range of physical-social outcomes for Mexico City in the next two decades. Thus, an alternative projecting current trends (growth without successful planning); stabilization for a variety of reasons (policy or private choice); decentralization based on policy success, with a possible resource reallocation; and the collapse into systems anarchy (perhaps already achieved!) are noted in our table. This table of alternatives lives in the fantasy land beyond actual history in the making. As Tim Campbell and David Wilk note in their article on "Plans and plan-making in the valley of Mexico" the 1985 earthquake was such that: "The Government has seized upon the earthquake rather arbitrarily as a pretext to suddenly remake the physical and bureaucratic landscapes of the city." Efforts to decentralize would come more naturally, at least as the peril of rebuilding on the old vulnerable lake bed were concerned. The perils of prediction must include the quirks of mother earth, but humans must translate this into a reason d'etre for planning. What ever it takes! These authors are not unaware of the political context of planning, and the need for simple excuses (see page 287).

Covering a dozen plans between 1970 (starting with Echeverria's administration) and 1985 they try to show what has led to an increased awareness of the dangers of the centripedal forces previously at work. Campbell and Wilk believe that 2 or 3 times as much has been spent tooling up for Mexico City's planning efforts, but has yet "failed to

# SCENARIOS FOR PLANNING EFFORT

| OUTCOME (NOT MUTUALLY EXCLUSIVE?) | POSSIBLE APPROPRIATE ROLE FOR PLANNING | COMMENTS |
|---|---|---|
| CONTINUED EXPLOSION AS TO SIZE DENSITY (WITH SLOW DETERIORATION OF LIVING CONDITIONS) | * KEEP PRESENTING A MASTER PLAN.<br>* TELL COMMUNITIES WHAT THEIR OPTIONS ARE.<br>* FORCE POLITICAL ISSUES. | MOST LIKELY SCENARIO |
| STABILIZATION OF SIZE, DENSITY. SERVICES REMAIN ADEQUATE, BUT NO IMPROVEMENT GENERALLY. | * WORK WITH FAVORED GROUPS (ECLECTIC PLANS)<br>* TRY TO ANTICIPATE DIRECTION OF DEVELOPMENT. | MOST HOPEFUL OUTCOME GIVEN PAST FORM |
| DECENTRALIZATION POLICIES ARE EFFECTIVE. OPEN AREAS ARE MAINTAINED. RESOURCE SUFFICIENCY ALLOWS FOR RESTRUCTURING | * REDO MASTER PLAN TO CATCH UP TO NEW PROSPECTS.<br>* LINK METROPOLIS TO ITS HINTERLAND IN MORE CONSTRUCTIVE WAYS. | LEAST LIKELY SCENARIO? GIVEN PAST PERFORMANCES |
| ECO-CATASTROPHY CAUSED BY POLITICAL DEFAULT | * TRIAGE!<br>* PLAN FOR EVACUATION<br>* MAINTAIN CADRE WITH IDEAS ABOUT A FRESH START ELSEWHERE. | LEAST DESIRABLE OUTCOME (USE AS A HORROR TALE!) |

make a discernable dent'' in shaping the future (p. 288). These authors note how planning for economic growth reduced the chances for other planning; centralization was built-in due to locational advantages (p. 280). Investment in infrastructure was 2 to 9 times higher in the central region, and the latter region has consistently received 40% of total public capital expenditure.

1970 marks a transition from "ad hoc solutions" to more deliberate approaches according to these authors. The process noted favored the 1500 square kilometers Federal district over the weaker, peripheral area of the State of Mexico with 900 s-ks. As with Peter Ward, Campbell and Wilk note the people and the interests which resisted planning. The 1968 "crisis in legitimacy" is seen as a turning point or one that motivated Echerverria to balance some aspects of the national process. Population control might also be part of the new equation, but legal issues must be met in order to enable the planning effort. An information base was also necessary for planning, or at least adequate planning. The present writer helped develop a tool the Minneapolis Housing and Redevelopment Authority in the 1950's which showed substandard housing in this city arrived at by dividing the census population figures into the assessor's "full and true" data. Previous to this easily arrived at data, the agency had been flying blind it seems.

Campbell and Wilk's summary concerning planning states (p. 295) that "an institutional build-up based on a planning-strategy" was achieved in the Echeverria sexenio. The "discovery" of vast oil reserves in the next, Portillo administration gave further impetus to planning. The years from 1978 to 1981 were growth years as to planning effort and implementation. The S.A.H.O.P agency after 1977 "functioned as an organizational umbrella." S.A.H.O.P. for instance looked at the growth picture for the whole nation and designated "growth priority" areas (Lazaro Cardenas) "consolidation" areas (Veracruz and Tijuana) and "control areas as the Federal district, Guadalajara, and Monterrey. The national Plan (PNDU) would focus on small to middle sized cities which eventually could hold 18% (versus 5%) of the nation's population (p. 298). Small cities must have their lives reinvigorated! Problems with the intent to limit "control" areas seemed to "cancel" PNDU's initiative, however.

We do not wish to repeat the excellent analyses of the planning process found in Ward, Juan R. Gill Elizondo, or Campbell and Wilk. We do see more optimism in the later two about the efficacy of planning, and the articles are realistic as well. For instance, the weaker State of Mexico is seen as being slow at planning, and they state that: "Most observers of Mexico agree that the centralized nature of the Mexican political system makes planning more of a record keeping exercise'' (p. 304). Mexican urban planning as seen by Campbell and Wilk was also seen as piecemeal, dissonant, even at cross-purposes.'' Then comes the bad news! ''The end of the Lopez Portillo administration marks the end of an era of optimism that prevailed for many years in Mexican development'' (p. 305). After 1982, issues seemed to be more centered on public participation, even though the fiscal downturn made progress less likely. More empty sounding terms like ''self-help,'' neighborhood councils, and local fiscal responsibility showed up. The shift to the more tractable issues of environmentalism also was a possible signal of impending failure. Although an increase in the ''technical corpus'' was to be found, and ''experimentation'' was the new modality, ''concrete action'' is no closer. Local action without real political power is described as ''wooden'' (p. 310). ''Legal formalism'' is also used to describe government structures.

All of these evaluations would seem to tend toward overall pessimism and perhaps favoring our theoretical alternative of collapse! Even with petrodollars coming out Mexico's pockets, planning did not achieve a regulatory status. Large metropolises seem beyond any human force, perhaps even for a Chinese, Roman or Russian autocrat!

## Planning and Terremoto

### Terremoto and the Future

Perhaps the most clear-cut example of how Mexico City's government has acted through physical design to reproduce social inequality and to (inadvertently) create social divisions that did not exist before is provided by the post-earthquake reconstruction program (Ward, 1990, page 194).

When a hurricane or tornado hits a highly populated area we have a likely human tragedy in the making. Cities are vulnerable to natural forces because of their particular qualities of concentration and their locked-in qualities. By the latter we refers mostly to architecture, environment and site layout. The San Andreas Fault running through California makes for a vulnerability that we almost are forced to give odds in favor of. Mexico and Mexico City have the vulnerability of a ''land of shaking earth'' as Eric Wolf entitled this country. Mexico City has another peculiar vulnerability—it is perched partly on an old lake bed.

The three lakes on which part of the current city of Mexico City are located were likened to a bowl of "jello" after the September 1985 earthquake. The savageness of nature's deal for Mexico City was felt long beyond the few seconds of earth movement on September 19th and 20th, 1985. As with other natural events it does not have a "random" outcome: there is unevenness in the results.

The part of Mexico City which lies in the old lake beds is reported to have reverberated and amplified the 8 point Richter scale quake. Worst of all, buildings on such poor subsoil were prone to banging against one another when the ground shook. They collapsed on top where many lived. Many of the deaths were the result of this peculiar habitation pattern where the top floors of otherwise occupied buildings had families jammed into them. The morning (7:19 horas) occurrence found many people dying at home, and who stayed there until dump-truck and scoops gave them an ignomineous funeral.

We all have a concern for this tragedy, because it highlights Mexico City's preexisting circumstances—as if a plague needed to be followed by a plague. Whole colonias and neighborhoods of central Mexico City (Doctores, Morelos, Cuauhtemoc, Juarez, Condesa, Tlataloco, Carranza, Roma, and others) were seriously impacted beyond the more spectacular wreckage elsewhere in the central area. From 20,000 to 100,000 people died in the following hours. Estimates ranged from 9,000 to 200,000 dead, depending on your perspective. Up to 60% of the housing in such colonias as Morelos was damaged. Ironically a week before the government nixed housing additions or improvements, and now there were many less units! (*Daily News*, Sept. 21, 1985.) The "killer quake" made possible a rearrangement of urban values and qualities whatever other cruelties it inflicted on Mexico City. The months and now, years since the quake have seen a variety of responses from government and assorted private sectors. We shall be concerned with their subsequent direction and impact on the city and it's people. An experimental approach to our concern is obvious; we want to know how events such as this quake effect the on-going process of activities in this urban center. We have human—and intellectual—concern for the outcomes given the immensity of this natural event.

## The extent of damages and future concerns

*The Atlas de la Ciudad de Mexico* has a whole volume on the effects of the 1985 earthquake (Fasciculo 6). We have their map showing earthquake occurrences in the 30 years before the 1985 event (p. 155). The two dozen quakes make for two average occurrences every three years! They will no doubt continue at the same rate, although ones as large as the 1985 quake are more rare by far. Other natural disasters, as from vulcanism, have a much lower probability, although a man-induced "ecological Hiroshima" may have a higher probability of occurring. The map in the *Atlas* is in a chapter by G. Suarez and Zenon Jimenez and its shows the previous decades quakes mainly as having their centers of intensity from Tlalpan in a south central region on to the northwest through the Chapultepec area on into the state of Mexico. Other quake centers were found in each direction of the compass, but this center to northwest corridor is likely to be revisited in the next two decades. Our predictive problem is not one of seismographic accuracy but of certainty of occurrence of a range of shocks.

The maps enclosed in this volume show the probable impact area to be of high population density (from 5000 per km in the south through 20,000 per km in the central to a growing figure of 10,000 plus in the northwest). Some of this area was on the old lake beds. The areas hit hardest contain a variety of lifestyles and income levels, although the 1985 quake seemed to hit lower income areas hardest because of the type of housing and work conditions.

The *Atlas* has a chapter on the socio-economic characteristics of the damnificadas (refugees) and these would presumedly match the personal qualities of those who perished. Perhaps future victims would be similar in composition as well. Fewer males were in the refugee group than females and 40% were children (p. 163). Obviously the poor would be over-represented because of the areas struck and their lack of personal resources after their initial structures collapsed. The total pyramid presented may still be close to the actual for the population in the areas hit hardest. Types of architecture, suspiciously vulnerable, did effect some groups more than others. Some workers who arrived early to their "sweat shops" also fell victims in certain kinds of buildings. What is also important is the consequences down the line which we will now focus upon.

Peter Ward writes about the R.H.P. program set up very shortly after the 1985 quake. It was focused upon rehousing low income residents (p. 194), and, although running against its older policy of deconcentration, it tended to rebuild in the same areas. The housing was very heavily subsidized, for a variety of humanitarian and political motives. The existing capital basis for the previous housing program was "eroded" despite world bank loans for half the amount needed (p. 195). Roughly

45,000 new or rehabilitated units were involved, and many traditional values were preserved. Pride of barrio was maintained for some but Ward notes that many with similar experiences and backgrounds were not included—thus creating a new class division. The government's expropriation decree was the main source of this divisiveness, although its behavior was seen as "inadvertent."

A number of implications for future planning can be drawn from the aftermath of the 1985 quake. First such catastrophes can derail plans already in place, as with respect to deconcentration and on-going housing programs. Secondly, efforts to earthquake-proof the existing architectural stock may or may not be furthered in the short run because of shifting priorities. Third, political mobilization (under world scrutiny) may reform the planning process. The author was in the city two months later and noted the intensity of the coverage of the tent cities of refugees. The last volume of the *Atlas* has an article devoted to "movimientos sociales" in the city and has a map showing the types in each delegacion (p. 391). Not least, nor last, the earthquake's residual impact seems to have been a heightened awareness of the necessity to planning the environment for better-safer living. Global and even catastrophic consequences can be obtained or avoided through the dedicated plan. People can avoid their own self contamination, mother nature can be foiled! The necessity for immediate (albeit emergency) action will not hurt the public's notion of the planning process either.

*Chapter 8*

# Conclusions

## Views of Mexico City's Alternative Futures

Conclusions:

> Of course form is sometimes turned upside down; history is full of sur-
> prises. But since surprises are, by definition unpredictable, it is best to rely
> on known form, past performances, the 'lessons' of history. (Knight, in
> Cornelius et al., page 451)

We have examined a wide range of characteristics concerning Mexico
City. Perhaps we could have picked other areas as well, but demography, economy, politics, environment and planning caught our attention.
In this section we want to reexamine our "findings" in relation to our
original predictive and theoretical models.

Demographic outcomes, for instance, might be best approached by
extrapolation. There will be shifts in the internal distribution, but total
size will continue to grow. We know this also by comparison with the
other mega-cities. A panel of experts would be hard-put to spot a
counter trend. Apriori "methods" might offer a "critical mass" or
"saturation point" type of metaphor that might hold out for a sudden
departure from this superconcentration, but this effort may be like bet-
ting on a 200 to 1 shot horse in the Derby. As to compatible theories,
the concentric zone offerings with their "natural history" underpin-
nings might be most compatible with extrapolation and comparisons.
Marxist theories might be more likely to match the assumptions of a
(selected?) Delphi panel or of A-priori (off the theoretical wall?) approaches. Demographic predictions may have the greatest certitude because they seldom predict population decline or dispersal (ancient societies almost all did this, however).

Mexico City will remain a mega-city based on the above kind of logic. Policy making, as well as individual decisions (to migrate, to seek greater amenities, to follow friends, to seek security, etc.) will also determine the mega-dynamic demographic outcomes. Policy making for Mexico City has been furthered by some decentralization efforts, attempts at birth control, agriculture and land reform decisions, capitalization and infrastructure focuses, as well as failures to fund rural amenities. Also the offer of good roads and transportation to the urban areas! Mega growth can be inhibited by these kinds of factors. Non-linear outcomes could be postulated based on the correct assumptions about these kinds of policy and individual decisions.

What about economic predictions for Mexico City? Economists are more likely to predict at the national or even international levels, and to see the urban areas as a sub-creature. In Chapter IV we noted a dozen variables, drawn from a variety of economic writings, that might impact Mexico City. Probably this list underestimated the "world system" type of developments which would impact Mexico City as a whole. Debt reduction, the world price of oil, and trade agreements are in the larger system which people like Immanuel Wallestein pointed us at. The domestic nature of the political-economy especially its probable regionalization would also need to be followed. In our Table on page 42 we did also follow five economists and their types of (national?) scenarios. These writers may be typical of the range available and that range is considerable in terms of variables and models. You pays your money and you takes your choice! Does our attempt here constitute a Delphi panel? Do these writers interact at all? Are they not a random group with well defined A-priori assumptions? Should we despair of economic predictions, or merely extrapolate growth, even with probable ups and downs and transformations in the type of economic activity?

In our section on political prediction we could rely on the Cornelius, et al., volume on the country's alternative future. However, only a few writers (Ward) focused on Mexico City, per se. Our political focus was on groups as viable actors, and the attempt was to assess their motivation and general efficacy. The plan was to look at the poor, students, workers, the business elite, the middle class, and the intellectuals for their potentials for change in the next two decades. We deliberately avoided the political parties, because we assume more democratization or at least groundswells. We assume new amalgrams and coalitions as well even through the outcomes may be regional versus national in scope. We might favor a "critical mass" model in seeing these constituent coalitions, with less "insight" being derived from strictly extrapolation or comparative approaches. We did make an effort as to what kind of approaches these authors in used in their 1988 symposium. The latter, over-all was an onsite Delphi technique, although few of the participants ventured significant change in Mexico or Mexico City's political status. Comments on papers did reflect their interactions.

Our chapter on Mexico City's environment was based in an extrapolation of technical means to improve it, and the increased consciousness of the problems. We do know from comparisons elsewhere that ecological consciousness rises, then may have a tendency to collapse. It may well be crisis-driven, and hence, fragile in its impact. Yet Mexico City is an on-going environmental crisis; no one would deny that, and the powers that be are concerned to some extent with it. Technical indicators of air quality are now in place and some policy changes have been implemented. Technological indicators can describe if not explain; they can show what happened in past periods. Day-to-day oscillations can be made into "moving averages." The latter can be smoothed out into "trends," and when the daily line *significantly* crosses the "moving average" then perhaps the "trend" is reversing itself—the latter can happen without much warning! (See U.S. News and World Report, January, 1990, page 63.)

Our long appendix on the history of Mexico City in maps has a purpose in the generation of basic background data on its development. The most unlikely case would be that we could predict the dimensions or form of the city at any appreciable point in the future. Yet the city in its present relationship to its environment will persist through time. Given our knowledge of the demographics, land use pattern, economic facts of life and policy attempts we might be able to extrapolate the basic shape of the city in the year 2010. There are built-in elements in this urban landscape (the valley surrounded by mountains, the drainage problems, the need for open areas, the routes for transportation, the relationship in external resources, and so forth) which will continue to shape the metro area. The map collection demonstrates a kind of environmental parameter setting. The Chicago-ecological school might be more resonant with a large scale view, while a Marxist may inspect the shifting land uses for motivations and forces that are more obscure. The city must be viewed in its spatial dimension, especially over time. Recent maps are more technically correct and provide the opportunity for sophisticated extrapolation. There are many theories about urban development between the naive optimism of ecological approaches and the realism (albeit with its own problems) of Marxist varieties. Most of the maps we offered were macro-views whereas detailed maps showing the processes at work may better relate to any legitimate theory. The

# APPROPRIATE METHODS

| Area | Best Mode of Prediction (First and Next Best) | Likelihood of an Accurate Prediction? |
|---|---|---|
| Demographic | Extrapolation > Comparative | — High as to Total Size; Less so as to Dispersal Pattern |
| Economic | Overall Process-Comp > Extrap. Specific Events: Apriori > Comparative | — Medium as to Growth Over Time <br> — Low as to Nature of the Pattern |
| Political | Process: Extrap. > Comparative Specific Events: Apriori | — Medium/Low as to "Trends" <br> — Zilch as to Impact on City's Future |
| Cultural Role | Delphi Techniques as to Content Otherwise Apriori | — Technological Spread & Centralization (Initially): High <br> — Nature of Content: Low |
| Planning Impact | Comparisons > Apriori | — Medium as to Likelihood of Recognition <br> — Low as to Level of Implimentation |
| Physical Structure (Maps) | Comparisons, Over Time & Between Mega Cities | — High as to Trend from Centripedal, then to Acentrifugal Pattern |
| Ecological | Comparisons with Other Urban Settings | — Technological Aspects-Extrapolation <br> — Elite & Public Readiness-Apriori |
| Overall | Few Reliable Extrapolations, Comparisons Very Instructive, Forget Experts | — Econ > Demo Growth Likely, not Primate Status, Planning Increase of Necessity (?) |

view of the total configuration is of most value to planners, but may be of less value to other specialties. In any case macro and micro views of the spatial-functional pattern are a basis for theoretical confirmation and possible prediction. In simple terms, to understand the city's future we need to know what is going on now! Peter Ward sees the growth of inequality both relative and absolute. There is no doubt about this, and it is demonstrable. Ward claims that, despite this perception, he is not a "Marxist." There are conservative observers who see the city as "going-to-hell-in-a-handcart" as well. The urban ecologists, or the Chicago school, were often critics of industrial capitalism—and may have introduced this theme into American sociology.

The appendix chapter on the long history of settlement in the valley attempts a kind of historical structural-functional analysis of the valley. What was important, how much so, and what are the continuing prerequisites for the functioning of this metropolis. Units like cities continue through time with similar priorities as to "functional prerequisites" we are told by archaeologists and other specialists. The extension of these needs being met and anticipated might allow prediction on some level. These materials were not put into the appendix because of their speculativeness or obtuseness, but because they represent a kind of date not easily triangulated (reinforced!) by other "data."

Comparative archaeology, especially of the cultural-evolutionary kind had achieved much success as to the prediction of sequences. We are using it to predict the nature of the continuing urban end of the "stages" or "sequences." If forces have carried civilization to a given point these surely must continue to have an impact over time. They do not disappear like a shooting star, but *may* persist as continuing prerequisites. "Mutation" may well occur in needs or structural processes to obtain them. We are afraid of the academic jibberish, and tautological thinking such structural functional requisite analysis has promulagated elsewhere, and, thus, consign it to our appendices. This kind of analysis has been accused of being synchronic, not sufficiently historical or diachronic. The author believes that the theory, used as a method can in fact predict change and its nature. (Julian Steward, the archaeologist, advocated this.) Change is as evident as is continuance in society's needs, and the elements involved can be specified. Archaeological analysis, especially the time oriented versions use all four of our "methods." It extrapolates on the basis of the appearance of certain sequences. The theory or model was tested by rigorous comparisons. The emergence was by a group of interacting digger-theoreticians. Their models involved much armchair, a-priori thinking as to the causes of stasis and change.

Our chapter on Mexico City as a mega-culture assumes that the new technology will expand the metro areas role especially given its geopolitical situation. The recent interim elections again stressed the role of a centralized media, which the coming satellite systems may augment. Extrapolation with a mixture of Macheavellian politics will tell you about the outcomes in terms of political communication. Mexico City as a fountain of popular culture is somewhat more problematic. Spontaneity from outlying areas that is successful would be coopted by the capital at least in form. Popular culture does retain its spontaneous, random origins, even though "manufactured" forms also thrive. High culture will remain centered on large urban elites of which Mexico City has a very large share.

Our chapters on the historic changes in the city and its environs and on planning do reveal increasingly successful attempts at organization and control. Water control would be an obvious case of success, whereas control of traffic, urban sprawl, etc. reveal less linear outcomes. What method of prediction would we then utilize? Some sociologists postulate increasing rationality (Weber?), but the optimism-pessimism dimension remains in great dispute. Let us complete this chapter by looking at current planning efforts, and the views of a range of current observers.

## Current Planning Efforts

The massive changes that I have observed during the many years that I have been acquainted with the city advise caution about the accuracy of any crystal ball gazing. (Ward, 1990, page 233.)

Planning may grow out of naive optimism, sheer necessity or mind blowing fear. Perhaps current efforts are a combination of these sources. Mexico City does have a cadre of planners at work in such agencies as the Secretaria General de Desarrollo Social, the Centro de Estudios Demograficos y de Desarrollo Urbano (El Colegio de Mexico), and the Coordinacion General de Reordinacion Urbana y Proteccion Ecologica. Outside of the agency domain there exists what many see as a "political card game" (Needler, 1982, cited in Ward, 1990, page 71). It is "inclusionary" but there are winners and losers. Our chapter on planning (p. 207–231) gives us a history of these activities. Our previous planning chapter could have stressed the successful planned response to the reconstruction after the 1985 earthquake, and the roles of SPP and SEDUE in this. Previously the uncontrolled growth of the city (illegal as well as "legal" developments) had spelled doom for planning (and political) efforts. The Federal district has its General Secretary of Public Works which handles such specific planning activities as transport, water, power and drainage. There is little of these activities that is not part of the "political card game." The latter agency constitutes the "big-spenders."

At this point in the planning cycle the metro area is well mapped. There are projected land use and development plans, what ever weight they may carry. Increasingly planning will have direct efficacy we would predict, and indirectly raise issues of legitimacy for the losers in the losers in the "card game." A Marxist theorist might predict sudden massive changes because of the obvious contradictions in this process. Others may see a "natural" pattern of the city's "development." But in either case the increased awareness of projected plans will eventually alter the rules of card playing.

## Summary of Views of M.C.S. Alternative Futures

We really need to ask what kinds of social scientists we should seek answers from. Obviously the focus would change if we asked cultural anthropologists versus economists or demographers instead of political scientists. We probably should ask people with different models of societal change as well. Functionalists see change as coming in a ceratin fashion-usually beneficial to most people. Believers in feedback systems now see positive feedback as a cause for growth of new forms (morphogenesis?). Catastrophe theorists see small changes as suddenly giving way to very different alternatives, which may or may not be predictable. P. M. Allen in 1982 write about predictable changes in early cities based on what was called self organization theory. Various activities in cities were modeled and seen as changing in response to demographic and multiple economic events. Many models of change are non-linear and do not allow for prediction. The punctuated equilibrium theories in evolutionary biology note long periods of stability preceding dramatic and relatively abrupt changes. Are there sociocultural equivalences to the build-up of potentially decisive point mutations, whose time may be coming?

A list of contributors to this section could show considerable variation in academic approach and models of change. At the outset we must confess a bias in favor of those who stress progressive and necessary changes for this great city. However we agree with Peter Ward that things may not change significantly, what ever the appearances pessimism may be called for. The latter is certainly self-fulfilling, and does not stimulate the imagination with respect to scenarios of positive change. Ward asks legitimately, "Has the position of the urban poor in Mexico City been helped or hindered by the existence of the 1980 master plan and associated zoning regulations?" (1990, p. 135). (See Footnote #1.)

Going back to our chapter on theory and methods we may conclude the following: 1) From our study on prehistory we may project the "functional prerequisites," the eternal varieties into the future, much beyond 2010. 2) Demographic extrapolation is a dicey game, and the extraneous variables are hardly knowable. Probably not all the delegacions will grow, but the ZMCM certainly will. 3) Many economic and political scenarios are possible, and theory will probably not guide us. Wallerstein's world system theory allows us to focus on critical variables beyond the city that will exert their influence. 4) Public services will expand, but as Ward notes, they can be new sources of inequality. The city's methods of financing had led to "bankruptcy" in the early 1980s. 5) Mexico City's environment must change, or an "ecological Hiroshima" will occur. Policy changes started here after 1985 will continue. 6) Mexico City will remain as a center of cultural, influence and may become "world class" on this basis. 7) Planning in the metro area will(is) occur(ing). Land use however, will still force the conurbation process which may well spread from Queretaro to Puebla, and has already gone south to Cuernavaca.

In this last section we hope to get the thoughts and information of known urbanologists—hopefully both on the areas we have tried to analyze and on areas omitted. We have not sufficiently discussed topics such as the class structure, the conflicting social values, the role of religion, personal motivations of elite or masses, the impact of the national (and urban) debt, the international pressures, the lopsided nature of development nor the social character of the various kinds of citizens. In a real sense our task was to outline a creature whose vital organs were left unexamined.

## Alternative Futures *Ward*

Again the paralysis of prognostication, even from those who know the metro area best, from an analytical point of view. We have already dealt with Ward's impressive knowledge of the planning process. He admits that in 1978 he did write a pretentious article on "Mexico City, the city the world will watch." Let me delineate his thoughts however tentative they are from his various writings.

p. 233, 1990     The ecological Hiroshima view may be exaggerated.
p. 234, 1990     The crisis is not new, but "ongoing."
p. 234, 1990     The lack of political commitment will continue as shown in the growing acceptance of inequality.
p. 235, 1990     The game will be won or lost depending upon planning in the state of Mexico, not in areas of previous growth.
p. 235, 1990     Planning processes have increased, and this is grounds for optimism. (Industry, vehicle users, and others have started to respond.)
p. 236, 1990     The beginnings of mass, counter-participation can be perceived, that may even force an end of "an anti-democratic political structure."

The City, because of all of these dimensions, may survive without thriving, but the tombstone need not be ordered.

## A Final Note on Prediction: A "Wild Card" Game?

Future studies help in the interpretation of present events. (Coates and Jarratt, "Exploring the future: A 200-year record of exploding competence." ANNALS, July 1992, Volume 522, page 12.)

Above all, predicting the future, assumes taking responsibility for future people. This is true even when events with a low probability of occurrence; so called wild cards, can change the total picture. Many social science disciplines have as their highest goal the prediction of events within their territory. Predictions whether improbable or not can, in fact, change the future by reason of showing us where we do or do not want to go. Earthquakes, assassinations, charismatic leaders, technological breakthroughs may be seen as wild cards, although the French probably had it right about things remaining the same. As Ward and others have noted there is much effort at keeping things more or less the same, despite the appearance of change.

The authors of this ANNALS compendium note that many researchers have been involved in future oriented research. In sociology there is an honored tradition from Sorokin to Bell and Etzioni. Heilbroner and Paul Kennedy have carried on the effort in history and economics. There are institutions whose efforts have gotten us into the wild card game with abandon, as the RAND Corporation's somewhat marginal military studies. What if there was a mad major? Is anything "fail safe"? Isn't there a safer activity for boys with bigger toys?

The attempt to note "Key Trends" may be safer realizing that multiple futures are possible, some things can be anticipated, and we can influence the future. Without predicting "Megatraumas" as former governor Richard Lamm did in this volume about the environment we can note an aging population for some countries; we can anticipate a changing sexual division of labor; we can predict that AIDS will cost us a lot of money (including in Mexico); and we can expect incremental changes in such areas as education, health, nutrition, and so forth. Dogan and Kasarda are sure that Mega-Cities will continue to grow, although we have tried to ask how that will occur (SAGE studies, #68). Yes there will be threats to the physical environments, as one of these "key trends" predicts. Do bears defecate in the woods?, as one wit put it. Will there be more individual responsibility as Grell and Gappert claim in this volume of the Annals? What will be the nature of future "demographic imbalances" as this volume, easily predicts? Will growth continue to be "irregular"? There assuredly will be competitive technology, fewer industrial jobs (in the great, post-industrial world). What will be the nature of the "crisis in welfare" as far as Mexico is concerned? Will the "new energy prices" favor Mexico's economy, and will they change its pattern of urban primacy? States, and regions within them, will continue to compete. Will the state's role change back from deregulation, so called, to a more interventionist position—or are these just mythological perceptions? Surely the international scene will become more "lawless"? Is there a sheriff in town? Social tensions not only will continue until the last quiver of the beast, but they will mark areas with lots of people—which means, of course, places like greater Mexico City.

# *Appendix A*

# First Metro Areas

## (Teotihuacan and Tenochtitlan)

## The New World's First Metro Areas

Villages and towns, no doubt, preceded true urbanism in Mexico, including the valley of Mexico. Between at least 1000 and 100 B.C., advancements beyond the primitive archaic life in skimpy villages came into being in several areas. On the gulf coast, at Monte Alban, at Tikal in Mayan territory, and in what was to become Teotihuacan, there were the beginnings of regional foci which became the centers of economic, political, and general cultural activity. It was true that after an early Olmec influence, there was a lapse in development in the valley of Mexico.

## Early Urbanism in Central Mexico

The long archaic and formative periods would lead in some regions to "true" urban buildups, and where this occurred, political, economic, demographic, and cultural processes were the causes and outcomes. Large complexes of monumental structures with associated signs of habitation and general human activity sprang up in the valley of Mexico, the Mayan lowlands, the Gulf Coast, in Oaxaca, and in parts of Central America. When the first great cities like Teotihuacan lost their momentum and collapse after 750 A.D., then some regional centers (like Xochicalco in the current state of Morelos) regain the hegemony of smaller (albeit militarized) units. The reasons for the collapse of the first classical urban areas into the post classic are not well known, but it was a significant transformation.

This chapter is based on archaeological field work done in the 1960's

163

and 1970's and reported on by such people as William Sanders and Eric Wolf. With their many colleagues, the valley or basin of Mexico had been well surveyed. Credit is given to earlier and contemporary work by Pedro Armillas, Robert Adams, Michael Coe, Rene Millon, Angel Palerm and a brigade of other notables. The effort by these workers has been to trace the nature and causes of transformation in this region. Major questions had to do with whether the materialist hypothesis was adequate, the role of hydraulic agriculture, how cultural factors correlated with one another, the problems with later urbanization, and more specific topics as control functions, warfare, and the effects of conquest (p. 3 in *The Basin of Mexico*, 1979).

Our task will be to review the hypothesized elements in this evolutionary development, and specifically to assess them for their *continuing* significance. The basic subsistence pattern of pre-Hispanic Mexico is not what supports contemporary life in Mexico City, but the continuing ingredients are not that different. If corn and beans come from 1500 km away rather than 15 km, it is still the result of an understandable economic process. The agricultural productivity of Chinampas in 1519 (12,000 hectares supporting 228,000 people, according to Sanders) may have nothing to do with current situations, but it is probably true than an extended family of 7 can still thrive on 1120 kilos of corn as it did in the "Late Horizon" period. The kilo-calories needed for work probably are not that different today either (p. 391 in Sanders, et al.).

What we can glean from such archaeological work is an appreciation of the basic parameters of social life at any "level" of development. The valley and its "well-watered plain with perennial springs" sustained for centuries the grandeur that was Teotihuacan. There are prerequisites for such levels of development. We can also get from archaeological sequences a sense of continuity about living social forms. Mexico City and its immediate environs grew out of such an intensification of effort, if not local, at least where linkages can be traced—and should be examined.

## Teotihuacan: An Earlier Prototype?

The major explanation for the development of Teotihuacan (T) is informed by an ecological model and the assumption the (T) was an Oriental-despotic state based upon irrigation agriculture. (Donald V. Kurtz, *Current Anthropology*, Vol. 28, #3, June 1987, page 329.)

A dozen centuries before Tenochtitlan, the Aztec capital was "founded," a city-state which greatly influenced central mesoamerica developed nearby to the north of the present metropolis of Mexico City. An economy, culture, society and body politic came into being that dominated millions of square miles and tens of thousands of people. It was a period in time called by archaeologists the "classic period." This culmination of evolutionary development involved the rise of true, high density urbanism, a cultural fluorescence, the solution of some political problems, and up to a point in time, a sufficient economy. More about the notions of the "classic period" will follow later in this volume.

The "causes" of this obviously spectacular urban growth have been widely investigated by archaeologists, urbanologists, and cultural historians of the New World. Probably a model exists to describe and occasionally predict the progress of such centers of human activity. It may be that such models also account for the sudden demographic and territory-wide collapse of such early urban experiments. Is the model one of "everybody fall down?" or is it more non-deterministic one, allowing for powerful, ideosyncratic influences on urban development.

This subsection, like many others in our study of greater Mexico City, must look at the academic-intellectual issues in each substantive area. If these separate issues contribute to Mexico City's current situation, then we might be pleasantly surprised; the current author is not holding his breath in anticipation of such an additive result. Mexico City's, as well as Teotihuacan's explanations for growth, fluorescence and dispersal are relevant to our current study of the surge toward primacy of the Federal district of Mexico (ZMCM, or MZMC in English).

Teotihuacan's emergence from a group of small towns around Mexico's central basin obviously involved:

1) centrality as to demographic developments
2) resource availability (water, climate, obsidian, or other raw materials)
3) an inward focus of the political and economic intents by thousands
4) an abeyance of competition—as one center functionally surpasses the less conscious neighbors
5) a successful economy (meeting local needs, and having potential to draw in what else was needed)

(After Diehl (1976), Millon (1973), Kurtz (1987), et al.)

Let us draft a list of what may be called functional prerequisites for these earlier urban areas and see which ones (in generic form) persist today. The latter may help us to project future needs and outcomes, although if these are described at too general a level, they become rather trite. In this chapter we will not get involved in issues between ecologists, economists, structuralists or whatever current fads of explanation exist. Our chapters on theory will perform some of these chores.

### *Elements Include:*

1. Internal local trade or tribute (surplus implied)
2. Rainfall or ground water (fluctuations occur—Sanders, p. 406)
3. Colonization of the lake bed (implies flood control, drainage)
4. Long distance trade (exports)
5. Control of Agricultural land (Chinampas; Sanders, et al, p. 400)
6. Efficiency of Transportation (Meyer/Sherman p. 237)
7. Non-human energy
8. Nature's cooperation
9. Mortality/Birth rates (vitals) as labor force
10. Local resources (obsidian, lime, basalt, chert, reeds, protein, salt, fine clay; p. 403, Sanders)
11. Exchange (vs. profit) markets
12. Political control (dual system; Wolf, for T and T)
13. Distinctive cultural style (imperial quality)
14. Appropriate technology (household-craft specialization, or machine)

With our "extrapolated" data we are using the arguable conclusions and data of experts on the valley of Mexico. It is arguable and problematic because research paradigms overlap—and deal with category-wise ambiguous data. As with geology, the "record is in the rocks" or the strata, but does it speak to us under oath? Without a supeona?

Many factors in cultural evolution seem necessary, but not sufficient to bring about a cultural "level" by themselves. There must be errors in logic where specific factors, from a matrix of related elements are seen as sufficient, rather than "necessary," "key," or "substitutable." Soem elements are in fact "necessary," and must remain that way until a "substitute" comes along (distant food sources versus local, etc.). We have made in this section assumptions about basic survival needs and their phase specific importance. The fact that there is continuity of social-economic-political forms in the basin of Mexico from 300 B.C. to the present allows questions about the continuing basis for their viability. The "data" we've synthesized and collected is put in the shape of an informed hypothesis, nothing more.

# EXTRAPOLATED ARCHAEOLOGICAL DATA

## The Continuing Economics/Ecology of Urbanization in the Basin of Mexico

**\*Based on the works of Sanders, Logan, Parsons, Millon, Santley, Price, Kurtz, and Armillas**

| Urban Manifestation | Functional/Material Prerequisites | Of Continuing Significance |
|---|---|---|
| Teotihuacan 300 B.C. – 100 B.C. | $1 = 2 = 8 = 10$ | + |
| Teotihuacan 300 A.D. | $12 = 10 = 9 = 11$ $14 > 4 > 6$ | 1, 2, 8 |
| Teotihuacan 600 A.D. | $12 = 13 = 10 = 4$ $= 6 = 9$ | 1, 2, 8 |
| Tenochtitlan– Tlatelolco – 1000 A.D. | $3 = 5 = 9 = 12 =$ $6 = 10$ | 1, 2, 8 |
| Tenochtitlan– Tlatelolco – 1500 A.D. | $3 = 5 = 9 = 12 =$ $13 = 10 = 11$ | 1, 2, 8, 9, 6 |
| Mexico City 1700 A.D. | $12 = 9 = 13 = 14$ $= 4 = 6$ | 10, 5, 1, 6, 11 |
| Mexico City 1900 A.D. | $14 = 12 = 9 = 7$ $= 13 = 4$ | 10, 5, 1, 6, 11 |
| Mexico City 1950 A.D. | $14 = 7 = 12 = 9$ $= 11 > 4 > 6 = 13$ | 10, 1, 2 |
| Mexico City 1990 A.D. | $12 = 14 = 6 = 7$ $4 = 13 = 9$ | 1, 2, 8 |
| Mexico City 2000 A.D. | $13 = 14 = 12 = 4$ $= 9 > 6$ | 1, 2, 8, 11 |
| Mexico City 2010 A.D. | $13 > 12 > 14$ | 1, 2, 8, 6, 11 4, 7, 9 |

Most prerequisites for a cultural manifestation have a way of being linked historically or elsewise of having a status short of explanatory clarity. Life, as most of us experience it, does not separate out into variables, causal or otherwise. It is also an act of sciencing, using your best judgement, to more or less correctly rank elements in their order of actual importance. Subsuming variables under umbrella headings, i.e., these are "economic," "ecological," or "political," is also fraught with risk. Donald V. Kurtz's article on "The economics of urbanization and state formation at Teotihuacan," is noted in our previous chapter on theory. His categories, he argues, (based on Jacobs' 1969 and 1985 works) are "economic" as opposed to "ecological" (p. 330, *Current Anthropology*, June, 1987). We have no quarrel one way or another with this debate, but want to use more specific elements in the total human history of the valley of Mexico. The latter may help us to predict the future in the sense of *continuing* elements. Which elements are of most importance are matters of choice ahead of time and available for informed evaluation after their time has passed. Will "style" be more important than "political control" or technology in the year 2010 as our table suggests? Will not the export of goods, an adequate labor force and sufficient energy be important. The latter (4, 7, and 9 on our chart) should be seen as "of continuing significance" but not on the cutting edge.

We'll end this chapter by noting a response by Kurtz to one of his critics, (p. 347)

> I concur with Stantley that the process may not have been as unilinear as I suggest. Still Jacobs' (1969, 1985) work indicates that certain socioeconomic conditions and formations are prerequisites for each successive step.

Going further, Kurtz discusses the need for studying the "interaction of economics,, politics, and ideology" in accounting for Teotihuacan. In our table we have put three related elements (style as ideology?, political control, and appropriate technology) in a ranking. The assumption here is that one must get one's act together *before* "political control" or appropriate technology are achieved.

## The Transition to Mexico City

T.R. Fehrenbach (*Fire and Blood*, 1973, p. 189) notes how Cortez proceeded to rebuild Tenochtitlan. Dragooned Mexica by the thousands laid the foundation for the new city. The background beauty of the overall site was not lost upon those involved. These native workers paid a great cost for these early efforts, and plazas, government and religious structures were soon built. The outline of the modern Zocolo was initiated during the early period and Cortez laid out the sites. The current national palace is on the site of the deposed Motechuhzoma II. Fehrenbach (p. 189) notes how broad avenues radiated out from the great plaza and the lesser conquistidores were allowed to build on these radii. The following quote from Fehrenbach details these early efforts:

> Broad avenues went out from the great plaza in all directions to the lake. The houses of the conquistadores were planned along these streets. Laborers sweated blocks of soft gray lava stone, and the red tezontle the Spaniards especially preferred into position for these great houses, and they brought down thousands of cedar and cypress logs from the mountains for beams. Within a few months, the outline of Cortez' capital was taking shape.

Fehrenbach goes on to note the effects of forced labor, the "transplanted hispanic civilization," the racial mixing, the Spaniard desire for town living, the impact of European Agro-husbandry, and the draining off of European's bottom of the human barrel! Fehrenbach (p. 191) notes the conflicts in Mexico City of this strange package of riff-raff (except for a few "true Spaniards"). Probably more critical than the historians objectivity is the cultural archaeology of a writer like Eric Wolf. The piercing archaeo-history of Mexico *Sons of the Shaking Earth* (p. 131, 1959) says that myths obscure the realities of living in the valley of Mexico. Cryptic histories of pre-spanish hegemony got the story wrong, especially about what made a difference. The control of the valley was based on control of food supply not ruthless militarism of the Mexica kind, at least in earlier periods. Hence Texoco not Tenochtitlan had dominated the valley under Hungry-Coyote (Netzahualcoyotl). Texcoco had opened lands for agriculture by its expansion of a tremendous system of canals and damns. Many other differences prevailed because of Texcoco's "secured Chinampa agriculture." They were more democratic, less militaristic, more intellectual, and less given to human sacrifices at an earlier point. The latter proving, perhaps, that prosperity need not be coerced nor development necessarily bloodily authoritarian. Unfortunately Tenochtitlan's militarism and that of the later Spaniards did prevail much like the rather universal demise from "classical" to "post classical" militaristic civilizations elsewhere.

Mexico City under the Spaniards, according to Eric Wolf, became a place where the "well connected" (p. 234, 1959) got what they wanted and formed the city in their own interests and images. The "unconnected" saw their fortunes erode and the barren hinterlands their only retreat. Fehrenbach notes the impact of this "immensely wealth leisure class" (p. 204) although much of this impact copied European affluence it did lead to "universities, palaces, printing presses and fancy dress balls," (p. 204). "Hispanicization" did not impact everything as students of indigenous survivals are well aware of. Of this early colonial impact on Mexico City Fehrenbach notes an upgrading (p. 228): "The capital did not approach the former size of Tenochtitlan, but it was well ordered, remarkably clean, and broad avenued." Much wealth was lavished on architecture, and earlier gothic catastrophes were replaced. These early "cities as yet contained not slums, they were the territory of a master class" (p. 228). Fehrenbach did see a "sterility" and a "somnolence" despite the buildings and colorful parks. The motive to avoid provincialism led the "encomenderos" to high culture elaborations (great libraries and classical learning), but also to a profligate imitation of grand living (expensive wine and horses). Mexico City for the next two centuries remained the center of Hispanic culture.

## Appendix B

# A Partial Inventory of Maps of Mexico City

No concept of geography is blanker on the map, yet richer with both invitation and peril, than terra incognita. It is why humans continue to map, and why as a civilization we need to map. Maps serve as a visual shorthand for how we conceptualize and integrate the unknown. (Stephen S. Hall, *Mapping: The next millenium*, 1992.)

In the best sense the future of Mexico City is terra incognita as are its maps. It is a different unknown than areas never visited before because in mapping the future of a known area we have many past features that will survive into the near and even distant future. In what sense can the future be perceived based on previous maps or a series of them? Now that Hubre is working again we may get some profound answers from the universe past! What features go forward—the natural features of hard rock will persist for the most part? The lines of concrete in streets, canals, dams, and highways have a tendency to persist, as do the functions which they serve. New forms can be laid down in relatively short order as the "super highways" replace the route 66s of the world. Perifericos, airport runways and underground metros can appear almost without warning. The concrete forms which are mapped, it can be argued, are not the city—but rather the frame or stages for human action.

The copies of parts of maps in the next pages are indicative of the history of those stages. Different aspects of the stage and of the action are stressed in the different maps. Some show process more than stasis, and some show processes that are still going on. Maps that are current do in a real sense predict the future because much will not change in a short time frame, and as for Mexico City much has preserved. One of the more interesting maps shows a dramatic transformation from Tenochtitlan to the city of Cortez. The scorched earth policy of the conquistadores was not the main mode of historical change, however.

171

# HISTORIC MAPS OF MEXICO CITY
## EXAMPLES: FORM AND PURPOSE

CIUDAD DE MEXICO E-14-A-39

There is much inertia in city forms, as with boundary designations, with changes often being accretions rather than erasures. Many kinds of data appear on these maps and some of them portend more for the future than do others. Our chapter on infrastructure is predicated on the idea that many subsequent changes follow from infrastructural investments.

Plans are maps of the future in the most likely, but not certain sense. Many plans are legitimatizations of the present it seems. We have included several plans in this collection. Our main problem is to decide upon a focus, and to consider which mapped information can be ex trapolated. Are radical departures revealed in the features we have observed on these maps?

## Map Makers Who Have Focused on Mexico City The 1500's

There have been many kinds of producers of maps for Mexico City. Agents of the Culhuacan, the spanish crown and individual cartographers constitute some of the earliest as far as our scope is concerned. Later on international private and governmental bodies became involved. Commercial firms depicted tourism, business features and basic information. Many of the early maps of Mexico City proudly proclaim the existence and status of the place. Depicting its architectural form, especially as a mirror of Europe, was an early goal, and idealized imagery abounded. Maps on ownership probably had the first definable accuracy as far as space was concerned. Often maps were privately circulated or limited on a need-to-know basis.

Yet modern map making for Mexico City seems to have lagged behind the state of the art elsewhere. The use to which ''maps'' were put determine their characteristics, of course, and maps of this city seemed to be trying to put it ''on the map'' in the 1500's. Bird's eye, idealized, over-Europeanized projections were common, and were meant to flatter some client it seems. The audience could have been potential investors in new Spain, in terms of money or power. Verbal descriptions could not have ignored the assaults to the senses, nor the dizzying visual impact of the place. Locations were vaguely depicted, there were few ways to measure distance or area with any accuracy. Routes of transport could not have been arrived at, except in a general sense of compass directions. The lakes in the valley of Mexico are variously depicted because of their changing levels, and a lack of orientation. The early maps do contain useable information however, and can be used in making some inferences. The relationships between places can be analyzed in many cases. Land use as with the Aztec Culhuacan chinampas can be located. Activities of cargo carrier or boatmen can be noted as can some land-use functions. These early maps were drawn by hand, occasionally with multicolors on parchment or primitive maguay paper. Titles or artists names did accompany some of these early renderings although (as with the Alonso de Santa Cruz) we do not know much about the actual producers. S. B. Elasser still sees this latter map of 1550 as an "excellent source." A bit earlier the Oztoipac Lands of Texcoco showed the horticultural properties and practices with much accuracy. Cline in 1966 analyzed these latter maps. Much early information was also taken from the surviving copies, which had a variety of other purposes.

The many fanciful, early maps include Munster's Bordone Map which may have been inspired by the search for Atlantis. The Clavijero Reconstruction features the location of the city in relationship to the lakes. There was a bird's-eye view of architecture in a Nuremberg publication, and a similar production in Ramusio Collection. The lakes, major structures, and some topographical information are shown in these maps. The main causeways or Calzadas are clear and probably in their actual locations. Trails up the mountain sides are also depicted, and drainage features, of which we will see more of later, are in evidence.

We must not underestimate the accuracy of these maps as the relative distances were probably generally correct. The Oztoipac Land Map of 1540 was evidently used in litigation over land, trees and other resources and must therefore have referred to real boundaries and points of departure. Panoramic views as in the Alonzo de Santa Cruz maps from 1550 had a sense of geographic integrity and offered a chance to gauge relative areas and distances.

## The 1600's

Inundacion of Mexico City in 1607 and again in 1629 and 1691 sparked much map making and hydrological activity. The Enrico Martinez map in 1602; The Dr. Zigneros Map depicting the status in 1618; The Anigada (flood) Map of the mid century showed the city and its watery problem. A 1607 description showing the work of draining the "Laguna" depicts major features of the valley and rivers, drainage features, and calcadas. Although the map is oriented top to bottom, east to west it is reasonably well calibrated. Not much detail of the city itself shows at this scale. The 1618 semi-Bird's eye view by Diego de Zisneros look down over "chapultepech" to the towers of "Mexico." The surrounding communities are depicted with their cluster of buildings centering on local cathedrals. The whole lake mass is shown to be connected from northwest to southeast.

The 1628 map by Juan Gomez de Trasmonte is one of the early semi-bird's eye maps to show the main city with buildings in their proper spatial relationships. The palace cathedral and Alameda are in their respective positions and the closeness of lake waters is apparent. Churches, hospitals and colleges are clearly located. A 1633 map of the "inundacion" really is a picture (dibujo) with "poco realista." Boatmen are shown right inside the Venice-like city. The Carlos de Siguenza map from a slightly later period seems to show the waters in remission, and also the direction of drainage flow at that time.

## The 1700's

Given the continued hydrological nightmares there were depictions of these features in 1700, 1753, and 1774. Early in this century the built-up area was small and self contained. However, a map in 1760 showed major buildings and architectural features. Maps in 1776 and 1793 showed major structures and the block pattern—with over 100 "blocks" developed. These maps are available, as are many other at the Museo de la Ciudad de Mexico and the Museo Nacional de Historia del Castillo de Chapultepec, Mexico.

By the late 1700's the maps of Mexico City were modern looking. Avenues, blocks, ad buildings were competently delineated. The block street pattern approximates the present form for El Centro. The 1760 and 1793 maps are keyed in order to locate major buildings and streets, although little other information is enscribed. The royalist decoration adorns the edges of these maps as well as hand lettering (instead of printing) at least into the 1800's. Not many maps of Mexico City have ever approached the artistic quality of European varieties, these stressing heraldry and spectacular architecture or scenery. The Seminario de Historia—Departario de Investigaciones Historicas—INAH has a series of block and structure maps of the city that give the plain truth about the layout of the city, and there appears to be less fantasy (see the 1753 INAH map for instance).

## The 1800's

The Plano General de la Ciudad de Mexico showing the city in 1807 is a detailed, keyed, modern type of map. A map with Humboldt's name on it from 1807 shows the valley very sketchily, but having location coordinates on its edges. ("Carte de la Vallee de Mexico") A fishbowl map from 1824 seems accurate as to scale but lacks location coordinates. There must have been many other maps for this particular year, as this was the one in which the Federal district was delineated. Another circular map "Croquis del Plano del Distrito Federal" from 1852 was, indeed a "rough sketch" as "croquis" means, but it showed haciendas, irrigated gardens; pueblos and ranchos. Artistic bird's eye sketches from the middle 1800's are also available.

After 1864, well detailed street maps are available. The extension of radiated streets and railways are shown in a map put out by the Minister of Public Works in 1885 (Carlos Pacheco). Henceforth (after 1874) the Mexican National, Interoceanic, Vera Cruz, and Mexican Central Railways form a spider-web pattern out of Mexico City.

The conscious planning efforts of the last quarter of the 1800's led to a range of types of maps other than for hydrological and transport purposes. Spread of the cities into the surrounding hill sides was to be the future and the street car network did its magic after 1899.

## The 1900's

The productivity of maps would obviously vary in this century of happenings. The last ten years of the Porfiriato found the city being celebrated as achievements in such areas as drainage and potable water came about (1902 and 1914). The 1914 map "Obras de Provision de Aguas Potables Para la Ciudad de Mexico" shows the settlement pattern moving southwest and west. The revolution did impact Mexico City in February of 1913 and the "Decena Tragica" seen barricades, trenches, artillery blasts and fires in the National Palace area. Meyer and Sherman describes the chaos, (*The Course of Mexican History*, 1978, page 519) but the shape of the city was not greatly altered.

The "constructive" phase of the revolution (1920–1940?) would have seen more developments throughout the country. Schools were built everywhere, and the muralists decorated public buildings. The domestic program of the 1920's also involved inoculations and food inspection, although moves to the left and right obscured much progress.

Probably what transformed Mexico City most was the incredible increase in trucks and buses by the mid-1930's. Mexico City grew to 1,726,858 people in 1940, an increase of one million since 1920. The cost of living in Mexico City more than doubled between 1939 and 1945 (Meyer and Sherman, 1978, page 629). Industrialization in the 1940's, the Pan American highway after 1951, and cheap electrical power, all would play a role in this exploding metropolis. A three mile square University City was dedicated in 1952 and this transformed a quadrant of the city. Much more effort did go into form than into content during the middle decades. U.S. "multinationals" did effect this visual dimension with their logos and presence. No one would say that the metro system or the new Museum of Anthropology after 1970 were form without substance, however.

Each government agency noted in our bibliography was a source of special purpose maps. Tourist maps came from most major publishers and the Ministry of Tourism as well. The city was no longer terra incognito, but it was still a surprise when you asked some natives of this city to locate themselves on a unfolded street map. The following tables note the data of these maps, their major purposes, and where one can learn about them. Next there will be an attempt to interpret their major "functions."

## A Note on Maps and Functions

In our Table on "Maps and Functions" we have periodized much of Mexican history and spelled out six types of functions that maps may perform. Certainly maps are used to claim territory. As plans they can be attempts to coerce the future of land use. Maps additionally try to legitimate behavior, give instructions to willing subjects, sell the image of the territory, and can actually can be used to locate specific places. With ranks on these six functions we have hypothesized about some less obvious purposes for these five centuries of maps. Legitimation of state behavior is always given a high priority, but territory claiming is more likely at certain moments when the flag is being planted. Planning for future circumstances may be a sometime thing. One of the more manifest purposes of maps are to relate the history of the unit, or more obviously to help people to locate themselves in political terms. Because we have no data to substantiate these rankings, we will not pursue them further here, but they do reflect on maps as plans.

# HISTORIC MAPS OF MEXICO CITY
## EXAMPLES: FORM AND PURPOSE

| MAP | DATE | PURPOSE | SOURCE |
|---|---|---|---|
| MATRICULA DE TRIBUTOS (CODEX MENDICINO) | 1511 | -TAXABILITY? | -BASIS FOR R. H. BARLOW'S "EXTENT OF CULHUA EMPIRE" |
| OZTOTICPAC LANDS OF TEXCOCO | 1540 | -PROPERTIES, HORTICULTURAL PRACTICES | -DEALS WITH LITIGATION OVER LAND, TREES (H. CLINE, 1966) |
| ALONSO DE SANTA CRUZ | 1550 | -GEOGRAPHICAL, ANTHROPOLOGY? | -SEEN AS EXCELLENT RECORD -(S.B. ELASSER, 19  ) |
| MUNSTER'S BORDONE MAP (CORTEZ?) | 1544 | -SENT TO CHAS. V. -WESTERN IMAGE OF ISLAND CITY | -A PLATONIC VIEW OF ATLANTIS? (A. TENNANT?) |
| CLAVIJERO RECONSTRUYE | 1519 | -GEOGRAPHIC, TOPOGRAPHIC | -LAKES PROMINENT (FERNANDO BENETIZ, 1984) |
| NUREMBERG PUBLICATION | 1324 | -SHOW URBAN ARCHITECTURE | -BIRD'S EYE, FANCIFUL (F. BENETIZ, 1984, page 38) |
| RAMUSIO COLLECTION | — | -VALLEY-LAKE AREAS | -ANOTHER VARIATION (BENETIZ, 1984, page 42) |
| FRANCESES TAMBIEN RECONSTRUC-tion | 1519 | SHOW LAKE AND ENVIRONS | (BENETIZ, 1984, page 44) |
| UPSALA COLORATION | 1550 | -GEOGRAPHIC, ANTHROPOLOGICAL? | 1897, SWEDEN COPY IN U OF M  FORD BELL ROOM |
| LAKE REGION DESCRIPTION, (DR. ZISNEROS) | 1618 | -APPRECIATION OF WATER RESOURCES | MEMORIA - SYSTEMS OF MAJOR DRAINAGE, TOMO II, NUMBER 5 |

# HISTORIC MAPS OF MEXICO CITY
## EXAMPLES: FORM AND PURPOSE

| MAP | DATE | PURPOSE | SOURCE |
|---|---|---|---|
| FORMA Y LEVANTADO JUAN GOMEZ DE TRASMONTE | 1628 | MAJOR INSTITUTIONS | MEMORIA--SYSTEMS OF DRAINAGE, TOMO II, # 6 |
| ANEGADA, SIGLO XVII | 1629-33 | INUNDATION, OBSTRUCTION | M. S. M. D., TOMO II, #7 |
| HYDROGRAPHIA CAHELO MEX... NELLE SUE LACUNE | 1700 | TOTAL VALLEY OF MEXICO | M. S. M. D., TOMO II, #10 |
| PROFILE--LATITUDE & DEPTH --PLAN DEL REAL DESAGUE HUHUETOCA | 1753 | SHOW DANGER OF"INUNDACIONES" | M. S. M. D., TOMO II, #11 BY JOS. DE PAEZ |
| PLANTA Y DES. DE LA IMPERIAL C. DE MEXICO | 1760 | MEXICO CHARACTERISTIC OF SIGLO XVIII + ARCHITECTURE | M. S. M. D., TOMO II, #12 |
| CARTA TOPOGRAPHICA QUE COMPREN DE EL TERRENO... | 1774 | SHOWS CANAL AND DRAINAGE TO THE NORTH WEST | M. S. M. D., TOMO II, #13, SEE # 14, 15 |
| PLANO GEOMETRICO DE LA IMPERIAL, NOBLE Y REAL C. DE MEX. | 1776 | EL CENTRO, MAJOR STRUCTURES | M. S. M. D., TOMO II, #16 |
| PLANO GENERAL DE LA C., DE MX. | 1793 | EL CENTRO AND VECINITY | M. S. M. D., TOMO II, # 17 ENGRAVED IN 1807 |
| CARTA DE LA VALLEE DE MEX. | 1804 | TOPOGRAPHICS, CLIMATE OF THE VALLEY | M. S. M. D., TOMO II #19 HUMBOLDT WAS INVOLVED |
| PLANO TOPOGRAPHICAL DE MEX. | 1824 | DISTRICT CENTERED ON MEX. CITY | M. S. M. D., TOMO II_ #20 |

# HISTORIC MAPS OF MEXICO CITY
## EXAMPLES: FORM AND PURPOSE

| MAP | DATE | PURPOSE | SOURCE |
|-----|------|---------|--------|
| CD DE MEXICO | 1811-1844 | ELCENTRO, BLOCKS COMPARED | |
| PLAN ICNOGRAPHICO DE LA CIUDAD DE MEXICO | 1842 | INTERIOR OF THE CITY, MAJOR STREETS, COMMUNITIES | BY ARQ IGNACIO CASTERA |
| PLANO GENERAL DE LA CIUDAD MEXICO | 1869 | EL CENTRO, MAJOR PUBLIC BUILDINGS, CHURCHES, PLAZAS DE MERCADO | SHOWN IN BENETIZ, PAGE 25 -NOTES POPULATION AT 269,534 |
| MEXICO CITY AND ENVIRONS THE MEXICAN GUIDE | 1885 | CITY AND VALLEY | PRODUCED BY CARLOS PACHECO, MINISTER OF PUBLIC WORKS |
| LOS TRANVIAS DE MULITAS SUBURBANOS, LOS FERRO-CARRILES DE VAPOR | 1896 | TRAINS SINCE 1874, with connect-ing LINES ACTUAL AND PLANNED TO 1910 | SEMENARIO DE HISTORIA URBANA, DEPTO. DE INVS. HISTORICAS-INAH |
| RED DE TRANVIAS (STREET CAR NETWORKS) | 1899 | PRINCIPALES TRANVIAS DE LA CAPITAL | INAH |
| OBRAS DE PROVISION DE AGUAS POTABLE — PLANO QUE MUESTRA LA LOCALI-ZATION....... | 1914 | SHOWS SOURCES OF FRESH WATER AND DISTRIBUTION | |

# MAPS AND FUNCTIONS

| PERIOD ⟶ FUNCTIONS | LEGITIMATION OF BEHAVIOR | TERRITORY CLAIMING | CONTROLLING FUTURE PLANS | INSTRUCTIONS TO LOYAL SUBJECTS | SELLING THE IMAGE OF THE TERRITORY | MANIFEST LOCATOR OR HISTORY |
|---|---|---|---|---|---|---|
| PRE COLONIAL - CODICES | 1 | 4 | 6 | 2 | 5 | 3 |
| EARLY COLONIAL | 2 | 1 | 3 | 5 | 4 | 6 |
| NATION BUILDING DIAZ | 1 | 6 | 2 | 5 | 4 | 3 |
| REVOLUTION 1920+ | 2 | 6 | 1 | 5 | 4 | 3 |
| INDUSTRIALIZATION | 4 | 6 | 2 | 5 | 1 | 3 |
| BALANCED DEVELOPMENT | 2 | 6 | 4 | 5 | 1 | 3 |

# EARLY MEXICO CITY IN MAPS

VISTA DE LA ʒ∩DAD DE MÉXICO CON SU LAGO

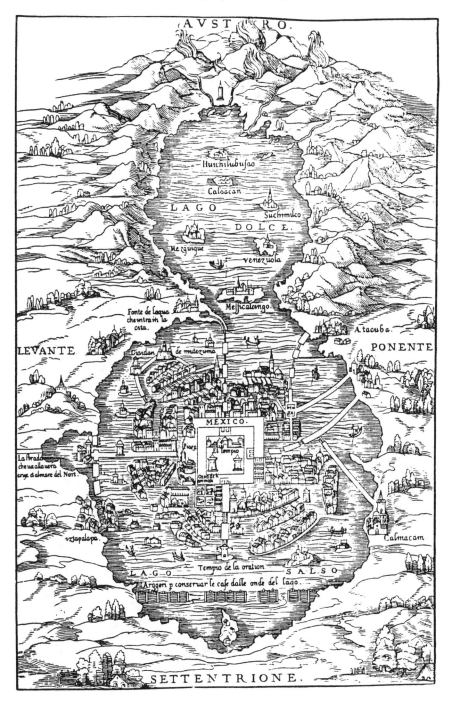

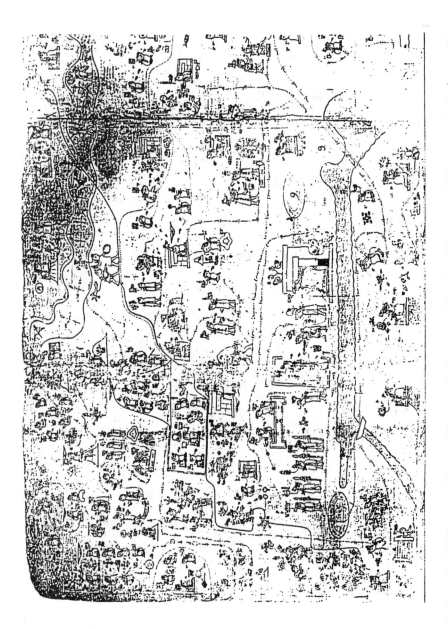

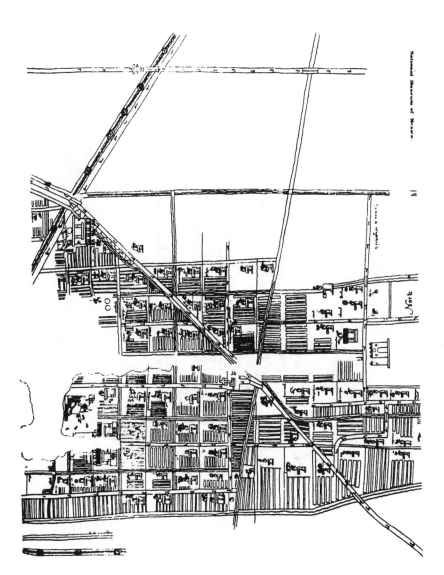

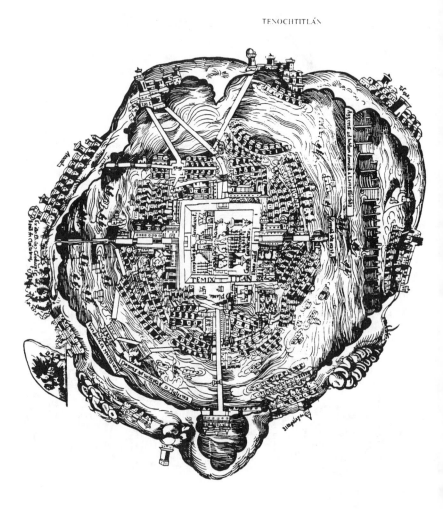

TENOCHTITLÁN

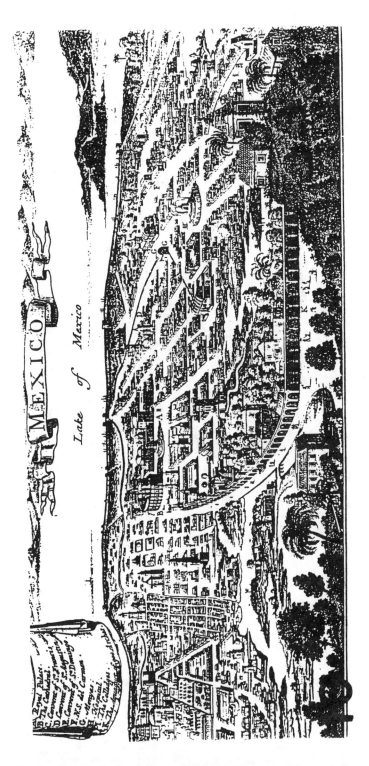

VISTA DE LA CIUDAD DE MEXICO A PRINCIPIOS DEL SIGLO XVIII.

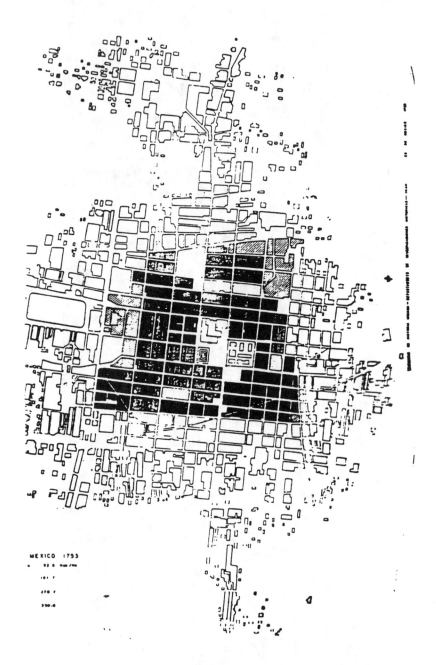

MEXICO 1753

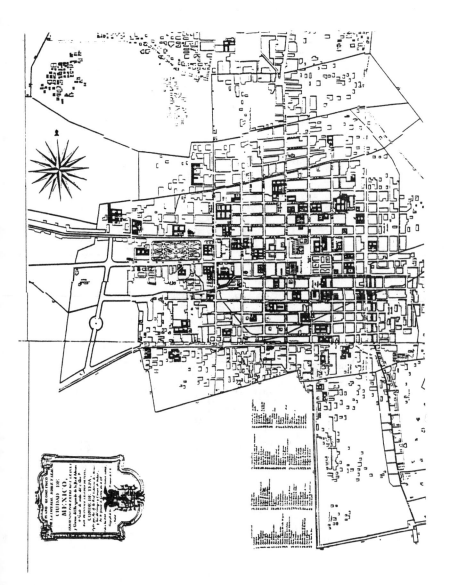

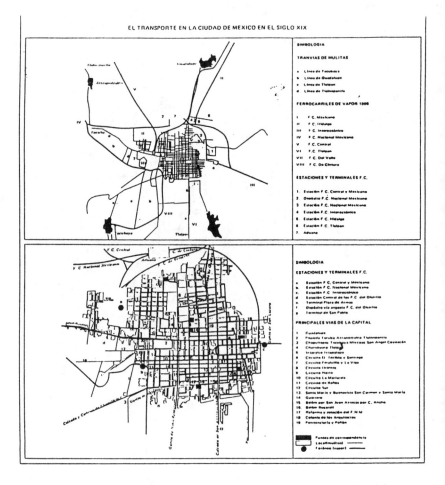

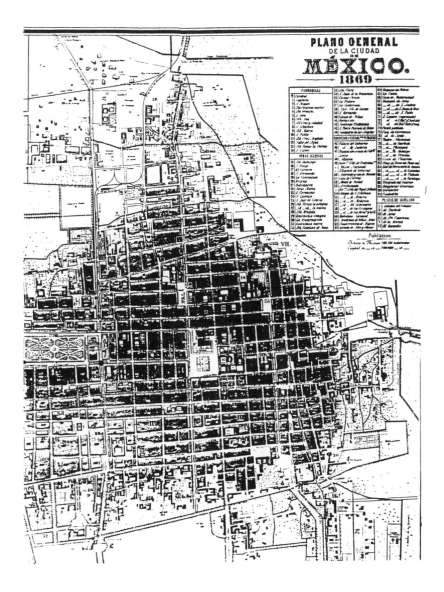

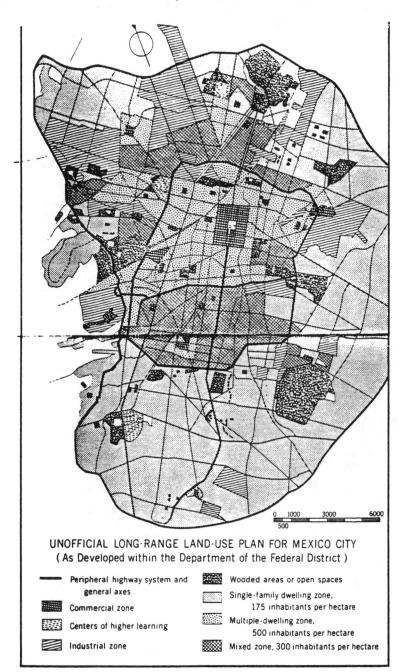

UNOFFICIAL LONG-RANGE LAND-USE PLAN FOR MEXICO CITY
( As Developed within the Department of the Federal District )

<table>
<tr><td>—— Peripheral highway system and general axes</td><td>Wooded areas or open spaces</td></tr>
<tr><td>Commercial zone</td><td>Single-family dwelling zone, 175 inhabitants per hectare</td></tr>
<tr><td>Centers of higher learning</td><td>Multiple-dwelling zone, 500 inhabitants per hectare</td></tr>
<tr><td>Industrial zone</td><td>Mixed zone, 300 inhabitants per hectare</td></tr>
</table>

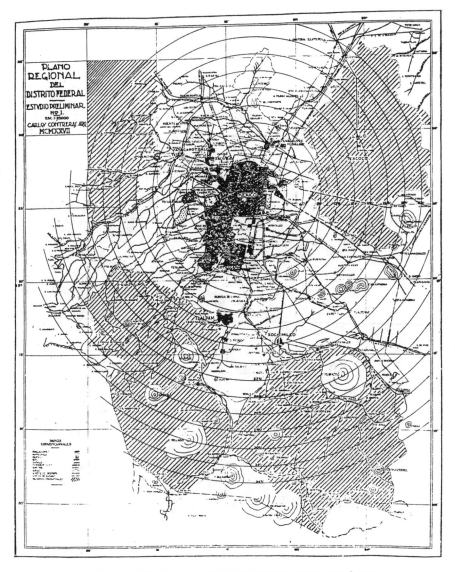

Plano Regional del Distrito Federal -- Sugestion de Reservas Forestales -- Arquitecto, Carlos Contreras

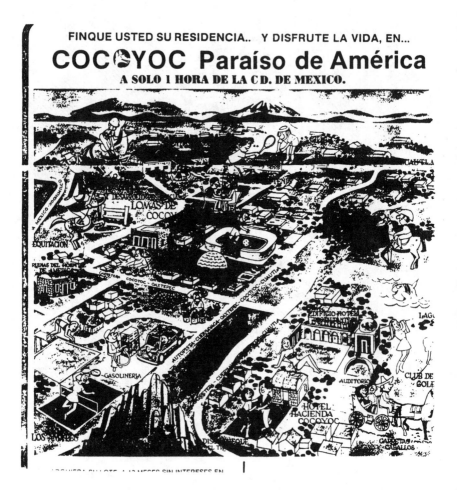

# A Select Bibliography On Mexico City

There are extensive works on all aspects of this Mega City. The *Historia de La Planificarion y la Administration Urbana de la Ciudad de Mexico* has 1000 items plus 25 sources. Peter Ward's 1991 volume has a current 500 item bibliography on Mexico City, stressing planning housing and political forces.

Our original 400 item version was trimmed to 50 items—trying to be representative, current and in most cases accessible. It stresses longer, academic studies and does slight current journal efforts. The supreme cataloging of the latter, allows quick printouts. We did not include much on such topics as maps or comparative works. The writer's included do represent people from the classics of the last 2 decades. I hope that it serves the reader well, in any case.

Revista Geografica #107—Enero-Junio 1988. Instituto Panamericano de Geografia E Historia, p. 29. Planeacion y proceso politico en la ciudad de Mexico el casa Central de Abastos. Adrian Guillermo Aguilar.

Aguilar, Martinez, G. (1988). "Community Participation in Mexico City: A Case Study, *Bulletin of Latin American Research*, 7 (1), pp. 22–46.

Apenes, Ola. *Mapas Antiguos del Valle de Mexico*. Instituto de Historia, U.N.A.M., 1947.

Barkin, David. (1978). "Regional Development and Interregional Equity: A Mexican Case Study." In Wayne Cornelius and Robert V. Kemper, eds. *Urbanization and Inequality: The Political Economy of Urban and Rural Development in Latin America*. Beverly Hills: Sage.

Bataillon, C., and Riviere D'Arc, H. (1973). La ciudad de Mexico (No. 99) Mexico, D.F.: SepSetentas.

Benitez, Fernando (1981). *La ciudad de Mexico: 1325–1982*. 3 volumes, Mexico, Salvat. (See also 9 volume version, 1989.)

Mexico: Problems Urbano Regionales Guillermo Boils Coordinador, Institute de Investigaciones Sociales Primera Edicion, 1987. Garcia Valades, editores. Note: 3 articles on Mexico City area: on food, cortage, and the metro.

Brambila, C., (1987). Ciudad de Mexico: La Urbe Mas Grand del Mundo? In *Elatlas de Ciudad de Mexico*, G. Garza, Mexico, D.F., Department del Distristo Federal and Colegio de Mexico.

Camacho, C. (1987). La ciudade de Mexico en la economia nacional. El atlas de la Ciudad de Mexico, Garza, (ed.), pp. 95–99. Mexico DF: Departamento del Distrito Federal and Colegio de Mexico.

Campbell, T. and Wilk, D. (1986). "Plans and Plan Making in the Valley of Mexico," *Third World Planning Review*, 8 (4), pp. 287–313.

Catells, M. (1977). The Urban question: A Marxist approach, Edward Arnold. Original French edition, 1972.

Cultura Urbana Tomo 5 Emilio Pradilla CoBos (Compilador). Part of a 7 part series, 1991.

Projectos Urbanos de Los Partidos Politicos, edited by Emilio Pradilla CoBos. Part of a larger 7 part series on "Democracia y Desaprollo Urbano en la Zona Metropolitana de la ciudad de Mexico, 1991.

La Modernization de Las Ciudadesen Mexico, Manuel Perlo Cohen, Compilador, Mexico, 1990. Note: This was based on a seminar at URAM Co-sponsored by the department of humanities, Sedue, and the faculty of architecture.

Connolly, P. (1982). Uncontrolled settlement and self-build: what kind of solution? The Mexico City case, in Ward, P., ed. *Self-help housing: a critique*, Mansell Publishing Co., 141–74.

Cornelius, Wayne (1975). *Politics and the Migrant Poor in Mexico City*, Stanford University Press.

Cornelius, Wayne A. and Robert V. Kemper (eds.) Latin American Urban Research (Vol. 6 Metropolitan Latin America: The Challenge and the Response). Sage Publications: Beverly Hills, CA, 1978.

Coulomb, R. (1989). Rental housing and the dynamics of urban growth in Mexico City. In housing and land in urban Mexico, A. Gilbert (ed.), pp. 39–50. San Diego: Centre for US- Mexican Studies, University of California, Monograph Series No. 31.

Revista Geografica #109—Enero-Junio 1989. Inst. Panamericano de Geografica E Historia. P. #45. El Desarrollo Espacial de las Ciudades en American Latin, Casode la Ciudad de Mexico. Miroslawa Czerny & Jerzy Makowske.

Delgado, J. (1988). "El Patron de occupacional territorial de la ciudad de Mexico a ano 2000. In Estructura Territorial de la Ciudad de Mexico. Terraza and Preciat (eds.). Dept. de Distrito Federal.

*Memoria de las obras del sistema de drenaje profundo del Distrito Federal.* 3 vols. Departamento del Distrito Federal. Mexico: UNAM 1975.

Dogan, Mattai and John Kasarda (1988). *The Metropolis Era*, Volume 2, "Mega Cities," Sage.

Domingues, 1. 1987. Sistema de transporte colectivo el metro. In el atlas de las Ciudad de Mexico, G. Garza, (ed.), pp. 198–201. Mexico DF: Departamento del Distrito Federal and Colegio de Mexico.

Drakakis-Smith, David (1987), *The 3rd World City*, New York, Methuen & Co.

Direccion General De Reordenacion Urbana y Proteccion Ecologica. *Historia de la Planificacion y La Administracion Urbana de La Ciudad de Mexico* (1990?).

Flores, Moreno J. (1988), "El Transporte en la Zona Metropolitana de la Ciudad de Mexico. In *Grandes Problems de la Ciudad de Mexico* by R. Benitez and J. Benigno, pp. 265–280.

Popular Movements and Political Change in Mexico, edited by Joe Foweraker and Ann L. Craig. Lynne Rienner, publishers. Note: 3 chapters have urban content.

Friedo, R.C. (1972). "Mexico City" in W.A. Robson (ed.), *Great Cities in the World: Their Government, Politics, and Planning*. Sage Publications.

Garza, Gustavo and Martha Schteingart (1978). "Mexico City: The Emerging Metropolis" in *Latin American Urban Research*, volume 6, edited by Cornelius and Kemper, Sage publications.

Garza, Gustavo. El proceso de industrializacion en la Ciudad de Mexico, 1821–1970. Mexico: Colegio de Mexico, 1985.

Gil, Elizondo, J. (1987). "El Futuro dela Ciudad de Mexico" in *El Atlas de la Ciudad de Mexico*, G. Garza (ed.), pp. 415–418.

Gilbert, Alan and Peter M. Ward (1985). *Housing, the State and the Poor: Policy and Practice in Three Latin American Cities*, Cambridge University Press.

Diccionario D.F. Ilustrado Fernandez Editores Hector Campilito Guautli 1988. Note: Just a dictionary but has some data on the federal district.

Guevara, S. and Moreno, P. (1987). "Areas Verdes de la Zona Metropolitana de la Ciudad de Mexico," in G. Garza, pp. 231–6, DDF and El Colegio de Mexico.

Hayner, Norman S. (1960). "Mexico City: Its Growth and Configuration, 1345–1960" in *Urbanization in World Perspective*, Sylvia Fava, (ed.), pp. 166–177.

Historia de la Planification y la Administracion Urbana de la Ciudad de Mexico. (A Bibliography with 24 major sources on last 3 pages.)

Kandell, J., *La Capital: The Biography of Mexico City*. New York: Random House.

Kemper, R. V. (1974). "Tzintzuntzenos in Mexico City: the anthropologist among peasant migrants," pp. 63–91 in G. M. Foster and R. V. Kemper (eds.) *Anthropologists in Cities*. Boston: Little, Brown.

Revista Geografica #113 Enero-Junio 1991. Inst. Panamericano de Geografica E Historia. "La politica de autoconstruccion dirigida en la ciudad de Mexico. Algunas Bases de Evaluacion. Adrian Guillermo Aguilar & Alicia Ledeyma.

Lizt, Mendoza S. (1988). "Respuetas del Transporte Urbano en las Zonas Marginadas," in *Grandes Problemas de la Ciudad de Mexico* by R. Benitez Zenteno and J. Benigno Morelos (eds.), pp. 215–242, Plazay Janes and DDF.

Mexico-DDF (1982). Sistema de Planificacion Urbana de Distrito Federal, DDF Publication.

Morales, M.D. (1987). La expansion de la Ciudad de Mexico (1858-1910). In El atlas de la Ciudad de Mexico, G. Garza (ed.), pp. 64–8. Mexico DF: Departamento del Distrito Federal and Colegio de Mexico.

Moreno Toscarno, Alejandra (1979). "La 'Crisis' en la Ciudad. In Pablo Gonzalez Casanova nd Enrique Florescano, eds., *Mexico, hoy*. Mexico: Siglo 21.

Oldman, Oliver, et al. (1967). *Financing Urban Development in Mexico City: A Case Study of Property Tax, Land Use, Housing, and Urban Planning*, Harvard University Press.

Partida, V. (1987a). El proceso de migracion a la ciudad de Mexico. In El atlas de las Ciudad de Mexico, G. Garza (ed.), pp. 134–40. Mexico DF: Departamento del Distrito Federal and Colegio de Mexico.

Rabinovitz, F. (1965). *The Political Feasibility of Metropolitan Planning: Mexico City, A Case Study*, Regional and Urban Planning Implementation, Inc., Cambridge, Mass.

Schteingart, M. (1987). "Mexico City," in *Mega Cities*, M. Dogan and J. Kasada (eds.), Vol. 2, pp. 268–93, Sage Pub.

Scott, I. (1982). *Urban and Spatial Development in Mexico*, Baltimore, John Hopkins Press.

Vaughan, Denton (1970). Urbanization in 20th Century Latin America: A Working Bibliography. Institute of Latin American Studies, Population Research Center, University of Texas, Austin.

Varley, Ann (1985). "Urbanization and Agrarian Law: the Case of Mexico City," Bulletin Latin American Research.

Historica Ciudad de Mexico, Publicado y Editado por Editor/S.A. 1993. Note: Mostly pretty pictures and one good map. Should not be ignored in the visualization of modern Mexico City. See also Pictoral Distrito Federal.

Unikel, I. and Lavell, A. (1979). "El Problema Urbano Regional En Mexico, Gaceta UNAM, Cuarta Epoca, Volume 3, Suplemento Numero 20, 9 de Agosto (impossible to get, but illustrates Unikel's relevant works).

Ward, Peter M. (1986). "Urban Problems and Planning" in Pacione, M. (ed.), *Urban Problems and Planning in the Modern World*, Croom Helm, pp. 28–64.

Ward, Peter M. (1986). *Welfare Politics in Mexico: Papering Over the Cracks*, Boston, Allen & Unwin.

# Index